Study Guide

for

American Government: Continuity and Change, 2004 Edition

to accompany Comprehensive, Alternate, and Texas Edition versions

prepared by

John Ben Sutter

Houston Community College

Longman

New York Boston San Francisco
London Toronto Sydney Tokyo Singapore Madrid
Mexico City Munich Paris Cape Town Hong Kong Montreal

Study Guide for American Government: Continuity and Change, 2004 Edition

Copyright ©2004 Pearson Education

All rights reserved. Printed in the United States of America. Instructors may reproduce portions of this book for classroom use only. All other reproductions are strictly prohibited without prior permission of the publisher, except in the case of brief quotations embodied in critical articles and reviews.

ISBN: 0-321-18688-5

3 4 5 6 7 8 9 10-BM –06 05 04 03

TABLE OF CONTENTS

Section I	Study Skills	1
Section II	Chapter By Chapter Guide	14
Chapter 1	The Political Landscape	15
Chapter 2	The Constitution	27
Chapter 3	Federalism	40
Chapter 4	State and Local Government	52
Chapter 5	Civil Liberties	64
Chapter 6	Civil Rights	79
Chapter 7	Congress	94
Chapter 8	The Presidency	109
Chapter 9	The Executive Branch and the Federal Bureaucracy	121
Chapter 10	The Judiciary	132
Chapter 11	Public Opinion and Political Socialization	146
Chapter 12	Political Parties	158
Chapter 13	Voting and Elections	171
Chapter 14	The Campaign Process	185
Chapter 15	The News Media	199
Chapter 16	Interest Groups	213
Chapter 17	Social Welfare Policy	226
Chapter 18	Economic Policy	239
Chapter 19	Foreign and Military Policy	254

Note: Chapters 20-26 are to accompany *American Government, Texas Edition, Second Edition*

20	The Context for Texas Politics and Government	274
21	The Texas Constitution	285
22	Local Government and Politics in Texas	293
23	The Texas Legislature	303
24	The Governor and Bureaucracy in Texas	316
25	The Texas Judiciary	328
26	Political Parties, Interest Groups, Elections, and Campaigns in Texas	338

SECTION I
STUDY SKILLS

This section is designed to give you a number of ideas about how you can learn better study skills. Studying is an individual thing--what works for some does not work for others. So please use these hints to help you think about what works for you and how you can improve your own skills.

If a suggestion doesn't work for you, try something else. But consciously think about how you study best, what kinds of settings work for you, what times of day help you to recall facts, and so on. Oftentimes, your study skills improve when you simply think consciously about how to study. If you need more help, see your professor, consult the suggested web pages at the end of this section, and or find out what kind of help is available on campus. Most campuses today offer tutoring and counseling, often including classes on studying.

- **Note-taking**

- **Reading**

- **Taking Tests**
    - **Essay Tests**
    - **Objective Tests**

- **"The Ten Traps of Studying"**

- **Web sites of Interest**

NOTE-TAKING

Good notes often make the difference between good and superior students. Bad note-taking often serves only to confuse. No one system works for everyone, but here I list a number of rules of thumb that should be helpful as you devise your own system.

The main rule of note-taking is to do what you find helpful and comfortable. Often comparing your notes to those of your colleagues or asking you professor to look at one day's notes will help you determine how well you perform this task.

1) **GO TO CLASS!!!** The single easiest way -- actually, the only way-- to figure out what the professor will emphasize on a test, is to attend class daily. Missing class and getting the notes from someone else is an extremely poor substitute for attendance. Besides, "repetition is the mother of learning," as the saying goes. And if you hear it AND write it, you will be more likely to remember it.

2) **Think about taking notes BEFORE you start.** In other words, have a plan. A common way of doing this is to draw a vertical line down the paper dividing it into two parts. Take notes to the right of the line. Save the left to add information that is given to you later, for your own thoughts on the subject and for notes about the information, as you study for tests later. An alternative is to use a spiral notebook (or similar style) and use the right hand page for notes and the left hand page for comments, etc. Or, use a loose leaf binder so you can sort your notes and add handouts. There are many ways to organize your notes.

3) **Sit up front!** This will help you concentrate (particularly in subjects that you do not find fascinating). You will also appear interested and excited to the professor; never a bad thing!

4) **Read and prepare for class IN ADVANCE!** It will be much easier to discern the important points in a lecture if you are already familiar with the material. You will also be able to answer questions asked in class. Plus, repetition is an excellent way to remember material. It also helps to review your notes from previous classes prior to each session. This will help you at exam time, and help you to reconnect with the material and see links among topics.

5) **Arrive early and stay for the whole class.** The first sentence or two uttered by the professor often tell you what the lecture will be about; the lecture will make less sense without the context. Also a large amount of information is often given out in the last ten minutes of class as a professor strives to cover the material. If you are putting your stuff away and zipping your book bag, not only are you being rude and making obnoxious levels of noise, but you are missing important material.

6) **LISTEN closely to the lecture or discussion.** In particular try to pick out the following:

> •ideas and concepts
> •signal words: " in contrast," "on the other hand," "What I mean here is," "The important idea is," and so on.
> •If something is unclear, ask a question!

7) **Take Notes, not Dictation!** Your job is not to take down every word but to summarize the points and note the facts. Use indentation, underlining, highlighting, and/or outlining to get the important information down.

> •Be brief, get main ideas down
> •Use your own words
> •Use symbols to emphasize important points, such as * or !
> •Leave spaces for words and ideas you missed or that are covered out of sequence

8) **You should always write down:**

> •names
> •dates and significant events
> •concepts, ideas, or phrases that are repeated
> •formulas, charts, drawings, etc. put on the board
> •examples given by the professor
> •professor's biases, if identifiable

9) **Find a way to make the subject interesting!** You won't remember what you consider boring and useless. You can make anything interesting with a positive attitude and a little creativity.

10) **Do not abbreviate unless** you will know later what the abbreviation stands for. Writing SC throughout your notes could mean social contract, Supreme Court, or Stanley Carpenter. Be consistent, whatever you choose. Standard abbreviations that might save you time include the following:

w/	=	with	Const	=	Constitution
w/o	=	without	dem	=	democracy
#	=	number	K	=	contract
vs	=	versus	pres	=	president
=	=	equals	nat'l	=	national
fed'l	=	federal			

11) **Review early and often!** I read my lectures notes before each session of class. Many people recommend you review them immediately after class, while the information is still fresh, so you can correct mistakes and spell out problematic abbreviations, etc. -- a good idea. Add to your notes. Jot down ideas you have had since class, how the information in chapter 2 relates to that of chapter 7, compare your notes from class with your reading notes and integrate them. I always found it helpful to outline my notes and keep a list of definitions as I went. Both made studying for tests easier.

READING

Yes, you are in college, so you know how to read. But how do you attack and comprehend boring or difficult material? Many students simply "get through" the reading assignment and then cannot answer questions in class and do not really understand the material. In order to read critically and analytically, you must be careful, thoughtful, and have a plan of attack before you dive in.

I strongly recommend that you do NOT use a highlighter. At least not in the way I see most students using them. They color huge passages thoughtlessly as they read. This is not helpful in the long run. I recommend a style of **active reading** that takes more time initially, but in the long run will save you time, because you will understand the material better, remember it longer, and be able to analyze what you have read.

Rules of Reading

- **Skim the chapter, book, or article first before you try to read it.** This provides you with a road map to the contents of the piece.

- **Use the guides provided by the author and publisher.** Tables of contents, appendices, tables of charts and graphs, glossaries, indices, etc., are there for you to use. They should help you get a handle on the material.

    - **Scan the table of contents.** Often textbooks provide more than one table of contents -- an abbreviated one and a complete one.
    - **Read the preface!!** In the preface, the author (or some other expert) tells you what they want you to get out of their book or why they wrote it.
    - **Use the end pieces:** appendices, indices, glossaries, etc.

- **Decide what you think you will learn from the work.** Think about what you are about to read. What questions do you have? Do you think the author has a bias? If so, what bias and why do you think there is one? Why did the professor assign this reading? What does he/she expect you to get out of it? Here, it is often helpful to look at your syllabus; the topic may give you some understanding of why this piece was assigned.

- **Read the piece fairly quickly** to get more information about main ideas and intent. Mark any passages that look particularly difficult. Circle unfamiliar words and phrases.

- **Now you are ready to really read the piece.**

    - **Take a notebook and a pen** and keep notes as you read. I outline on paper and use marginal notes in the book to argue with (or sometimes agree with) the author.

- I never read for more than an hour or two without a break, and if my eyes glaze or I start to fall asleep, I stop and **take a break**. (This means you cannot do your reading immediately prior to class -- you need to plan ahead.)
- At the end of each section or subsection, **stop and ask yourself what you just read.** Does it make sense? What were the main ideas? Any definitions you may need to know on a test? If you can't answer those questions, you need to reread the passages with more concentration.
- At the end of the whole piece, you should be able to **identify the author's main points**. If not, you need to reread the piece or, if you took good reading notes, reviewing your notes should be sufficient.

- Most texts offer **summaries and questions** at the end of a chapter or in a study guide such as this one. Use them to ensure your understanding of the material. You should be able to answer the questions posed and be able to flesh out the information provided in a summary. If not, again that is a signal that you need to review the material again.

- The best way for me to know that I have mastered the material is to try to explain it to someone else. Think of this as a self-test. Discuss the material with your classmates, tell your roommate or spouse about it, or make your folks listen to your summaries.

Taking Tests

ALWAYS

- **Read or go over the entire test** before beginning to answer questions. You could read the whole essay exam, but I do not mean for you to read an entire 10 page multiple choice exam. But you should go over it so you know what to expect. If it is a multi-page exam and is mostly multiple choice but has an essay buried at the end, you're in trouble if you find that out 5 minutes before the end of class!

- **Make choices** if they are offered.

- **Allot your time** carefully and **be aware of time during the** test, but PLEASE do not set watch alarms; they will disturb others. If a question is worth 20%, you should spend only 20% of your time on it.

- Depending on your style and level of test anxiety, **choose the order** in which you will address the questions. Answer the easiest question first if you need a confidence builder, or answer the most difficult if you need to get it out of the way while you are fresh.

- **Be neat and legible.**

- **Ask questions** if you are unclear about content or procedure.

- Save time to **proofread and double check** your answers at the end.

HINTS for Essay Exams

1) **TIME**

The most challenging part of taking essay exams is often the management of time during the exam. This is extremely important, especially for those of you who often have trouble finishing an exam. Exams are more than just tests of knowledge. They teach and reinforce important lessons about discipline, organization, and your ability to communicate what you know. Exams place a premium on your ability to make up your mind about issues and concepts, as well as to organize your thoughts and write <u>concisely</u> and <u>lucidly</u> (clearly) about topics within a given time period.

Hint 1: Start with the questions that are ***worth the most points***. Then if you run out of time, you can quickly jot down identifications and short answers. You cannot write an essay in 5 minutes!

Hint 2: ***Organize and think before you start to write***, preferably before you come to class to take the exam. You should study by thinking of possible questions so that you are half-way there while still studying. This will save you time during the exam period.

2) **CLARITY**

Clarity is essential to earning a good grade on an essay. It is not enough to simply jot down all of the facts you have studied. You must address the question as asked. For example, if the question says to address the impact of the Anti-Federalists on the U.S. government, do not include a discussion of Congressional committees.

A competent exam answer will be clear and well organized. You must have a point or an argument, as well as convey the facts.

Hint 3: Be sure you *know what the question means* before you start writing!
Hint 4: Use an outline to *organize* your thoughts before writing.
Hint 5: Pay attention to *keywords* within the question and use them to understand the question and formulate the answer. For example:
    Analyze
    Compare and contrast
    Discuss
Hint 6: Keep your *focus;* do not wander off the subject.
Hint 7: Read and respond to *all parts* of the question. Often students neglect to answer part of a question.

3) **LANGUAGE**

A good exam must be legible and readable in terms of grammar, etc. If your grammar and syntax are too convoluted, your meaning will be hopelessly obscured.

Hint 8: Do not use words you can not define, and be sure to define all concepts you use. For example, if the question asks you to discuss the nature of federalism, ALWAYS begin with a definition and discussion of what that word means.
Hint 9: Keep your sentences simple and your ideas will come through more clearly.
Hint 10: Avoid symbols and abbreviations. The professor may not be able to decipher them.
Hint 11: Do not use slang or colloquialisms. Do not write as you speak. An essay or essay exam is a formal means of conveying information.
Hint 12: Organize! Use paragraphs and essay format to make your essay clear and understandable. Start at the beginning and end at the end; do not jump around. If you are confused, your answer will be confused, and your grade will reflect that confusion!

4) **CONTENT**

The single most important part of any exam is the content. You must have facts, theories, and a basic understanding of the material to do well.

Hint 13: Always choose to answer the questions you know best if a choice is given on an exam. Do not just answer the questions in order!
Hint 14: <u>Be specific and precise</u>. For example, if you are asked to identify Bill Clinton, do not simply say he is President of the U.S. There have been many of those. What did he do that was important? Why do we study him? When did he serve and how well did he govern? What is he famous for?
Hint 15: Be concise but not too concise. In other words, clarity and brevity are good, but do not overdo it and leave out important information.
Hint 16: <u>Do not assume</u> that the professor knows anything! This is your opportunity to demonstrate that YOU know it. Too often students tell me, "Well, I didn't include that because you already know that." You need to show me YOU know it.

Hints for Objective Tests

1) **Reconnoiter the test**. Briefly look over the entire test. Read the directions carefully. How long is it? Are there sections worth different amounts of points? Plan your strategy and allot your time.

2) **Read each item carefully.** Don't lose points because you didn't notice a "not" or an "except" in the question. Always read every possibility. Even if (a) seems to be the most logical response, it may not be.

3) **Answer only the questions you know cold on your first run through**. This will help you warm up and may jar your memory on tougher questions. It will also reduce your test anxiety and build your confidence.

4) **Do not read too much into or out-think the question.** Most professors are not trying to trick you; we simply want to find out how much you have learned.

5) **Answer every question** unless there is a severe penalty for guessing. And when guessing, use some common sense. Things are rarely "always" or "never". If you can choose only one answer and two are virtually identical, you can probably rule out those two.

6) Always proofread and check your work. But **be careful about changing your first response** unless you are absolutely sure. First instincts are often correct.

"THE TEN TRAPS OF STUDYING"

reproduced with the permission of the Counseling and Psychological Services of the University of North Carolina, Chapel Hill

1. "I Don't Know Where To Begin"

Take Control. Make a list of all the things you have to do. Break your workload down into manageable chunks. Prioritize! Schedule your time realistically. Don't skip classes near an exam -- you may miss a review session. Use that hour in between classes to review notes. Interrupt study time with planned study breaks. Begin studying early, with an hour or two per day, and slowly build as the exam approaches.

2. "I've Got So Much To Study…And So Little Time"

Preview. Survey your syllabus, reading material, and notes. Identify the most important topics emphasized and areas still not understood. Previewing saves time, especially with non-fiction reading, by helping you organize and focus on the main topics. Adapt this method to your own style and study material, but remember, previewing is not an effective substitute for reading.

3. "This Stuff Is So Dry, I Can't Even Stay Awake Reading It"

Attack! Get actively involved with the text as you read. Ask yourself, "What is important to remember about this section?" Take notes or underline key concepts. Discuss the material with others in your class. Study together. Stay on the offensive, especially with material that you don't find interesting, rather than reading passively and missing important points.

4. "I Read It. I Understand It. But I Just Can't Get It To Sink In"

- Elaborate. We remember best the things that are most meaningful to us. As you are reading, try to elaborate upon new information with your own examples. Try to integrate what you're studying with what you already know. You will be able to remember new material better if you can link it to something that's already meaningful to you. Some techniques include:

- Chunking: An effective way to simplify and make information more meaningful. For example, if you wanted to remember the colors in the visible spectrum (Red, Orange, Yellow, Green, Blue, Indigo, Violet), you would have to memorize seven "chunks" of information in order. But when you take the first letter of each color and spell the name "Roy G. Biv", you reduce the information to three "chunks"

- Mnemonics: Any memory-assisting technique that helps us to associate new information with something familiar. For example, to remember a formula or equation, we may use letters of the alphabet to represent certain numbers. Then we can change an abstract formula into a more meaningful word or phrase, so we'll be able to remember it better. Sound-alike associations can be very effective, too, especially while trying to learn a new language. The key is to create your own links, so you won't forget them.

5. "I Guess I Understand It"

Test yourself. Make up questions about key sections in notes or reading. Keep in mind what the professor has stressed in the course. Examine the relationships between concepts and sections. Often, simply by changing section headings you can generate many effective questions. For example, a section entitled "Bystander Apathy" might be changed into questions such as: "What is bystander apathy?" "What are the causes of bystander apathy?" and "What are some examples of bystander apathy?"

6. "There's Too Much To Remember"

Organize. Information is recalled better if it is represented in an organized framework that will make retrieval more systematic. There are many techniques that can help you organize new information, including:

Write chapter outlines or summaries; emphasize relationships between sections. Group information into categories or hierarchies where possible.

Information Mapping. Draw up a matrix to organize and interrelate material. For example, if you were trying to understand the causes of World War I, you could make a chart listing all the major countries involved across the top, and then list the important issues and events down the side. Next, in the boxes in between, you could describe the impact each issue had on each country to help you understand these complex historical developments.

7. "I Knew It A Minute Ago"

Review. After reading a section, try to recall the information contained in it. Try answering the questions you made up for that section. If you cannot recall enough, re-read portions you had trouble remembering. The more time you spend studying, the more you tend to recall. Even after the point where information can be perfectly recalled, further study makes the material less likely to be forgotten entirely. In other words, you can't over-study. However, how you organize and integrate new information is still more important than how much time you spend studying.

8. "But I Like To Study In Bed"

Context. Recall is better when study contexts (physical location, as well as mental, emotional, and physical state) are similar to the test context. The greater the similarity between the study setting and the test setting, the greater the likelihood that material studied will be recalled during the test.

9. "Cramming Before A Test Helps Keep It Fresh In My Mind"

Spacing. Start studying now. Keep studying as you go along. Begin with an hour or two a day about one week before the exam, and then increase study time as the exam approaches. Recall increases as study time gets spread out over time.

10. "I'm Gonna Stay Up All Night 'til I Get This"

Avoid Mental Exhaustion. Take short breaks often when studying. Before a test, have a rested mind. When you take a study break, and just before you go to sleep at night, don't think about academics. Relax and unwind, mentally and physically. Otherwise, your break won't refresh you and you'll find yourself lying awake at night. It's more important than ever to take care of yourself before an exam! Eat well, sleep, and get enough exercise.

WEB SITES OF INTEREST

These are simply starting points. There are many free and quite a few commercial sites on the Internet devoted to learning, study skills, etc. A little surfing will yield many more. And remember, the more conscious you are about your coursework and studying, the better you are likely to do.

Some College and University Web Pages on Study Skills:

Middle Tennessee State University offers strategies for success in college from note-taking to memory and learning styles.
www.mtsu.edu/~studskl

The **University of North Carolina** web site offers "Study Habits and the Ten Traps of Studying" plus more on skills and success in college.
www.unc.edu

Southern Illinois University offers study help on-line as well as numerous links to other sites with similar goals.
www.siu.edu

Virginia Tech's Division of Student Affairs offers many tips for studying, reading, taking notes, etc.
www.ucc.vt.edu

SECTION II

This section of the study guide will help you study each chapter of the O'Connor text. Each chapter is broken down into several parts to help you understand and remember the material:

- **Chapter Goals and Learning Objectives**

- **Chapter Outlines and Key Points**

- **Research Ideas and Possible Paper Topics**

- **Websites**

- **Practice Tests**
    - **Multiple Choice**
    - **True/False**
    - **Compare and Contrast**
    - **Essay and Short Answer Questions**

CHAPTER 1
THE POLITICAL LANDSCAPE

Chapter Goals and Learning Objectives

One of the first things you might ask someone you have just met is, "Where are you from?" To better know someone and understand them more fully, it is important to learn something of their personal history. The same holds true of our government. The government we have didn't just plop down from the sky suddenly one day perfectly formed. It had its roots in the past. So, in order to understand the present, we must understand our history. Where did we come from? What were and are our goals? Why does our government look, act, and function the way that it does? Why *this* form of government and not some other form?

You may be one of the many students holding this book, looking at the first chapter at the start of the new semester with the thought, "I don't like politics and I'm not interested in government!" Stated bluntly, while you might not be interested in government, government is very interested in *you*. From the moment of your very conception until you die and every moment in between, the government is involved in all aspects of your life. When does life begin? Will abortion be legal or illegal? What kind of education will a child get? Will I be sent to a war in a far-off country? Is my sexual choice legal? Will terrorists strike my community and will my civil liberties be curtailed as a result? Will there be a decent job for me in the future? Will Social Security be there when I'm old? Should the terminally ill be euthanized upon request?

Who makes these decisions? Legislatures, courts, governors, presidents: The government. From the standpoint of self-interest alone, apathy is perhaps an unwise attitude to hold about government and politics.

In our country, the government is, essentially, made up of the people who understand it and take part in it. Can you make a difference? Can you protect yourself from the abuses of government? Can you improve your community? Do you have a role in politics and government? You cannot answer these questions unless you have an understanding of our government, its structure, and its foundations.

Equipped with such understandings, you can be better citizens and, in turn, make your life, your community, and your government better. This nation is changing, as it always has. Many Americans are not satisfied with the workings of government and many do not understand how the government works. A thorough understanding of the system, its history, and structure are essential to improving and reforming the system. Armed with this knowledge, you will be better informed and a more active participant in the political process.

This chapter is designed to give you an overview of the subject of the text as well as a look at the theories and ideas that underpin our political and economic system. The main topic headings of the chapter are:

- The Roots of American Government

- Characteristics of Democracy
- The Changing Political Culture and Characteristics of the American People
- Characteristics and Political Culture in America
- Political Culture and Views about Government

In each section, there are certain facts and ideas that you should strive to understand. Many are in boldface type and appear in both the narrative and in the glossary at the end of the book. Other ideas, dates, facts, events, people, etc., are more difficult to pull out of the narrative. (Keep in mind that studying for objective-[multiple choice, T/F] style tests is different than studying for essay tests. See the Study Guide section on test taking for hints on study skills.)

In general, after you finish reading and studying this chapter, you should understand the following:

- the philosophies that underpin our system of government
- the seven characteristics of democracy that define and influence our system of government
- who the American people are and how they are changing
- American political culture and our views about government
- How the American dream has changed as our ethnic and racial makeup have changed

Chapter Outline and Key Points

In this section, you are provided with a basic outline of the chapter and any key words/points you should know. Use this outline, in your own notebook, to develop a complete outline of the material. This will help you study and remember the material in preparation for your tests, assignments, and papers.

The Political Landscape

The Roots of American Government

Aristotle to the Enlightenment

natural law—

Thomas Aquinas--

Reformation--

Enlightenment--

Popular Consent

    social contract theory --

    Thomas Hobbes and *Leviathan* --

    John Locke and *Second Treatise on Civil Government*--

    life, liberty, and property--

Devising a National Government

    monarchy--

    oligarchy--

    aristocracy--

    democracy--

The Theory of Democratic Government

    direct democracy--

    indirect democracy--

    republic --

Why a Capitalist System?

    free market economy--

    Adam Smith--

    capitalism--

    mercantilism--

    laissez-faire economics--

Other Economic Systems

    socialism--

    Karl Marx--

communism--

totalitarianism--

Characteristics of American Democracy

Popular Consent--

Popular Sovereignty--

Majority Rule--

Individualism--

Equality--

Personal Liberty--

Civil Society--

The Changing Political Culture and Characteristics of the American People

political culture --

Changing Size and Population

from 4 million to 286 million people--

Changing Demographics

the "graying" of America--

Changes in Racial and Ethnic Composition--

Changes in Age Cohort Composition--

Changes in Family and Family Size--

Implications of These Changes

culture conflict--

Ideology of the American Public

political ideology--

conservatism--

liberalism--

libertarianism --

Problems with Political Labels

<u>Political Culture and Views of Government</u>

Drudge Report--

competition for news stories and pressure of journalists to be "the first"--

easier for press to focus on Clinton/Lewinsky than substantive news--

High Expectations

peoples' expectations of federal government in country's first 150 years--

A Missing Appreciation of the Good

Mistrust of Politicians

Voter Apathy

the "conversation of democracy"--

Ralph Nader--

<u>Redefining our Expectations</u>

politics--

Research Ideas and Possible Paper Topics

1) Further examine the Enlightenment and some of the political philosophers who developed concepts which the Founders incorporated into our system of government. What were some of the key ideas that formed the predicates for the government we have today?

2) Some people contend that America is not a democracy. Research this point of view and then debate the merits of both sides in essay form.

3) Discuss the nature of the challenges to America posed by the changing racial, ethnic, and age distribution in society. Look at historical precedents as well as more philosophical arguments. Has the meaning of the phrase "We the People" from the Preamble to the

United States Constitution changed from the meaning vested in that statement by the Founders?

4) Are Americans cynical about government and politics? Why or why not?

Websites

U.S. Census Bureau offers information on the demographic, geographic, and economic make-up of our country. Includes the ability to search for state-level data.
   www.census.gov/

GALILEO is a website developed by the University of Georgia that provides a one-stop academic research site for students. Its Demographics and Census Data page lists numerous links to sites to assist in researching political, racial, ethnic, social, and other demographic information.
   www.usg.edu/galileo/internet/census/demograp.html/

The **Gallup Organization** offers up-to-date and historical perspectives on the opinions of the American public.
   www.gallup.com

Louisiana State University's Political Philosophy Resources webpage provides links to a variety of websites for further study in the philosophy of politics and government. Similarly, **Brandeis University's** Political Philosophy Internet Resources webpage provides links to numerous sites of interest in political philosophy.
   www.artsci.lsu.eud/poli/theoryx.html
   http://people.brandeis.edu/~teuber/polphil.html

To better understand the Enlightenment, go to a marvelous website developed by a high school history teacher in Mesquite, Texas titled **TeacherOz.com**. The Enlightenment page lists scores of resources. (The TeacherOz.com website received a recommendation by The History Channel.)
   www.teacheroz.com/Enlightenment.htm

Yahoo.com. Yahoo is a commercial search engine that has a wide variety of information. For our purposes, there is a government subheading of Yahoo that will provide you with links to many topics on government, regime type, ideology, political thought, and more.
   www.yahoo.com/government

	Practice Tests

MULTIPLE CHOICE

1. The first to articulate the notion of natural law--the doctrine that human affairs should be governed by certain ethical principles--was

    a. Hobbes.
    b. Newton.
    c. Socrates.
    d. Aristotle.

2. The idea that men form governments largely to preserve life, liberty, and property comes from

    a. John Locke.
    b. Thomas Hobbes.
    c. Baron de Montesquieu.
    d. Jean Jacques Rousseau.

3. A form of government in which the right to participate is always conditioned on the possession of wealth, social status, military position, or achievement is called

    a. aristocracy.
    b. oligarchy.
    c. monarchy.
    d. democracy.

4. A system of government in which representatives of the people are chosen by ballot is called

    a. hegemonic democracy.
    b. tutellary democracy.
    c. indirect democracy.
    d. direct democracy.

5. A system that binds trade and its administration to the national government is called

    a. capitalism.
    b. mercantilism.
    c. socialism.
    d. republicanism.

21

6. The U.S. government took a much larger role in the economy due to the

    a. Progressive Era.
    b. administration of Herbert Hoover.
    c. populist movement.
    d. Great Depression.

7. The right of the majority to govern themselves is called

    a. popular sovereignty.
    b. popular consent.
    c. personal liberty.
    d. equality.

8. The attitudes that people have toward the political system and its parts, and attitudes toward the role of self in the system are often referred to as

    a. public opinion.
    b. norms.
    c. ideology.
    d. political culture.

9. For the first time, the U.S. population is getting

    a. younger.
    b. older.
    c. more female.
    d. more male.

10. Many parties in American history have opposed immigration as their primary plank. Among those parties were the

    a. Dixiecrats.
    b. Reform Party.
    c. Know Nothings.
    d. Libertarians.

11. An individual's coherent set of values and beliefs about the purpose and scope of government are called

    a. individualism.
    b. attitude.
    c. political culture.
    d. ideology.

12. One who favors a free market and no governmental interference in personal liberties is called a

    a. libertarian.
    b. conservative.
    c. liberal.
    d. mercantilist.

13. In the first 150 years of American history, the federal government

    a. expanded rapidly.
    b. had few responsibilities.
    c. was more powerful than the state governments.
    d. did not grow at all.

14. Many Americans say they don't vote because they

    a. have no time.
    b. have no real choice.
    c. are content.
    d. all of the above.

15. The process by which policy decisions are made is called

    a. representation.
    b. government.
    c. politics.
    d. science.

TRUE/FALSE

1. The Reformation altered the nature of government as people began to believe they could also have a say in their own governance.

2. John Locke argued that man's natural state was war and government was necessary to restrain man's bestial tendencies.

3. A republic is an economic system based on the market.

4. The American system tries to balance the ideals of majority rule and minority rights.

5. A single member of the House of Representatives represented 30,000 people in the 1790s and as many as 882,000 in 2000.

6. Since 1970, the number of female-headed households in the United States has decreased dramatically.

7. Liberals favor local and state action over federal action, and emphasize fiscal responsibility, most notably in the form of balanced budgets.

8. A libertarian is someone who favors the free market with no governmental interference in personal liberties.

9. Federal government programs proliferated in almost every area of American life due to the New Deal programs of Franklin Roosevelt in the 1930s in response to the Great Depression.

10. The Watergate scandal and resignation of President Richard Nixon in the 1970s led to stricter governmental ethics laws.

COMPARE AND CONTRAST

natural law and social contract theory

the theories of Thomas Hobbes and John Locke

monarchy, oligarchy, aristocracy, and democracy

direct democracy and indirect democracy

capitalism, mercantilism, socialism, communism, and totalitarianism

majority rule and minority rights

elite theory, interest group theory, bureaucratic theory, and pluralist theory

conservatism, libertarianism, and liberalism

ESSAY AND SHORT ANSWER QUESTIONS

1) The United States, following its operations to remove the Taliban from control of Afghanistan following the 9/11 attack, has made efforts to assist in the economic redevelopment of that country. The U.S. has also worked toward the development of a democratic government in that country. What success has been achieved toward that goal and what measures has the U.S. used to foster the institution of democracy in Afghanistan? What type of governmental system existed under the Taliban?

2) What is popular consent and what are its historical roots?

3) What impact has, and will, the Internet have on our democracy and system of government?

4) What is political culture in general and what is American political culture?

5) Discuss the roots of the American government. Discuss what philosophies guided the founders of our country as they created a new system of government.

6) What are some of the characteristics of democracy in the United States? Compare democracy in the U.S. to other democracies in the world.

7) In order to understand the nature of the American government, one must know who the American people are. Discuss the demographics of the United States and their effects on the political system.

8) Many Americans seem displeased with their government and politicians. Discuss if this is the case and why.

9) Discuss the changing nature of America. What does it mean to be an American, particularly in the post-9/11 world?

10) What expectations do you believe most Americans have of their government and its leaders? What expectations do you have toward your government and its leaders? Are those expectations realistic? What is the role of government in meeting the needs of the people of this country and do you believe it is meeting those functions?

ANSWERS TO STUDY EXERCISES

multiple choice answers

1.	d	p. 3
2.	a	p. 5
3.	b	p. 7
4.	c	p. 6
5.	b	p. 7
6.	d	p. 8
7.	a	p. 10
8.	d	p. 12
9.	b	p. 16
10.	c	p. 18
11.	d	p. 22
12.	a	p. 23
13.	b	p. 25
14.	d	p. 29
15.	c	p. 30

true/false answers

1.	T	p. 3
2.	F	p. 4
3.	F	p. 6
4.	T	p. 11
5.	T	p. 12
6.	F	p. 18
7.	F	p. 22
8.	T	p. 23
9.	T	p. 25
10.	T	p. 27

CHAPTER 2
THE CONSTITUTION

Chapter Goals and Learning Objectives

You don't build a house or a building without a foundation. The foundation buttresses the structure, gives it support and definition. You build your house directly atop the foundation. Anything not build on that foundation will surely fall.

The foundation of our system of government is the Constitution. Our nation and its laws are built on it. The U.S. Constitution is one of the longest lasting and least amended constitutions in the world. It has endured despite changing demographics, changing technology, and changing ideas. The problems encountered and compromises made by the Framers continue to affect our nation and our political process. Yet the structure created and supported by our Constitution still stands. It is important to understand why. So, an understanding of the Constitutional era is essential to understanding our political system.

This chapter is designed to give you a basic understanding of the colonial era and the events that led to the writing of the Declaration of Independence, the main grievances of the colonists against the Crown and Parliament, the first American government under the Articles of Confederation, the writing of the Constitution, the nature of the U.S. Constitution, and the ratification debate.

The main topic headings of the chapter are:

- The Origins of a New Nation
- The Declaration of Independence
- The Articles of Confederation
- Drafting a New Constitution
- The U.S. Constitution
- The Drive for Ratification
- Formal Methods of Amending the Constitution
- Informal Methods of Amending the Constitution

In each section, there are certain facts and ideas that you should strive to understand. Many are in boldface type and appear in both the narrative and in the glossary at the end of the book. Other ideas, dates, facts, events, people, etc., are more difficult to pull out of the narrative. (Keep in mind that studying for objective-[multiple choice, T/F] style tests is different than studying for essay tests. See the Study Guide section on test taking for hints on study skills.)

In general, after you finish reading and studying this chapter, you should understand the following:

- why colonists came to the New World
- the nature of the American colonies under British rule and how they changed from the 1600s to the mid-1700s
- the break with Great Britain and the circumstances surrounding the eruption of the Revolutionary War
- the Declaration of Independence and its philosophical underpinnings
- the first American government under the Articles of Confederation and the failings of that document
- the Constitutional Convention--who was there, what they did, why they did it
- the U.S. Constitution. What does it say?
- the controversy over ratification, the ratification debates--Federalists and Anti-Federalists
- the process for amending the Constitution, including the first ten amendments or Bill of Rights
- constitutional change through judicial interpretation and cultural/technological change

Chapter Outline and Key Points

In this section, you are provided with a basic outline of the chapter and any key words/points you should know. Use this outline, in your own notebook, to develop a complete outline of the material. This will help you study and remember the material in preparation for your tests, assignments, and papers.

The Origins of a New Nation

Trade and Taxation

French and Indian War --

mercantilism--

Stamp Act--

Samuel Adams--

Sons of Liberty--

First Steps Toward Independence

Stamp Act Congress--

Committees of Correspondence--

Tea Act--

Coercive Acts (Intolerable Acts)--

The First Continental Congress

First Continental Congress—

The Second Continental Congress

Second Continental Congress--

Common Sense--

The Declaration of Independence

confederation--

Declaration of Independence--

Thomas Jefferson

A Theoretical Basis for a New Government

John Locke--

social contract theory--

The First Attempts at Government: Articles of Confederation

confederation--

Articles of Confederation--

    Key provisions of the Articles of Confederation--
    1)
    2)
    3)
    4)
    5)

Problems Under the Articles of Confederation--
1)
2)
3)

4)
5)
6)
7)
8)
9)

Shays's Rebellion--

Miracle at Philadelphia: Writing a Constitution

Constitutional Convention of 1787--

The Framers

"Founding Fathers"--

Charles Beard's *An Economic Interpretation of the Constitution*--

The Virginia and New Jersey Plans

Virginia Plan--

New Jersey Plan--

Constitutional Compromises

Great Compromise--

Three-Fifths Compromise--

Unfinished Business

Committee on Unfinished Portions--

Executive--

Electoral College--

Federalist No. 68--

removal of the chief executive--

The U.S. Constitution

The Preamble--

"We the People"--

Basic Principles

    Federalism--

        James Madison--

        the Federal System--

    Separation of Powers (and 3 key features)--

    Checks and Balances--

The Articles of the Constitution

    Article I: The Executive Branch

        enumerated powers--

        necessary and proper clause (elastic clause)--

        implied powers --

    Article II: The Executive Branch

        President--

        State of the Union Address--

    Article III: The Judicial Branch

        Supreme Court

        appointments for life--

        good behavior--

    Articles IV through VII--

        Full Faith and Credit Clause--

        Defense of Marriage Act--

        Supremacy Clause--

        No Religious Test for Public Office--

The Drive for Ratification

Federalists--

Anti-Federalists--

The Federalist Papers --

Formal Methods of Amending the Constitution

Madison Amendment--

Bill of Rights (Why added? When? What major provisions?)--

The Amendment Process

Article V--

two-stage amendment process--

two methods of proposal--

ratification--

ERA--

reaction to *Texas v. Johnson*--

Informal Methods of Amending the Constitution

Judicial Interpretation

Marbury v. Madison--

Social, Cultural and Legal Changes

Great Depression and the New Deal

Research Ideas and Possible Paper Topics

1) Read the Articles of Confederation and pose an argument that they were not flawed and should have been maintained as the American form of government. Examine some of the arguments by conservatives and those who propose a further downsizing of the federal government and the return of many now federal powers back to the states. How do these arguments compare to the Articles of Confederation?

2) Research the historical and political importance of the Federalist Papers with regard to the interpretation of the Constitution. Do the Federalist Papers provide a complete and sound explanation of the Framers' thinking in writing the Constitution or are the Federalist Papers a polemic written to sell the new constitution to a skeptical public?

3) The text gives a few examples of how the Constitution has changed due to interpretations by the judiciary and others. Think about other ways in which the Constitution has changed or will soon change and write a paper.

Websites

Official government site with full text of Constitution.
www.house.gov/house/constitution/constitution.html

Cornell University site offers the complete text of the Constitution. Many terms are hyperlinked and cross-referenced to other key issues.
www.law.cornell.edu/constitution/constitution.table.html

The U.S. Constitution OnLine offers many documents, including the Articles of Confederation, Declaration of Independence, the Constitution, and many other links.
www.usconstitution.net

Kingwood College Library offers links to constitutions of the world.
www.nhmccd.cc.tx.us/contracts/lrc/kc/constitutions-subject.html

Search and download the text of the **Federalist Papers** from **Thomas**, the Internet research and information website of Congress.
http://memory.loc.gov/const/fed/fedpapers.html

PBS.org has an impressive database on American history, including information on the Founding Fathers, the early national period, the Constitution, etc.
www.pbs.org/history/american.html

The **Manuscript Division of the Library of Congress** offers a wide variety of documents from the 15th to 20th centuries on American history.
lcweb2.loc.gov/ammem/mcchtml/corhome.html

National Museum of American History offers timelines, virtual exhibits, music, and other information from American history.
www.americanhistory.si.edu/

Practice Tests

MULTIPLE CHOICE

1. Colonists came to the New World for a variety of reasons, including

    a. to escape religious persecution.
    b. to acquire land.
    c. to be more independent of government.
    d. all of the above.

2. The first official meeting of the colonies and the first step toward a unified nation was/were the

    a. Stamp Act Congress.
    b. First Continental Congress.
    c. Committees of Correspondence.
    d. Colonial Parliament.

3. The type of government in which the national government derives its powers from subsidiary units is called

    a. shared sovereignty.
    b. unitary government.
    c. confederacy.
    d. federalism.

4. The Articles of Confederation failed due to a number of weaknesses, including that the national government was not allowed to

    a. coin money.
    b. tax its citizens or the states.
    c. pass laws.
    d. all of the above.

5. A Constitutional Convention was held in Philadelphia in 1787. Every state except participated.

    a. Rhode Island
    b. Maine
    c. Vermont
    d. Georgia

6. The proposal that called for a bicameral legislature at the Constitutional Convention was called the

   a. New Jersey Plan.
   b. Virginia Plan.
   c. New York Plan.
   d. Connecticut Plan.

7. In general, at the Constitutional Convention, most of the small states felt comfortable with

   a. a stronger central government to deal with the crisis at hand.
   b. three branches of government.
   c. a bicameral legislature.
   d. the Articles of Confederation.

8. Reflecting the attitude of many of the Framers of the Constitution, including Alexander Hamilton, the election of the president of the United States would be removed from the hands of the "masses" through the creation of

   a. a bicameral legislature.
   b. the Senate, which would be elected by the states' legislatures.
   c. the Committee on Unfinished Portions.
   d. the electoral college.

9. The phrase included by the Framers in the Preamble to the Constitution, "in order to form a more perfect union," reflects the concerns, which were corrected by the new Constitution, the Framers had with the

   a. Declaration of Independence.
   b. New Jersey Plan.
   c. Federalist Papers.
   d. Articles of Confederation.

10. The powers vested in Congress by the Framers to govern the nation are enumerated in

    a. Article I, Section 8.
    b. the Preamble to the Constitution.
    c. Article II.
    d. the Supremacy Clause of Article VI.

11. Over the course of the nation's history under the Constitution, Congress has often coupled the "necessary and proper" clause with a particular enumerated power in order to dramatically expand its authority (e.g., to regulate airlines and railroads, which did not exist when the Constitution was written, and thus, any power to regulate them would be implied). Which of the following is an enumerated power?

    a. to levy taxes
    b. to regulate commerce
    c. to coin money
    d. to control immigration

12. Article III establishes

    a. the power of judicial review.
    b. the Supreme Court.
    c. all federal courts.
    d. the state and national judicial system.

13. Article VI creates the supremacy and also requires

    a. that the federal government create no ex post facto laws.
    b. all states to honor the laws and official acts of the other states.
    c. that states may not coin money.
    d. that no religious test for public office be required for holding any public office.

14. In general, the Anti-Federalists

    a. feared the power of a strong central government.
    b. argued that a president would be become far too powerful.
    c. feared the powerful new national government would usurp the individual rights and liberties of the citizens of the states.
    d. all of the above

15. An example of constitutional modification, without amendment, through social change occurred during the Great Depression with the adoption by Congress and approval by the Supreme Court of

    a. the New Deal programs.
    b. the doctrine of judicial review.
    c. the Supremacy Clause.
    d. the declaration of war against Japan.

TRUE/FALSE

1. Thomas Paine's *Common Sense* was instrumental in arousing colonists' support for the new Constitution.

2. The Articles of Confederation worked fairly well throughout the Revolutionary War.

3. The phrase "we the people" is found prominently in the Declaration of Independence.

4. The political philosopher John Locke heavily influenced the Framers of the Constitution through his writings, which advocated a separation of powers and a system of checks and balances.

5. Article I, section 8 enumerates the powers of the president to direct and manage the government of the United States.

6. The Constitution establishes the federal district court system in Article III.

7. The Bill of Rights was added to the Constitution in part as a way to garner support for the ratification of the Constitution from the Anti-Federalists.

8. *The Federalist Papers* were designed to explain the new Constitution and encourage people to favor ratification.

9. The Twenty-Seventh Amendment gives young people, aged eighteen to twenty-one, the right to vote.

10. The Constitution can only be changed through a formal amendment process.

COMPARE AND CONTRAST

Stamp Act Congress and Committees of Correspondence

the First Continental Congress and the Second Continental Congress

federation and confederation

Articles of Confederation and the U.S. Constitution

Virginia Plan, New Jersey Plan, and the Great Compromise

the three main compromises at the Constitutional Convention: the nature of the legislature, the executive branch, and representation

separation of powers and federalism

separation of powers and checks and balances

the Supremacy Clause and the Tenth Amendment

Federalists and Anti-Federalists

methods of amending the Constitution

formal and informal techniques for amending the Constitution

ESSAY AND SHORT ANSWER QUESTIONS

1) Discuss three events that led up to the Declaration of Independence.

2) What impact did the publication of *Common Sense* have on the revolutionary process?

3) What type of government did the Articles of Confederation set up and what powers did each institution of government have?

4) How was slavery treated in the Constitution? Why was it treated in this way?

5) What powers did the U.S. Constitution allocate to the executive branch and why?

6) Discuss the route that the American colonies took toward independence.

7) Explain the Articles of Confederation, its successes, and the problems that led to its abandonment and the Constitutional Convention.

8) Explain the "Miracle at Philadelphia" and the compromises that had to be made in order to adopt the Constitution.

9) Discuss the controversies over the ratification of the Constitution.

10) Fully explain the basic principles of the Constitution.

ANSWERS TO STUDY EXERCISES

multiple choice answers

1. d p. 36
2. a p. 38
3. c p. 40
4. b p. 42
5. a p. 44
6. b p. 45
7. d p. 47
8. d p. 48
9. d p. 49
10. a p. 52
11. b p. 53
12. b p. 54

13. d p. 54
14. d p. 56
15. a p. 64

true/false answers

1. F p. 40
2. T p. 42
3. F p. 49
4. F p. 50
5. T p. 52
6. F p. 54
7. T p. 58
8. T p. 56
9. F p. 61
10. F p. 65

CHAPTER 3
FEDERALISM

Chapter Goals and Learning Objectives

The Founders inherently distrusted a strong, central government and its powers, understandably, given the problems the colonies had with the King of England. When framing their own government, they reasoned it necessary to divide power as much as possible to prevent tyranny. They accomplished this horizontally with separation of powers and checks and balances, the three branches of government divided and sharing powers under this system. They accomplished this vertically through federalism, a system in which the national government and the states share powers. Because of these two basic divisions of power, according to James Madison in the *Federalist* #51, "a double security arises to the rights of the people." The Founders concluded that the national government needed more power than it was allotted under the Articles of Confederation, but the Framers never intended to gut the powers of the states. Instead, they intended to divide powers so that no one branch or level of government got too powerful. The rest of U.S. history and politics has included battles over the way in which the Constitution divvies up these powers, what the vaguely worded passages mean, and the constantly shifting relationship between the national and state governments. From the ratification of the Tenth Amendment to *McCulloch v. Maryland*, the Civil War to the New Deal, the Reagan Revolution to the Contract with America, all the way to the expansion of the federal government to deal with terrorism, the tug of war between the federal government and the states continues unabated.

This chapter is designed to introduce you to our system of federalism. The main topic headings of the chapter are:

- The Roots of the Federal System
- The Powers of Government in the Federal System
- The Evolution and Development of Federalism
- Federalism and the Supreme Court

In each section, there are certain facts and ideas that you should strive to understand. Many are in boldface type and appear in both the narrative and in the glossary at the end of the book. Other ideas, dates, facts, events, people, etc., are more difficult to pull out of the narrative. (Keep in mind that studying for objective-[multiple choice, T/F] style tests is different than studying for essay tests. See the Study Guide section on test taking for hints on study skills.)

In general, after you finish reading and studying this chapter, you should understand the following:

- the definition of federalism and why it divides powers between one national and several state governments
- how the federal system was created by the Framers
- the allocation of the powers of government
- the evolution and development of federalism

- the changing nature of federalism and how the Supreme Court plays a major role in those changes

Chapter Outline and Key Points

In this section, you are provided with a basic outline of the chapter and any key words/points you should know. Use this outline, in your own notebook, to develop a complete outline of the material. This will help you study and remember the material in preparation for your tests, assignments, and papers.

The Roots of the Federal System

federalism--

Federalist No. 51--

supremacy clause--

The Powers of Government in the Federal System

Article I, section 8--

enumerated powers--

necessary and proper clause--

implied power--

reserve or police powers--

national powers (Fig. 3.3)--

concurrent powers--

state powers (Fig. 3.3)--

Denied Powers

bill of attainder--

ex post facto law--

Guarantees to the States

privileges and immunities clause--

Relations among the States

    full faith and credit clause--

    final authority to decide controversies between states--

    interstate compacts--

    Emergency Management Assistance Compact--

The Evolution and Development of Federalism

    McCulloch v. Maryland (1819)--

    Gibbons v. Ogden (1824)--

Dual Federalism--

    Dred Scott v. Sandford (1857)--

The Civil War and Beyond

    Plessy v. Ferguson (1896)--

    Civil War Amendments--

The Sixteenth and Seventeenth Amendments

    Sixteenth Amendment--

    Seventeenth Amendment--

Cooperative Federalism

    The New Deal--

    FDR's Court-packing plan--

The Changing Nature of Federalism

    layer cake analogy--

    marble cake analogy

cooperative federalism--

Federal Grants--

categorical grants--

Creative Federalism--

LBJ's Great Society programs--

Reagan Revolution

New Federalism--

block grants--

changed nature of state politics due to Reagan--

intergovernmental lobbies --

The Devolution Revolution

Preemption--

Contract with America--

devolution revolution--

mandates --

Unfunded Mandates--

<u>Federalism and the Supreme Court</u>

Education

Morrill Land Grant Act of 1862--

Brown v. Board of Education (1954)--

commerce clause --

Garcia v. San Antonio Metropolitan Transit Authority (1985)--

The Devolution Revolution and the Court

U.S. v. Lopez (1995)

sovereign immunity --

Boerne v. Flores (1997) --

Printz v. U.S. (1997) --

Bush v. Gore (2000) --

Research Ideas and Possible Paper Topics

1) Read the *Federalist Papers* on the topic of federalism. Note down the important features of federalism and its intent. Next, do some research on federalism today. How well does what you see today conform to the "intent of the Founding Fathers"? In a paper, discuss your conclusions and why you think federalism today is similar to or different than what was envisioned in 1787.

2) Using the library or the Internet, find information on another federal system and compare the division of powers they use to the one that we use. What can such a comparison tell us about our system of government?

3) What do you think are the most important federal issues today and why? Some possibilities include "full faith and credit"--particularly regarding same-sex marriages and tinted windows in cars--the use of the "commerce clause," reproductive rights, term limits, child support issues, and many others.

4) Consider this idea and be prepared to argue in favor or against:
"Federalism, the separation of powers, and checks and balances are all institutional arrangements designed to make government move in a slow and cumbersome manner--in other words, the gridlock we often complain about is intentional--so that the government cannot infringe on our rights and liberties. If we had an efficient government, our liberties would be greatly reduced."

Websites

National Council of State Legislators site offers analyses and information on intergovernmental relations.
    www.ncsl.org/statefed/afipolcy.htm

NGA On-Line. The **National Governors' Council is** a non-partisan organization that looks at solving state-focused problems and provides information on state innovations and practices. The website has stories and articles of interest on the states and provides links to similar issues and organizations.
    www.nga.org/nga/1,1169,,00.html

Center for the Study of Federalism at Temple University. The Center publishes *Publius: The Journal of Federalism* and *The Federalism Report* and the website offers a variety of links as well.
    www.temple.edu/federalism/

Publius: The Journal of Federalism. *Publius,* published by Lafayette College, offers academic articles on federal issues in the U.S. and abroad. They do periodic special issues on the state of federalism in the U.S.
    ww2.lafayette.edu/~publius/

The General Services Administration gives you the ability to search for information on hundreds of federal grants.
    www.gsa.gov

Project Vote-Smart has a site on federalism/states' rights.
    www.vote-smart.org/issues/FEDERALISM_STATES_RIGHTS/

The Brookings Institution, a moderate-to-liberal think-tank in Washington, has a policy brief on federalism titled: "The Devolution Revolution: Why Congress Is Shifting a Lot of Power to the Wrong Levels."
    www.brook.edu/comm/policybriefs/pb003/pb3.htm

American Enterprise Institute, a conservative think-tank, conducts the Federalism Project, which "explores opportunities to restore real federalism--that is, a federalism that limits the national government's power and competes for their citizens' assets, talents, and business."
    www.federalismproject.org/masterpages/about%20us/inded.html

The Urban Institute, a "nonprofit policy research organization established in Washington D.C. in 1968" has prepared a number of articles and reports relating to federalism.
    www.urban.org/content/Research/NewFederalism/AboutANF/AboutANF.htm

The Constitution Society provides access to the text of the Federalist papers as well as links to other sites relating to states' rights.
   www.constitution.org/cs_feder.htm

Eurplace.org is a site which includes documents and articles about federalism from a European perspective.
   www.eurplace.org/federal

The Nelson A. Rockefeller Institute of Government at the State University of New York conducts research on the role of state and local government in American federalism and on the management and finances of states and localities.
   www.rockinst.org

This site from **Infidels.org** contains links to articles and organizations with information on federalism.
   www.infidels.org/~nap/index.federalism.html

Practice Tests

MULTIPLE CHOICE

1. Three arguments articulated by the Federalists in support of the new Constitution and its concept of federalism were: (1) the prevention of tyranny, (2) provision for increased political participation, and (3) the

   a. creation of a unitary system.
   b. prevention of speculative experimentation by the states.
   c. guarantee of the protection of personal liberties by the national government.
   d. use of the states as testing grounds or "laboratories" for new programs and policies.

2. When is the supremacy clause applicable?

   a. when a state and national law concur
   b. when a state law exists where no national law exists
   c. when state and national law conflict
   d. when national law exists and no similar state law exists

3. The Sixteenth Amendment to the Constitution, adopted in 1913, gave what power to the national government that had not existed under the original Constitution?

    a. the power to levy taxes
    b. the power to borrow money
    c. the power to tax personal income
    d. the power to regulate intrastate commerce

4. A power that is not stated explicitly in the Constitution but is considered to reasonably flow from a power stated in Article I, Section 8, is called a(n)

    a. derivative power.
    b. implied power.
    c. enumerated power.
    d. concurrent power.

5. The guarantee of states rights' was provided in the Constitution by

    a. Article I, Section 8.
    b. the supremacy clause.
    c. the necessary and proper clause.
    d. the Tenth Amendment.

6. Article I denies certain powers to the state governments, including

    a. passing bills of attainder.
    b. entering into contracts.
    c. involvement in elections.
    d. the power to tax.

7. Article IV requires that states recognize judicial proceedings, records, and laws of other states. This is known as the _____ clause.

    a. commerce
    b. full faith and credit
    c. contract
    d. necessary and proper

8. The first major decision of the Marshall Court (in 1819) to define the federal relationship between the national government and the states (by upholding the necessary and proper clause and the supremacy clause) was

    a. *Marbury v. Madison.*
    b. *Gibbons v. Ogden.*
    c. *McCulloch v. Maryland.*
    d. *Dred Scott v. Sandford.*

9. The Supreme Court ruled in 1824 that Congress had wide authority under the commerce clause to regulate interstate commerce, including commercial activity, in

   a. *Marshall v. New York.*
   b. *Gibbons v. Ogden.*
   c. *McCulloch v. Maryland.*
   d. *Fulton v. New Jersey.*

10. In 1937, the Supreme Court reversed its series of decisions against New Deal programs, afterward approving broad extensions of the use by Congress of the commerce clause to regulate and bolster the economy. The Supreme Court reversed its anti-New Deal trend as a result of

    a. the worsening of Great Depression conditions.
    b. the increased participation of city government in federal affairs.
    c. the imminent threat of war with Nazi Germany and Imperial Japan.
    d. the Roosevelt court-packing plan.

11. "Marble Cake" federalism is also known as _____ federalism.

    a. cooperative
    b. dual
    c. competitive
    d. mixed

12. A broad grant of monies given to states by the federal government for specified activities is called a _____ grant.

    a. creative
    b. categorical
    c. block
    d. federal

13. The practice of the federal government overriding state actions in some areas is called

    a. supremacy.
    b. preemption.
    c. confiscation.
    d. mandation.

14. The 1995 Supreme Court case, *U.S. v. Lopez* is significant because it was the first decision by the Court in many decades in which it

    a. restrained Congress's use of the commerce power and, thus, shifting power from the national government to the states.
    b. expanded Congress's use of the commerce clause in enhancing federal power.
    c. questioned the use of the power of judicial review by the Court.
    d. declared that federal preemption was unconstitutional.

15. The ruling in *Bush v. Gore* (2000) was surprising because

    a. it did not follow traditional liberal/conservative lines.
    b. the Court majority had never shown reluctance to intervene in state issues.
    c. it dealt with elections.
    d. the historically states' rights majority used federal law to justify their decision denying states' rights.

TRUE/FALSE

1. Some 87,000 state and local governments are bound by the provisions of the Constitution.

2. The Framers chose federalism to imitate the British centralized governmental system.

3. Federalism allocates powers among the national, state, county, and local governments.

4. The Supremacy Clause states that all powers not specifically granted in the Constitution are reserved to the states.

5. Police powers are those powers reserved to the states.

6. *McCulloch v. Maryland* was a Supreme Court case about the conflict between New Jersey and New York over their ability to grant a steamship monopoly on the Hudson River that was decided on the basis of the commerce clause.

7. The Supreme Court decision in the *Dred Scott* case contributed to the advent of the Civil War.

8. The Civil War forever changed the nature of federalism.

9. The first federal grant program came in the 1930s as a response to the Great Depression.

10. The current Supreme Court is opposed to federal excursions into the powers reserved to the states.

COMPARE AND CONTRAST

powers of the national government, concurrent powers, and powers of the state governments

enumerated, implied, and denied powers

supremacy clause and reserve (police) powers

dual federalism and cooperative federalism

layer cake and marble cake federalism

categorical and block grants

ESSAY AND SHORT ANSWER QUESTIONS

1) Why did the Framers choose federalism? (hint: remember to define federalism)

2) Discuss the nature and ramifications of the supremacy clause to intergovernmental relations between the states and the national government.

3) Explain the doctrine of implied powers.

4) What is the role of the states in our federal system? How is it dealt with in the Constitution? Is the question of states' rights settled now or is it ongoing?

5) Describe the nature of relations among the states.

6) Explain the distribution of power in the federal system.

7) Discuss how *McCulloch v. Maryland* and *Gibbons v. Ogden* contributed to the development of federalism. Be sure to include the facts and ruling in each case.

8) Discuss the various stages of federalism this country has gone through, from dual federalism to today. What does the evolution of federalism tell us about our system?

9) Explain the uses of preemption and unfunded mandates. How have these methods been used to alter the nature of federalism and what is their current status?

10) Explain the role of the U.S. Supreme Court in defining federalism.

ANSWERS TO STUDY EXERCISES

multiple choice answers

1. d   p. 73
2. c   p. 73
3. c   p. 73
4. b   p. 73
5. d   p. 74
6. a   p. 74
7. b   p. 75
8. c   p. 77
9. b   p. 77
10. d   p. 82
11. a   p. 83
12. c   p. 86
13. b   p. 87
14. a   p. 96
15. d   p. 99

true/false answers

1. T   p. 70
2. F   p. 70
3. F   p. 73
4. F   p. 73
5. T   p. 74
6. F   p. 77
7. T   p. 78
8. T   p. 78
9. F   p. 83
10. T   p. 98

CHAPTER 4
STATE AND LOCAL GOVERNMENT

Chapter Goals and Learning Objectives

Most of your day-to-day experiences with government are with local and state government. You bathed in water delivered to your home by your municipal government. You drove to school on state highways and city streets. You may attend a state university. You were stopped on the way home by a county sheriff or state trooper for speeding; all state and local government functions. Yet, the federal government may have provided funds to assist in many of these activities or have coinciding laws or regulations affecting your local and state governmental services.

The relationships between the various governments in our country are dynamic. The multiple levels allow citizens a variety of access points where they can get their voices heard; however, it also makes finding the appropriate place to make an argument a complex process that sometimes reduces a citizen's ability to effectively lobby government. Recent events have strengthened the hand of state governments in the federal bargain and the Supreme Court seems to be on a trend toward limiting the powers of the national government and enhancing those of the states. Therefore, it is becoming even more important to understand the nature of state and local governments.

This chapter is designed to introduce you to the nature and institutions of state and local governments. The main topic headings of the chapter are:

- The Evolution of State and Local Governments
- Grassroots Power and Politics
- State Governments
- Local Governments
- Relations with Indian Nations
- Finances

In each section, there are certain facts and ideas that you should strive to understand. Many are in boldface type and appear in both the narrative and in the glossary at the end of the book. Other ideas, dates, facts, events, people, etc., are more difficult to pull out of the narrative. (Keep in mind that studying for objective-[multiple choice, T/F] style tests is different than studying for essay tests. See the Study Guide section on test taking for hints on study skills.)

In general, after you finish reading and studying this chapter, you should understand the following:

- the history of state, local, and tribal governments
- the nature of power and politics at the community level
- the development of state constitutions

- the major institutions of state government
- types of local governments and the bases of their authority
- the budgeting process and finances at the state and local levels

Chapter Outline and Key Points

In this section, you are provided with a basic outline of the chapter and any key words/points you should know. Use this outline, in your own notebook, to develop a complete outline of the material. This will help you study and remember the material in preparation for your tests, assignments, and papers.

The Evolution of State and Local Governments

local government created by--

Baker v. Carr (1962) --

one-person, one-vote --

U.S. v. Lopez (1995)--

South Dakota v. Dole (1987)--

Grassroots Power and Politics

nonpartisan election--

sunshine law--

State Governments

State Constitutions

state constitution --

The Northwest Ordinance of 1787--

Missouri Compromise of 1820-1821--

Progressive Movement--

state constitution amendments--

Governors

governor --

package or general veto--

line-item veto--

methods of limiting gubernatorial power--

pardon--

commute--

parole--

extradite--

State Legislatures

citizen legislators--

one-person, one-vote rule--

Baker v. Carr (1962)--

sunset laws--

term limits --

State Courts

inclusion--

common law--

criminal law--

civil law--

Missouri Plan--

Elections

single party dominant --

majority party rule --

Direct Democracy

direct initiative--

indirect initiative--

direct or popular referendum--

advisory referendum--

Local Governments

Charters

Dillon's Rule--

charter--

special charter--

general charter-

classified charter--

optional charter--

home rule charter--

charter school--

Types of Local Government

counties--

towns--

municipalities--

special districts--

Executives and Legislatures

town meetings--

elected executive--

elected council or commission--

appointed manager--

political machines--

mayor and city council--

professional managers--

at-large election--

district-based election--

commission government--

public corporations or authorities--

Relations with Indian Nations

domestic dependent nation--

trust relationship--

compacts--

reservation and trust lands--

Finances

state governments rely primarily on what taxes?--

local government rely primarily on what taxes?--

segregated funds--

progressive tax--

regressive tax--

Research Ideas and Possible Paper Topics

1) Find a copy of your state's constitution and another state constitution from outside of your geographic region (i.e., Midwesterners look for a Western state, Southerners look for a New England state, etc.) and compare them. Are they similar or different? Why and how?

2) Go to the Internet and find the homepages of several different cities around the country. Compare the information you find on their methods of government, priorities, and revenues.

3) Does your community have direct democracy (initiative, referendum, and recall)? If so, research its use in your community and the rules regarding its use. If not, find a community that has these powers and do the same.

4) Using the library or the Internet, find out information on at least three Indian tribes. At least one tribe must not run casinos. Make sure they are from several different regions of the country as well. Discuss the quality of life of these three tribes. What kinds of decisions can tribes make? What is tribal life like? How are they governed? Compare the similarities and differences you find.

5) Find out how your community deals with finances. From where does their money come and where does it go? Is their budget balanced? What constraints does the local government operate under? How easy or difficult is it to get this information?

Websites

The website for **Governing Magazine**, a magazine on state and local government, contains a good index of state and local government links.
http://governing.com

This site, created by the **Piper Group**, a private consulting firm, lists links to all 50 state governments, along with federal sources, multi-state sources, national organizations, and other entities involved in state and local government.
www.statelocalgov.net/index.cfm

The **Internet Law Library** has links to all 50 state constitutions; also includes Indian treaties and compacts as well as territorial laws.
www.lawguru.com/ilawlib/17.htm

The **Council of State Governments** website has news stories pertaining to the states that is updated every weekday.
www.csg.org

National Council of State Legislators site offers analyses and information on intergovernmental relations.
www.ncsl.org/statefed/afipolcy.htm

NGA On-Line. The **National Governors' Council is** a non-partisan organization that looks at solving state-focused problems and provides information on state innovations and practices. The website has stories and articles of interest to the states and provides links to similar issues and organizations.
www.nga.org/governors/1,1169,00.htm

The **Pew Center on the States** offers a wide variety of information on the states. You can identify any state and find information about current hot issues, recent reforms, political makeup (who's in the legislature and executive, etc.), links to that state's websites, as well as state data on crime, taxes, education, and other key issues. You also have the ability to compare states' approaches to issues and their relative situations. You can also search by issue: welfare reform, utility deregulation, health care, taxes, budgets, and education.
www.stateline.org/

The **National Organization of Counties** collects information on county governments such as county officials, courthouse addresses, county seats, cities in a county, and maintains a collection of demographic data on counties.
www.naco.org/counties/counties/index.cfm

The **National City Government Resource Center** serves as a collection of municipal-related URL's from throughout the US in the following categories: General City Links, Functional City Links, Regional City Links and Other City-Related Links. You can access sites on most cities in the US on this page by using City Guide or CityNet. This is a personal website maintained by a university professor who is also a professional city manager.
http://www.geocities.com/CapitolHill/1389/

Practice Tests

MULTIPLE CHOICE

1. The requirement that state legislative districts have approximately the same number of people so that legislative representation would be equitable was established in *Baker v. Carr* (1962). This decision led to decreased control in state legislatures by

    a. rural areas.
    b. big city political machines.
    c. the federal government.
    d. the Democratic Party.

2. The most powerful and influential people in a state or community are

    a. those who hold public office.
    b. governors and mayors.
    c. the traditional elites.
    d. all of the above.

3. The groups most prevalent at the local and state levels are

    a. groups interested in general issues.
    b. ad hoc and oriented to specific issues.
    c. organized and hierarchical.
    d. local affiliates of national interest organizations.

4. State governments have primary responsibility for

   a. education.
   b. economic development.
   c. public health.
   d. all of the above.

5. The first state constitutions provided for

   a. limits on the authority of each state institution.
   b. checks and balances.
   c. strong executives.
   d. all of the above.

6. Direct voter participation was advocated by the

   a. Populists.
   b. Progressives.
   c. Republican Party.
   d. Whigs.

7. In forty-three states, governors have the power to

   a. propose budgets.
   b. veto an entire bill.
   c. line-item veto.
   d. package veto.

8. The most extensive and creative use of the line-item veto has been by Governor

   a. George W. Bush (TX).
   b. Gray Davis (CA).
   c. Tommy Thompson (WI).
   d. John Engler (MI).

9. In 1962, the Supreme Court decided the case *Baker v. Carr*, the result of which was

   a. representational equity: one man, one vote.
   b. that each legislative district had to have equal population.
   c. the reduction of rural power in state legislatures.
   d. all of the above.

10. State election campaigns are generally

    a. candidate-centered.
    b. extremely partisan.
    c. media-centered.
    d. all of the above

11. The principle that municipalities owe their origins and derive their powers from the states is called

    a. federalism.
    b. Dillon's Rule.
    c. charter power.
    d. the township rule.

12. There are approximately _____ local governments in the United States.

    a. 35,000
    b. 59,000
    c. 72,000
    d. 87,000

13. Of cities with populations in excess of 1,000,000 people, most choose the _____ form of municipal government.

    a. mayor-council
    b. council-manager
    c. commission
    d. town meeting

14. Under U.S. law and the Constitution, Indian tribes are

    a. given the same rights and responsibilities as states.
    b. ignored completely.
    c. treated as totally foreign nations.
    d. considered domestic dependent nations.

15. Local and state government budgets rely on _____ as sources of revenue.

    a. sales taxes
    b. property taxes
    c. income taxes and fees
    d. all of the above

TRUE/FALSE

1. States recognize and authorize the creation of local governments.

2. Political participation at the state and local level is less issue-oriented than national politics.

3. The intent of the authors of the original state constitutions was to empower state governments.

4. State constitutions are relatively easy to amend; this is an action that occurs frequently.

5. All governors have line-item and package veto powers.

6. Originally, most states had part-time, citizen legislatures.

7. Judges in the state courts are selected by nonpartisan elections.

8. Indian tribes retain their individual identity and sovereignty but must rely on the U.S. federal government for the interpretation and application of treaty provisions.

9. Reservations and trust lands are exempt from federal taxes, but must pay state levies.

10. State governments rely primarily on income taxes for their revenues.

COMPARE AND CONTRAST

nonpartisan and partisan elections

the goals of the writers of the state constitutions vs. those of the national constitution

compacts, reservation land, and trust land

the powers of state governors and those of state legislatures

state and federal laws

methods of judicial selection: elections (partisan and nonpartisan), chosen by legislature or governor, merit plans

initiative, referendum, and recall

county, municipality, and special district

municipal governments: mayor-council, mayor-manager, commission, town meeting

package, line-item, and general veto

ESSAY AND SHORT ANSWER QUESTIONS

1) Discuss the nature of state constitutions.

2) What was the Northwest Ordinance of 1787 and why was it important?

3) How are state courts structured?

4) Discuss charters. What kinds are there and what impact do they have on local governments?

5) Compare and contrast the various forms of municipal government and their effectiveness.

6) Which people and what groups tend to exercise power at the state, local, and community levels and what kinds of power do they wield?

7) For what policy areas do states have primary responsibility and how do these responsibilities relate to the constitutions they have adopted?

8) Discuss the legal status, treaty obligations, and relationships between the national government and Indian nations.

9) What are the roles, powers, and prerogatives of state governors?

10) The Constitution grants states the power to regulate elections. Discuss the various types of elections held including state level, judicial, local, and federal elections. What impact do states have on these processes? Have patterns of party competition changed over the years and, if so, how?

ANSWERS TO STUDY EXERCISES

multiple choice answers

1. a p. 106
2. c p. 106
3. b p. 107
4. d p. 107
5. a p. 107
6. b p. 109
7. c p. 110
8. c p. 110
9. d p. 113

10.	a	p. 120
11.	b	p. 123
12.	d	p. 123
13.	a	p. 123
14.	d	p. 128
15.	d	p. 130

true/false answers

1.	T	p. 104
2.	F	p. 106
3.	F	p. 107
4.	T	p. 108
5.	F	p. 11
6.	T	p. 113
7.	F	p. 115
8.	T	p. 128
9.	F	p. 128
10.	F	p. 126

CHAPTER 5
CIVIL LIBERTIES

Chapter Goals and Learning Objectives

Civil liberties are the individual rights and freedoms enumerated in the Bill of Rights that the federal government cannot abridge. They place limits on the power of government to restrain or dictate how people may act. The civil liberties we possess, however, are not absolute nor are these liberties simple to explain and understand. They are interpreted and reinterpreted by the Supreme Court and common practice over time. The Court tries to balance rights between competing interests. For example, the Court has generally ruled that your right to free speech ends when you incite a riot that would cause immediate harm to others. They are balancing your individual right with the rights of the public at large. Each liberty interest faces a similar balancing act in its interpretation. In this chapter, we explore what the government may and may not do and which interests are being balanced at a given time.

This chapter is designed to inform you about the individual rights and freedoms granted to you by the Bill of Rights. The main topic headings of the chapter are:

- The First Constitutional Amendments: The Bill of Rights
- First Amendment Guarantees: Freedom of Religion
- First Amendment Guarantees: Freedom of Speech and Press
- The Right to Keep and Bear Arms
- The Rights of the Accused or Criminal Defendants
- The Right to Privacy

In each section, there are certain facts and ideas that you should strive to understand. Many are in boldface type and appear in both the narrative and in the glossary at the end of the book. Other ideas, dates, facts, events, people, etc., are more difficult to pull out of the narrative. (Keep in mind that studying for objective-[multiple choice, T/F] style tests is different than studying for essay tests. See the Study Guide section on test taking for hints on study skills.)

In general, after you finish reading and studying this chapter, you should understand the following:

- the Bill of Rights and the reasons for its addition to the Constitution
- the application of some rights in the Bill of Rights to the states via the incorporation doctrine
- the meaning of the First Amendment's religion clauses:
    - the establishment clause
    - the free exercise clause
- the meaning of the First Amendment's free speech and press clause
- the interpretation and controversy over the Second Amendment; the right to bear arms
- rights of the accused or criminal defendant's rights in the 4th, 5th, 6th, and 8th Amendments
- the meaning of the right to privacy and how it has been interpreted by the Court

Chapter Outline and Key Points

In this section, you are provided with a basic outline of the chapter and any key words/points you should know. Use this outline, in your own notebook, to develop a complete outline of the material. This will help you study and remember the material in preparation for your tests, assignments, and papers.

The First Constitutional Amendments: The Bill of Rights

      civil liberties--

      Bill of Rights--

      Anti-Federalists' concerns--

      Ninth Amendment--

The Incorporation Doctrine

      Barron v. Baltimore (1833)--

      due process clause--

      substantive due process --

      incorporation doctrine--

      Gitlow v. NewYork (1925)--

      Near v. Minnesota (1931)--

      selective incorporation--

Selective Incorporation and Fundamental Freedoms

      Palko v. Connecticut (1937)--

      double jeopardy--

      fundamental rights--

First Amendment Guarantees: Freedom of Religion

      Article VI religious test--

      First Amendment--

establishment clause--

free exercise clause--

The Establishment Clause

Engel v. Vitale (1962)--

Lemon v. Kurtzman (1971)--

three-part *Lemon* test for establishment issues:
--1)
--2)
--3)

Agostini v. Felton (1997) --

Zelman v. Simmons-Harris (2002)--

The Free Exercise Clause

free exercise clause--

1990 peyote case (*Employment Division, Dept. of Human Resources of Oregon v. Smith)*--

Religious Freedom Restoration Act--

Santeria Church case (*Church of the Lukumi Babalu Aye v. Hialeah*)--

First Amendment Guarantees: Freedom of Speech and Press

thoughts versus motives--

prior restraint--

Attempts to Limit Speech

The Alien and Sedition Acts

Slavery, the Civil War, and Rights Curtailment

Ex parte McCardle (1869)--

Anti-Governmental Speech

clear and present danger test--

direct incitement test-

Libel and Slander

libel--

slander--

New York Times v. Sullivan (1971)--

actual malice--

Obscenity and Pornography

Chaplinsky v. New Hampshire (1942)--

Roth v. U.S. (1957)--

Miller v. California (1973)--

Congress and Obscenity

Reno v. ACLU (1997)--

Ashcroft v. Free Speech Coalition (2002)--

What Types of Speech are Protected?

Prior Restraint

New York Times v. United States (1971)--

Symbolic Speech

symbolic speech--

Stomberg v. California (1931)--

Tinker v. Des Moines Independent Community School District (1969)--

Texas v. Johnson (1989)--

Hate Speech

R.A.V. v. City of St. Paul (1992)--

free speech zones--

The Right to Keep and Bear Arms

Second Amendment--

U.S. v. Miller (1939) --

Quilici v. Village of Morton (1983) --

Million Mom March--

The Rights of Criminal Defendants

due process rights (aka procedural guarantees, rights of defendants)--

The Fourth Amendment and Searches and Seizures

Fourth Amendment--

immediate control--

reasonable suspicion--

warrant--

warrantless searches--

probable cause--

"open fields doctrine"--

thermal imager case--

automobile searches--

2002 border patrol officer case--

Drug Testing and DNA Sampling

Chandler v. Miller (1997) --

The Fifth Amendment and Self-Incrimination

Fifth Amendment--

self-incrimination--

Use of Voluntary Confessions

Miranda v. Arizona

Miranda v. Arizona (1966)--

The Fourth and Fifth Amendments and the Exclusionary Rule

Weeks v. U.S. (1914)--

exclusionary rule--

good faith exception --

inevitable discovery--

The Sixth Amendment and Right to Counsel

Sixth Amendment--

Gideon v. Wainwright (1963)--

2002 case involving suspended sentence for minor crime--

The Sixth Amendment and Jury Trials

exclusion of African-Americans from jury (*Batson*)--

Maryland v. Craig (1990) --

The Eighth Amendment and Cruel and Unusual Punishment

Eighth Amendment--

Furman v. Georgia (1972)-

Gregg v. Georgia (1976)--

McKleskey v. Kemp (1987)--

McKleskey v. Zant (1991)--

2002 mentally retarded convicts case (*Atkins v. Virginia*)--

Illinois moratorium on executions--

DNA testing and executions--

The Right to Privacy

Birth Control

Griswold v. Connecticut (1965)--

"penumbras" of the Constitution--

Abortion

Roe v. Wade (1973)--

Webster v. Reproductive Health Services (1989)--

Planned Parenthood of Southeastern Pennsylvania v. Casey (1992)--

Stenberg v. Carhart (2000)

Homosexuality

Bowers v. Hardwick (1986)--

Boy Scouts of America v. Dale (2000) --

The Right to Die

Cruzan by Cruzan v. Director, Missouri Department of Health (1990)--

1997 Supreme Court case on physician-assisted suicide (*Vacco v. Quill*)--

US Attorney General Ashcroft and Oregon assisted suicide law--

Research Ideas and Possible Paper Topics

1) Find out if your campus has a "speech code." (If it doesn't, find a nearby college or university with one.) Would this code stand up to a constitutional test? Why or why not? According to your understanding of the First Amendment, are speech codes constitutional? Do some research at the campus newspaper and see if there was any controversy surrounding the adoption of the speech code and discuss it in class.

2) Explore the current docket of the Supreme Court. What civil liberties issues are going to be heard this term? How do you think they will be decided and why? Follow the process until the rulings are made and see if you are right.

3) Under Chief Justice Rehnquist, the Court has reduced many of the due process rights granted under the Warren and Burger Courts. Find examples of how these rights have changed and why. What has the role of public and political opinion been in these changes?

4) Call your local branch of the American Civil Liberties Union. Visit or ask for written information about their activities and issues. Find out what they do and why. Also check their website (see below) for information.

5) Find out more about the Federal Communications Decency Act that regulates speech on the Internet. What issues are at stake? What rights are being balanced? Should the Internet be regulated? If so, how and by whom? What measures are currently being considered to regulate Internet content?

Websites

The **Legal Information Institute** of Cornell University has an excellent site that offers extensive information about civil liberties. There is a section focused on the First Amendment with definitions, historical background, Supreme Court decisions, and links to numerous First Amendment-related sites. There are also sites at LII for prisoners' rights, employment rights, and constitutional rights generally.
www.law.cornell.edu/topics/first_amendment.html

American Civil Liberties Union (ACLU) offers information on the entire Bill of Rights including racial profiling, women's rights, privacy issues, prisons, drugs, etc. Includes links to other sites dealing with the same issues.
www.aclu.org

Cornell University Law School offers the full text of the Bill of Rights and other constitutional documents.
www.law.cornell.edu/constitution/constitution.billofrights.html

The **Cato Institute,** a Libertarian think-tank, hosts a Constitution Studies page on its website, examining Amendments 1, 2, 4, 5, 9 and 10.
www.cato.org/ccs/issues.html

First Amendment Cyber-Tribune (FACT) is a website hosted by the Casper Star-Tribune and is an extensive resource on the many liberty guarantees of the First Amendment. The site is continually updated and expanded.
http://w3.trib.com/FACT/

PBS offers a webpage that presents the background and issues relating to *Texas v. Johnson* and *U.S. v. Eichman*, the flag-burning cases, freedom of expression cases.
www.pbs.org/jefferson/enlight/flag.htm

Freedom Forum is an organization that studies and reports on First Amendment issues, particularly matters relating to freedom of the press.
www.freedomforum.com

Americans United for Separation of Church and State monitors church-state separation issues and promotes protection of the First Amendment establishment clause in Congress and state legislatures.
www.au.org

Professor Eugene Volkh of the **UCLA Law School** maintains a list of links to sources on the Second Amendment. You can also click on a link to his homepage to find a list of scholarly articles he has written on the Second Amendment and other Bill of Rights issues.
http://www1.law.ucla.edu/~volokh/2amteach/sources.htm

The James Madison Research Library and Information Center website is hosted by **The National Rifle Association** to detail their understanding of the Second Amendment.
www.madisonbrigate.com

The Brady Campaign to Prevent Gun Violence, created by Nancy Brady after the debilitating gunshot wound to her husband, James Brady, during the Reagan assassination attempt, hosts a website detailing their national fight against the NRA to enact gun control measures in Congress and the state legislatures. The Second Amendment page on the site contends that the NRA is wrong in its interpretation of history and Supreme Court decisions that individual private gun ownership is broadly protected by the Second Amendment.
www.handguncontrol.org/facts/issuebriefs/second.asp

Fighting Terrorism/Protecting Liberty is a site by the **National Association of Criminal Defense Lawyers.** This site monitors the many bills in Congress and proposals by the Department of Justice to increase the powers of law enforcement in the face of terrorism. The NACDL and other organizations concerned with civil liberties track these measure to ensure the least possible intrusion on liberties consistent with protection from terrorist attacks.
www.criminaljustice.org/public.nsf/freeform/terrorism1?OpenDocument

NoloPress provides a webpage which offers a tour of the ways in which the Bill of Rights attempts to ensure fair treatment for those accused of crimes by the government.
www.nolo.com/lawcenter/ency/article.cfm/objectID/6410CC94-3E8F-4A37-A5F85E3348E6431F/catID/D4C65461-8D33-482C-92FCEA7F2ADED29A

The Center for Reproductive Law and Policy website has an extensive Guide to the Supreme Court and Choice, highlighting the right to privacy cases regarding abortion and other related issues from a pro-choice position.
www.crip.org/crt_roe_primer.html

The American Life League website also has a list of Supreme Court cases and links to information regarding the abortion issue from a pro-life position.
>   www.all.org/issues/abscotus.htm

LAMBA Legal is a national organization working for the civil liberties and civil rights of homosexuals. Its legal webpage has news about court decisions in this area and offers links to federal and state court cases along with legal briefs for those cases (click on "library").
>   www.lambdalegal.org/cgi-bin/iowa/index.html

Findlaw is a searchable database of S.C. decisions plus legal subjects, state courts, law schools, bar associations, and international law.
>   www.findlaw.com

Practice Tests

MULTIPLE CHOICE

1. The Bill of Rights, as added to the Constitution originally,

    a. was a compromise between the Federalists and the Anti-Federalists.
    b. listed a number of individual and states' rights to be protected.
    c. was designed to serve as protection against infringement of rights by the new national government.
    d. all of the above.

2. The Constitution was ratified in 1789; Amendments 1 through 10 were ratified

    a. over the course of 20 years, following the adoption of the Constitution.
    b. in 1789 (Amendments 1-5) and 1792 (Amendment 6-10).
    c. in 1791.
    d. in 1789.

3. The Supreme Court ruled that the Bill of Rights limited only the federal government and not the states in

    a. *Barron v. Baltimore.*
    b. *McCulloch v. Maryland.*
    c. *Cantwell v. Connecticut.*
    d. *Reynolds v. U.S.*

4. The Due Process clause is located in the _____ Amendment.

   a. Fifth
   b. Sixth
   c. Fourteenth
   d. Fifth and Fourteenth

5. The rationale for selective incorporation, the judicial application to the states of some of the rights in the Bill of Rights via the Fourteenth Amendment, was set out in

   a. *Cantwell v. Connecticut.*
   b. *Reynolds v. Sims.*
   c. *Near v. Minnesota.*
   d. *Palko v. Connecticut.*

6. The clause in the Bill of Rights that prohibits the national government from establishing an official religion is called the

   a. establishment clause.
   b. free exercise clause.
   c. religious freedom clause.
   d. freedom to choose clause.

7. The Supreme Court has ruled that in church/state questions, a law is constitutional if it does not foster excessive government entanglement with religion. The ruling comes from the case

   a. *Mapp v. Ohio.*
   b. *Agostini v. Felton.*
   c. *Stenburg v. Carhart.*
   d. *Chaplinsky v. New Hampshire.*

8. The guarantee of free speech in the First Amendment is not absolute. Among the limitations on speech are

   a. sedition and treason.
   b. slander and libel.
   c. obscenity.
   d. all of the above.

9. The Supreme Court first acknowledged symbolic speech in the case

   a. *Chaplinsky v. New Hampshire.*
   b. *Roth v. U.S.*
   c. *Stromberg v. California.*
   d. *Miller v. California.*

10. The amendment that requires the police to get a search warrant to conduct searches of your home in most cases is the _____ Amendment.

   a. Fourth
   b. Fifth
   c. Sixth
   d. Eighth

11. In 1966, the Court ruled that suspects must be apprised of their rights once arrested in the case of

   a. *Gideon v. Wainwright.*
   b. *Michigan v. Tyler.*
   c. *Mapp v. Ohio.*
   d. *Miranda v. Arizona.*

12. In *Weeks v. U.S.* (1914), the Supreme Court barred the use of illegally seized evidence at trial. This is called the

   a. warrant rule.
   b. exclusionary rule.
   c. Weeks test.
   d. search and seizure doctrine.

13. Death penalty cases are usually dealt with under the _____ Amendment.

   a. Fourth
   b. Fifth
   c. Sixth
   d. Eighth

14. The right to privacy was first cited in

   a. *Furman v. Georgia.*
   b. *McCleskey v. Zant.*
   c. *Griswold v. Connecticut.*
   d. *Roe v. Wade.*

15. Where is the right to privacy found in the U.S. Constitution?

   a. in the 4th Amendment
   b. in the 6th Amendment
   c. in the "Right to Privacy Amendment"
   d. in the "penumbras" of the Constitution

TRUE/FALSE

1. The Federalists put forward the idea of a Bill of Rights in order to protect the liberty of individual citizens from the state governments.

2. The Court first ruled that prayer in public school was unconstitutional in *Engel v. Vitale*.

3. *New York Times v. Sullivan* made it much easier to prove libel which is not constitutionally protected speech.

4. Burning the American flag is considered constitutionally protected symbolic speech.

5. In *New York Times v. United States*, the Supreme Court ruled that the U.S. government could prevent the publication of papers harmful to national security.

6. The Fourth Amendment's purpose was to deny the national government the authority to conduct general searches.

7. Police officers do not need a warrant if they have consent to search.

8. The Sixth Amendment guarantees citizens an attorney under all circumstances, civil and criminal.

9. The Supreme Court has held that jury trials must be available if a prison sentence of six months or more is possible, according to the Sixth Amendment.

10. The death penalty has more public support today than ever before.

COMPARE AND CONTRAST

civil liberties and civil rights

the Bill of Rights and the Incorporation Doctrine

free exercise and establishment clause

clear and present danger and direct incitement tests

symbolic speech, prior restraint, and hate speech

Due Process Rights: 4th, 5th, 6th and 8th amendments

Furman v. Georgia, Gregg v. Georgia, and *McCleskey v. Kemp*

Privacy Rights: birth control, abortion, homosexual rights, the right to die, medical records, etc.

ESSAY AND SHORT ANSWER QUESTIONS

1) What is the Bill of Rights and why was it added to the Constitution?

2) Explain the establishment clause and its current application.

3) What is the incorporation doctrine and how has it been used?

4) What is the exclusionary rule and why is it important?

5) What has the Supreme Court ruled in "right to die" cases?

6) Explain the First Amendment. What rights and liberties are covered by this amendment, how has the Supreme Court interpreted its meanings, and what rights/liberties is the Court trying to balance in making its rulings on these issues? Be sure to cite cases.

7) Explain our rights to free speech, freedom of the press, and freedom to petition and assemble. What limits exist on these rights? Be sure to cite cases.

8) Discuss the Fourth Amendment fully. Cite cases.

9) Discuss due process rights stemming from the fifth, sixth, and eighth amendments. How have these protections changed over time? Be sure to cite cases.

10) What is the right to privacy? What are the constitutional bases of this right? How has this right been applied and to what might it be applied in the future?

ANSWERS TO STUDY EXERCISES

multiple choice answers

1.	d	p. 139
2.	c	p. 139
3.	a	p. 139
4.	c	p. 140
5.	d	p. 141
6.	a	p. 143
7.	b	p. 144
8.	d	p. 148
9.	c	p. 153
10.	a	p. 157
11.	d	p. 159
12.	b	p. 160
13.	d	p. 163
14.	c	p. 165
15.	a	p. 170

true/false answers

1. F p. 139
2. T p. 143
3. F p. 150
4. T p. 153
5. F p. 152
6. T p. 158
7. T p. 158
8. F p. 161
9. T p. 162
10. F p. 166

CHAPTER 6
CIVIL RIGHTS

Chapter Goals and Learning Objectives

Civil rights concern the positive acts that governments take to protect certain classifications of individuals against arbitrary or discriminatory treatment by government or individuals. The Framers were most concerned with creating a new, workable, and enduring form of government than with civil rights. The Fourteenth Amendment introduced the idea of equal protection of the laws and has generated more litigation to determine and specify its meaning than any other constitutional provision. This chapter explores how African-Americans, women, and other disadvantaged political groups have drawn ideas, support, and success from one another in the quest for equality under the law.

This chapter is designed to inform you about the struggle of women and minorities for civil rights and the privileges of citizenship, including equal protection of the laws and voting rights. The main topic headings of the chapter are:

- Slavery, Abolition, and Winning the Right to Vote, 1800-1890
- The Push for Equality, 1890-1954
- The Civil Rights Movement
- Other Groups Mobilize for Rights

In each section, there are certain facts and ideas that you should strive to understand. Many are in boldface type and appear in both the narrative and in the glossary at the end of the book. Other ideas, dates, facts, events, people, etc., are more difficult to pull out of the narrative. (Keep in mind that studying for objective-[multiple choice, T/F] style tests is different than studying for essay tests. See the Study Guide section on test taking for hints on study skills.)

In general, after you finish reading and studying this chapter, you should understand the following:

- slavery, abolition, and the efforts of abolitionists, African-Americans, and women to gain the vote and expand civil rights
- the push for equality by women and African-Americans from 1885 to 1954
- *Plessy v. Ferguson* to *Brown v. Board of Education of Topeka, Kansas*
- the civil rights movement
- its techniques, strategies, and leaders
- the Civil Rights Act of 1964
- the development of a new women's rights movement
- the push for an equal rights amendment
- efforts of other groups to expand the definition of civil rights further such as Native Americans, Hispanic Americans, Gays and Lesbians, and Disabled Americans

Chapter Outline and Key Points

In this section, you are provided with a basic outline of the chapter and any key words/points you should know. Use this outline, in your own notebook, to develop a complete outline of the material. This will help you study and remember the material in preparation for your tests, assignments, and papers.

Civil Rights

civil rights--

Federalist No. 42--

Three-Fifths Compromise--

Slavery, Abolition, and Winning the Right to Vote, 1800-90

Slavery and Congress

Missouri Compromise of 1820--

The Abolitionist Movement: The First Civil Rights Movement

abolitionist movement--

NAACP--

women's rights tie-in--

Seneca Falls Convention (1848)--

franchise--

Uncle Tom's Cabin (1852)--

Dred Scott v. Sandford (1857)--

The Civil War and its Aftermath: Civil Rights Laws and Constitutional Amendments

causes of Civil War:
1)
2)
3)
4)

Civil War Amendments (13th, 14th, and 15th)

    Thirteenth Amendment--

    Black Codes--

    Jim Crow Laws--

    Civil Rights Act of 1866 --

    Fourteenth Amendment--

    Fifteenth Amendment--

Civil Rights and the Supreme Court

    The Slaughterhouse Cases (1873)--

    Bradwell v. Illinois (1873)--

    Minor v. Happersett (1875)--

    Jim Crow laws--

    privileges and immunities clause--

    Civil Rights Cases (1883)--

    three ways Southern states excluded African-Americans:
        1)
        2)
        3)

    grandfather clause--

The Push for Equality, 1890-1954

    Plessy v. Ferguson (1896)--

    separate but equal--

The Founding of the National Association for the Advancement of Colored People

    NAACP--

Key Women's Groups

    NAWSA--

NCL--

suffrage movement--

Muller v. Oregon (1908)--

Nineteenth Amendment--

Litigating for Equality

test cases--

Gaines (1938)--

Thurgood Marshall--

NAACP-LDF--

Sweatt and McLaurin (1950)--

amicus curiae briefs--

Brown v. Board of Education of Topeka, Kansas (1954)--

equal protection clause--

The Civil Rights Movement

School Desegregation After Brown

Brown II (1955)--

Cooper v. Aaron (1958)--

A New Move for African-American Rights

Rosa Parks--

Montgomery Bus Boycott--

Dr. Martin Luther King, Jr.--

Formation of New Groups

Southern Christian Leadership Council (SCLC)--

Student Nonviolent Coordinating Committee (SNCC)--

Woolworth sit-in--

freedom rides--

March on Birmingham--

The Civil Rights Act of 1964

Civil Rights Act of 1964--

March on Washington, August 1963--

"I Have A Dream" speech--

President Lyndon B. Johnson--

Elements of 1964 Civil Right Act:
1)
2)
3)
4)
5)
6)

Malcolm X--

1965 Selma, Alabama, march--

The Impact of the Civil Rights Act of 1964

Education

Swann v. Charlotte-Mecklenburg School District (1971)--

de jure vs. *de facto* discrimination--

Employment

Title VII--

Duke Power Company case (1971)--

"business necessity"--

The Women's Rights Movement

Hoyt v. Florida (1961)--

The Feminine Mystique--

Equal Opportunity Employment Commission (EEOC)--

addition of sex to Civil Rights Act of 1964--

National Organization of Women (NOW)--

The Equal Rights Amendment

ERA--

Litigation for Equal Rights

The Equal Protection Clause and Constitutional Standards of Review

suspect classification--

strict scrutiny--

standard of review (see Table 6.1)--

fundamental freedoms--

Reed v. Reed (1971)--

Craig v. Boren (1976)--

practices which have been found to violate the Fourteenth Amendment--

governmental practices and laws upheld by the Court--

Statutory Remedies for Sex Discrimination

Title VII--

Title IX--

sexual harassment allegations against Clarence Thomas--

Equal Pay Act--

Other Groups Mobilize for Rights

Hispanic Americans

MALDEF--

LULAC--

public school discrimination cases--

Native Americans

Dawes Act--

Bury My Heart at Wounded Knee--

Gays and Lesbians

Bowers v. Hardwick (1986)--

Don't Ask, Don't Tell policy--

1996 Colorado discrimination case (*Romer v. Evans*)--

Disabled Americans

ADA of 1990--

four Supreme Court cases in 1999 affecting and limiting ADA--

Affirmative Action

affirmative action--

Regents of the University of California v. Bakke (1978)--

Civil Rights Act of 1991 and affirmative action--

1996 US Supreme Court case on affirmative action in Texas higher education (*Texas v. Hopwood*)--

2003 US Supreme Court case on affirmative action in Michigan higher education (*Grutter v. Ballinger*)--

Research Ideas and Possible Paper Topics

1. Look at the current Supreme Court docket. What civil rights cases do you see? What are their constitutional arguments and how do they differ from the cases the book discusses in the 1950s and 60s?

2. The use of *amicus curaie* briefs has increased dramatically in the last several decades and many people now argue that public opinion plays a role in Supreme Court decisions. Analyze and discuss these two issues. How would you characterize the role of such influence in civil rights cases?

3. Choose one civil rights issue and research it in depth. What constitutional issues are used, what arguments, etc.? How do you feel the current Court would rule on this issue and why?

4. Look at the current Supreme Court. Do some biographical and case research on each of the nine justices in the area of civil rights. Build a typography (classify the judges into groups of like-minded individuals) on how the current justices rule on civil rights. (example: the simplest typography would be liberal--moderate--conservative. But be sure to define each of those categories! A more complex system would provide better analysis of the Court.)

5. Congress also plays a role in civil rights. Do some research to determine what types of civil rights issues Congress has been dealing with in the last decade years. What are the separate roles of Congress and the courts in civil rights?

Websites

Civil Rights Division, U.S. Department of Justice website offers an overview of the activities and programs of the DOJ on civil rights as well as links to documents, legislation, cases, and the Civil Rights Forum Newsletter.
www.usdoj.gov/crt/crt-home.html

U.S. Commission on Civil Rights is a bi-partisan fact-finding agency established within the executive branch. The website offers news releases, publications, a calendar of events, and multimedia coverage of civil rights events.
www.usccr.gov/

The **Legal Information Institute** of Cornell University has an excellent site that offers extensive information about the legalities and definitions of civil rights. It begins with a prose definition of a civil right and includes links to U.S. Government laws, state laws, Supreme Court rulings, international laws on civil rights, and more.
www.law.cornell.edu/topics/civil_rights.html

The **National Association for the Advancement of Colored People** (NAACP) website offers information about the organization, membership, and issues of interest to proponents of civil rights. Has sections on the Supreme Court, Census 2000, the Education Summit, and includes links to other websites.
www.naacp.org

The **Southern Poverty Law Center (SPLC)** is a non-profit group dedicated to fighting hate and intolerance. Their website includes information on the center and their activities including a program titled "Teaching Tolerance," the Klanwatch, and Militia Task Force. They also have a state-by-state listing of "hate incidents".
www.splcenter.org

National Organization of Women (NOW) website offers information on the organization and its issues/activities, including women in the military, economic equity, reproductive rights, and so on. They offer an email action list and the ability to join NOW on-line. Also has links to related sites.
www.now.org

Mexican-American Legal Defense and Education Fund (MALDEF) website offers information on Census 2000, scholarships, job opportunities, legal programs, regional offices information, and more.
www.maldef.org

Native American Rights Fund (NARF) website offers profiles of issues, an archive, resources, a tribal directory, and treaty information as well as a lot of other information.
www.narf.org

80-20 Initiative is a non-profit group working to further civil rights for Asian-Americans. Its webpage presents information related to legal and political issues central to the organization's activities.
www.80-20initiative.com

America with Disabilities Act (ADA) offers information on this legislation and rights of the disabled.
www.usdoj.gov/crt/ada/adahom1.htm

EthnicMajority.com is a website promoting equal rights and opportunities for African, Latino and Asian-Americans. Its page on affirmative action gives an extensive background on the issue and numerous links to organizations promoting and protecting affirmative action.
www.ethnicmajority.com/affirmative_action.htm

Arab-American Institute offers a webpage detailing discrimination problems facing Arab-American citizens following 9/11.
    www.aaiusa.org/discrimination.htm

Anti-Defamation League's webpage on civil rights focuses on several issues, including anti-Semitism.
    www.adl.org/main_civil_rights.asp

The **Legal Information Institute** of Cornell University has an excellent site that offers extensive information about the legalities and definitions of employment discrimination law. It begins with a prose definition of employment law and includes links to U.S. Government laws, state laws, Supreme Court rulings, and more.
    www.law.cornell.edu/topics/employment_discrimination.htm

Findlaw is a searchable database of SC decisions plus legal subjects, state courts, law schools, bar associations, and international law.
    www.findlaw.com

Practice Tests

MULTIPLE CHOICE QUESTIONS

1. Congress banned the slave trade in

    a. 1787.
    b. 1791.
    c. 1808.
    d. 1860.

2. Slavery and involuntary servitude were banned by the _____ Amendment.

    a. Tenth
    b. Thirteenth
    c. Fifteenth
    d. Seventeenth

3. In *Bradwell v. Illinois.* (1873), the Supreme Court ruled that

    a. the Fourteenth Amendment did not protect women.
    b. monopolies deprive citizens of their privileges and immunities and are unconstitutional.
    c. Jim Crow laws were unconstitutional, according to the Fourteenth Amendment.
    d. women were not allowed to serve on juries.

4. The doctrine of "separate but equal" was first enunciated in the case

   a. *Dred Scott v. Sandford.*
   b. *Bradwell v. Illinois.*
   c. *Minor v. Happersett.*
   d. *Plessy v. Ferguson.*

5. Women were granted the right to vote in 1920 through the _____ Amendment.

   a. Fifteenth
   b. Seventeenth
   c. Nineteenth
   d. Twenty-First

6. During the 1930s, the NAACP decided it was time to launch a challenge to the precedent set by *Plessy*. To do so, they used a strategy of

   a. litigation.
   b. strikes and protests.
   c. boycotts.
   d. all of the above.

7. The following state laws (no longer in effect) are examples of what kind of laws?

Lunch Counters No persons, firms, or corporations, who or which furnish meals to passengers at station restaurants or station eating houses, in times limited by common carriers of said passengers, shall furnish said meals to white and colored passengers in the same room, or at the same table, or at the same counter. *South Carolina*
Libraries Any white person of such county may use the county free library under the rules and regulations prescribed by the commissioners court and may be entitled to all the privileges thereof. Said court shall make proper provision for the negroes of said county to be served through a separate branch or branches of the county free library, which shall be administered by [a] custodian of the negro race under the supervision of the county librarian. *Texas*
Education [The County Board of Education] shall provide schools of two kinds; those for white children and those for colored children. *Texas*
Theaters Every person...operating...any public hall, theatre, opera house, motion picture show or any place of public entertainment or public assemblage which is attended by both white and colored persons, shall separate the white race and the colored race and shall set apart and designate...certain seats therein to be occupied by white persons and a portion thereof, or certain seats therein, to be occupied by colored persons. *Virginia*

   a. civil rights laws
   b. affirmative action laws
   c. constitutional laws
   d. Jim Crow laws

8. In 1964, a full decade after the Supreme Court ordered desegregation with "all due deliberate speed", ___ percent of southern African-American children attended integrated schools.

    a. 1
    b. 6
    c. 12
    d. 21

9. In *Craig v. Boren*, the issue at stake was

    a. single-sex public schools.
    b. different drinking ages for men and women.
    c. that only women were allowed to receive alimony.
    d. that women could be barred from jury service.

10. In 1970, the Ford Foundation helped to fund the creation of the

    a. Lambda Legal Defense Fund.
    b. Legal Defense Fund for Women.
    c. Native American Rights Fund.
    d. Equal Opportunity Employment Commission.

11. U.S. policy toward Native Americans in the Dawes Act of 1887 favored

    a. dependent status.
    b. foreign status.
    c. separation.
    d. assimilation.

12. In 1984, MALDEF filed a suit in Texas state court on the funding of public schools. The court ruled that the state's method of financing public schools was

    a. in compliance with the Texas constitution.
    b. in compliance with the equal protection clause of the U.S. Constitution.
    c. discriminatory but constitutional.
    d. unconstitutional under the state constitution.

13. The Supreme Court ruled against the rights of homosexuals in the case of

    a. *Gregg v. Georgia.*
    b. *Bowers v. Hardwick.*
    c. *Furman v. Georgia.*
    d. *Missouri v. Jenkins.*

14. Disabled people, fueled largely by a group of veterans, won greater protection against discrimination through

    a. the Americans with Disabilities Act.
    b. the Civil Rights Act of 1964.
    c. *Griggs v. Duke Power Co.*
    d. *Texas v. Hopwood.*

15. In 1978, the Supreme Court first addressed the issue of affirmative action in *Regents of the University of California v. Bakke*. They ruled that

    a. affirmative action is unconstitutional.
    b. race could not be taken into account in admissions decisions.
    c. race could be taken into account, but strict quotas were unconstitutional.
    d. if affirmative action policies discriminated against a member of the majority who was more qualified, they were unconstitutional.

TRUE/FALSE

1. Black Codes were laws of the Reconstruction South that allowed blacks to vote and exercise their constitutional rights.

2. Some women opposed the Fourteenth Amendment because it introduced gender to the Constitution for the first time.

3. In the 1870s, it was ruled constitutional to bar women from practicing law due to their "natural and proper timidity and delicacy."

4. Groups such as the NAACP preferred to lobby the federal Congress in their challenges to segregation and equal rights.

5. In *Brown*, a number of groups filed *amicus curaie* briefs in favor of desegregation and equal rights including trade unions, religious groups, and the U.S. government.

6. The Montgomery Bus boycotts were started by Dr. Martin Luther King, Jr. when he refused to give up his seat on a public bus to a white woman.

7. The Civil Rights Act of 1964 created the Equal Employment Opportunity Commission.

8. Southern states argued that Congress had overstepped its bounds in passage of the Civil Rights Act. The Supreme Court, on expedited review, agreed that Congress did not have the constitutional powers to remove control over elections and citizens from the states.

9. In 1961, the Court ruled that a Florida law that automatically registered men for jury duty but required women to personally visit the courthouse and petition for jury duty was ruled unconstitutional.

10.   *Roe v. Wade* basically managed to kill the Equal Rights Amendment.

COMPARE AND CONTRAST

slavery and abolition

African-American suffrage movement and the women's suffrage movement

Plessy v. Ferguson and *Brown v. Board of Education, Topeka, Kansas*

Thirteenth, Fourteenth, Fifteenth Amendments

Black Codes, grandfather clauses, and Jim Crow

NAACP and NAWSA

Civil Rights Act of 1964 and Voting Rights Act of 1965

de jure and *de facto* discrimination

suspect classification and strict scrutiny

ESSAY AND SHORT ANSWER QUESTIONS

1)   Define civil rights and discuss their constitutional bases.

2)   What was the abolitionist movement?

3)   Discuss the Civil War Amendments.

4)   Compare and contrast the rulings and reasoning of *Plessy* and *Brown*.

5)   Define and discuss affirmative action.

6)   Discuss the process the U.S. went through from 1800-1890 in civil rights.

7)   Discuss the history of the women's suffrage and rights movement up to and including the ERA and its ratification drive.

8)   The NAACP chose to use a litigation strategy to achieve desegregation and equal rights. How did they implement this strategy and what were their other choices?

9)   Explain the equal protection clause and the constitutional standards of review. Use examples of SC cases.

10) Once African-Americans and women had some success in the battle for equal rights, other groups mobilized to gain their rights. Discuss these groups, the tactics they used, and how successful they have been.

ANSWERS TO STUDY EXERCISES

multiple choice answers

1.	c	p. 179
2.	b	p. 181
3.	a	p. 182
4.	d	p. 184
5.	c	p. 187
6.	a	p. 187
7.	d	p. 187
8.	a	p. 194
9.	b	p. 198
10.	c	p. 203
11.	d	p. 203
12.	d.	p. 207
13.	b	p. 207
14.	a	p. 209
15.	c	p. 209

true/false answers

1.	F	p. 181
2.	T	p. 182
3.	T	p. 183
4.	F	p. 186
5.	T	p. 189
6.	F	p. 191
7.	T	p. 193
8.	F	p. 194
9.	F	p. 195
10.	T	p. 196

CHAPTER 7
CONGRESS

Chapter Goals and Learning Objectives

Since the first days of our country, a national Congress has existed in one form or another. First the colonies were represented by the Continental Congress, which had little to no authority over the colonies. Then, the Congress under the Articles of Confederation, a national legislature that had but a few more powers than before. Article I of the Constitution, however, vests the governing powers of the United States squarely in the hands of "the first branch of government," Congress. Indeed, Congress alone was given the power to create legislation, control the purse, declare war, raise an army, control commerce as well as other national governing authority under Article I, Section 8. The president, the Chief Executive officer, had not existed until the Constitution, and even under the Constitution, the Executive came in second place (Article II).

Constitutionally, these powers have not been diminished. However, few would argue today that the president of the United States stands preeminent over the Congress in many ways. Co-equal branches of government, the Congress, nevertheless, were preeminent for much of our county's history. Today, the president is, in terms of real and perceived power, the chief policymaker of the county. What has changed over the course of our history regarding Congress? Why can virtually all Americans readily name the president but few can identify their own representatives in Congress?

The Congress of the United States consists of the House of Representatives and the Senate. It enacts our federal laws and sets the federal budget. Members of Congress work to represent their states and districts within their states. Individually, each member of Congress shares power with his or her colleagues. As a body, Congress, the institution, makes laws and policy. Individually, its members work to better the conditions of their states and districts. It is important to understand their role, why they were set up and their constitutional powers. This chapter discusses how Congress is organized and how they make laws as a body and how the individual members of Congress make decisions, as well as the relationship between Congress and the Executive Branch.

This chapter is designed to inform you about the institution of Congress. The main topic headings of the chapter are:

- The Roots of the Legislative Branch
- The Constitution and the Legislative Branch of Government
- The Members of Congress
- How Congress is Organized
- The Lawmaking Function of Congress
- How Members Make Decisions
- Congress and the President

In each section, there are certain facts and ideas that you should strive to understand. Many are in boldface type and appear in both the narrative and in the glossary at the end of the book. Other ideas, dates, facts, events, people, etc., are more difficult to pull out of the narrative. (Keep in mind that studying for objective-[multiple choice, T/F] style tests is different than studying for essay tests. See the Study Guide section on test taking for hints on study skills.)

In general, after you finish reading and studying this chapter, you should understand the following:

- the roots of the legislative branch
- the Constitutional arguments about representation in Congress
- Article I, the Constitutional basis for Congress and the powers granted to Congress by the Constitution
- nature of representation in the House of Representatives and the consequences of redistricting in the House
- the membership of Congress, how they are elected, and how they spend their days
- how Congress is organized
- how the Senate and House of Representatives are similar and different and how this affects legislation
- how Congress makes laws
- how members of Congress make decisions
- the relationship between the Congress and the president and how that relationship has changed over time
- the changes and reforms working their way through Congress today

Chapter Outline and Key Points

In this section, you are provided with a basic outline of the chapter and any key words/points you should know. Use this outline, in your own notebook, to develop a complete outline of the material. This will help you study and remember the material in preparation for your tests, assignments, and papers.

The Roots of the Legislative Branch

    First Continental Congress --

    Second Continental Congress --

    Articles of Confederation --

The Constitution and the Legislative Branch of Government

        bicameral legislature--

terms of Representatives and Senators--

how Senators elected under Article I--

17th Amendment--

Apportionment and Redistricting

size of House--

redistricting--

Constitutional Powers of Congress

bill--

Article I, Section 8 powers (Table 7.1)--

necessary and proper clause --

impeachment--

key differences between House and Senate (Table 7.2)--

The Members of Congress

Members of Congress must appease two constituencies--

casework --

Running for Office and Staying in Office

incumbency--

Term Limits

term limits--

state-imposed term limits on Members of Congress--

What Does Congress Look Like?

"Millionaires Club"--

better educated, more white, more male and richer--

The Representational Role of Members of Congress

trustee--

delegate--

politico--

minority representation in Congress--

How Congress is Organized

The House of Representatives

   The Speaker of the House

      Speaker of the House--

      majority party--

      minority party--

      Newt Gingrich--

   Other House Leaders

      majority leader--

      minority leader--

      whips--

      Tom DeLay--

The Senate

   vice president of the United States--

   president pro tempore--

   majority leader--

   "Gentleman's Club"--

The Role of Political Parties in Organizing Congress

   control by majority party--

   party caucus--

party conference--

Senator Jim Jeffords--

The Committee System

the work of Congress is done in committees--

Types of Committees

standing committee--

conference committee--

joint committees--

ad hoc, special, or select committees--

discharge petition--

Committee Membership

value of committee assignments to members--

pork barrel--

committee membership and parties--

Committee Chairs

powers of chairs--

The Lawmaking Function of Congress

How a Bill Becomes a Law: The Textbook Version

Committee of the Whole --

hold--

filibusters--

cloture--

conference committee (a bill must pass both houses in the same language to go to the president)--
veto--

pocket veto--

line-item veto--

How a Bill Really Becomes a Law: The China Trade Act of 2000

How Members Make Decisions

Constituents

Colleagues

logrolling --

Party

divided government--

Caucuses

Interest Groups and Lobbyists

primary function of most lobbyists--

grassroots appeals--

Political Action Committees

Staff and Support Agencies

CBO--

CRS--

GAO--

Congress and the President

the relationship before and after the 1930s--

The Shifting Balance of Power

FDR and Congress--

Congressional Oversight of the Executive Branch

    oversight--

    congressional review--

    legislative veto--

    Immigration and Naturalization Service v. Chadha (1983)--

Foreign Affairs Oversight

    Constitution's division of foreign policy powers among:

        President--

        Congress--

        Senate--

    War Powers Act--

    2001 joint resolution authorizing president to use force against terrorists--

Confirmation of Presidential Appointments

    Senate's special oversight (advise and consent power)--

    senatorial courtesy--

Impeachment Process

    impeachment--

    "high crimes and misdemeanor"--

    removal--

    the process (role of House, role of Senate)--

Research Ideas and Possible Paper Topics

1. Do some research and compare how different or similar the 108th Congress is to the 107th in terms of party majority, leadership, representation, minorities, women, structure, incumbency advantage, and rules. What accounts for the similarities and differences?

2. Using the Congressional website or government documents, research the transition between the 107th and 108th Congresses. What happened from election day 2002 to office-taking in January 2003? How are new members introduced to the rules, protocols, and traditions of the House and Senate? What happens to staff if their member is defeated? How do new members recruit staff? How are leaders chosen? How are rules made? Are there any "left-over issues" from the 107th? What impact has the 108th Congress had on the country?

3. Pick a piece of legislation from the 108th Congress. Write a legislative history of that bill or law. Outline the steps it took, who supported it, who opposed it, and various other influences on its passage. Were there hearings? witnesses? controversy? Does this compare with what you learned in the text about the lawmaking process? How?

4. Most Americans claim to dislike and distrust Congress but like and trust their own member of Congress. What explains this paradox? Do some research on public opinion and voting behavior, analyze the media coverage of Congress, think about what members of Congress do, and why this would be the case. Prepare a presentation explaining this phenomenon for class. See if you can determine how your own U.S. Representative is perceived in your area as well.

5. There have been a number of high profile scandals in the Congress throughout history. Americans now seem quite concerned about the ethics of the legislature. Do some research on scandals in Congress. How many have there been? How severe have they been? How widespread have they been? Is it a few bad apples or the whole barrel? Be sure to look at how the media have covered these scandals and the lack thereof in your discussion of the ethical nature of Congress.

Websites

Official site of the **House of Representatives**.
www.House.gov

Official site of the **Senate**.
www.Senate.gov

YourCongress.com is an expansive, easily accessible website about Congress, its members, its issues, its lobbyists, and how you can influence it. The site states that it "combines irreverent articles, behind-the scenes information, and the revolutionary Congress.Watch tracking services to give everyone an easy and entertaining way to find out what's going on in Congress."
  www.yourcongress.com

C-SPAN provides the most extensive coverage of Congress available on television over its three cable channels. Its website allows you to follow Congressional action as it is broadcast on C-SPAN with streaming video or audio. The website is sponsored by C-SPAN and Congressional Quarterly and has headings such as Write to Congress, Directory of Congress, Vote Library, Capital Questions, Live Hearings and many more.
  www.c-span.org/capitolspotlight/index.asp

Congressional Quarterly is a non-partisan publication whose mission is to inform the electorate. Site includes information on Congress including bios, votes, election information, and so on. They also have a link to their state and local level publication.
  www.cq.com/

GPO Access by the U.S. Government Printing Office offers the full text of many federal government publications on the web, including the Congressional Record. Among the growing list of titles available are the Federal Register, Congressional Bills, United States Code, Economic Indicators and GAO Reports.
  www.gpo.gov/su_doc/index.html

The Hill: The Capital Newspaper. " The Hill reports and analyzes the actions of Congress as it struggles to reconcile the needs of those it represents with the legitimate
needs of the administration, lobbyists, and the news media. We explain the pressures confronting policymakers, and the many ways - often unpredictable - that decisions are made. But Capitol Hill is more than the focal point of the legislative branch of government. It is also a community not unlike a small city, and we report on its culture, social life, crime, employment, traffic, education, discrimination, shopping, dining, travel, and recreation. Our editorial viewpoint is nonpartisan and nonideological." Published on Wednesdays.
  www.hillnews.com

RollCall On-Line. "Roll Call is widely regarded as the leading source for Congressional news and information both inside the Beltway and beyond." RollCall On-Line publishes many of the same stories, classifieds, etc. that the print edition publishes. Published on Mondays and Thursdays.
  www.rollcall.com

Congress.Org is a joint venture of two Washington, D.C. area firms with expertise in communicating with Congress. Capitol Advantage and Issue Dynamics (IDI) teamed up to produce Congress.Org in 1996. Some search engines refer to it as a "one stop shop" for legislative information including contact information on members, committee assignments, etc.
  www.congress.org

Public Citizens' Congress Watch is a consumer interest group that monitors and lobbies Congress. Its webpage reports on its actions and issues in the current Congress.
www.citizen.org.congress/

The Washington Post. Check out the "Today in Congress" section, including committee hearings and votes. Also click "OnPolitics" for the latest in-depth political news of Congress.
www.washingtonpost.com

Official government website from the **Library of Congress** with information on legislation, the *Congressional Record*, links to Congress-related sites.
thomas.loc.gov

Project Vote-Smart is a non-partisan information service funded by members and non-partisan foundations. It offers "a wealth of facts on your political leaders, including biographies and addresses, issue positions, voting records, campaign finances, evaluations by special interests." It also offers "CongressTrack," a way for citizens to track the status of legislation, members and committees, sponsors, voting records, clear descriptions, full text, and weekly floor schedules, as well as access to information on elections, federal and state governments, the issues, and politics. Includes thousands of links to the most important sites on the Internet.
www.vote-smart.org/

Practice Tests

MULTIPLE CHOICE QUESTIONS

1. The first truly national legislature in the colonies was the

    a. House of Burgesses.
    b. Colonial Assembly.
    c. First Continental Congress.
    d. U.S. Congress.

2. The Senate was originally chosen by state legislators. This was changed to direct election in 1913 with the passage of the _____ Amendment.

    a. Seventeenth
    b. Eighteenth
    c. Nineteenth
    d. Twentieth

3. The clause of the Constitution that has allowed Congress to expand its powers without constitutional amendment is called the

   a. supremacy clause.
   b. necessary and proper clause.
   c. enumerated powers clause.
   d. executive powers clause.

4. From 1980 to 1990, an average of _____ percent of incumbents who sought reelection won.

   a. 75
   b. 80
   c. 88
   d. 95

5. A member of Congress who sees their role as voting how their constituents would want them to is called a

   a. politico.
   b. delegate.
   c. trustee.
   d. representative.

6. Among the main differences between the House and the Senate are that

   a. House members are highly specialized.
   b. the Senate is less centralized and formal.
   c. the House has a Rules Committee.
   d. all of the above.

7. The only House officer specifically mentioned in the Constitution is the

   a. president pro tempore.
   b. majority leader of the Senate.
   c. speaker of the house.
   d. sergeant at arms.

8. The Speaker in the 107th Congress is

   a. Dennis Hastert.
   b. Bob Livingston.
   c. Dick Armey.
   d. Joseph Cannon.

9. The presiding officer of the Senate is the

   a. vice president of the United States.
   b. president pro tempore of the Senate.
   c. majority leader of the Senate.
   d. speaker.

10. The first and last places that most bills go in Congress is the

    a. joint committee.
    b. subcommittee.
    c. standing committee.
    d. party caucus.

11. Approximately _____ bills are introduced in each session of Congress.

    a. 4,500
    b. 5,000
    c. 7,500
    d. 9,000

12. A tactic by which a senator asks to be informed before a particular bill is brought to the floor, in effect stopping the bill, is called a

    a. discharge petition.
    b. cloture.
    c. block.
    d. hold.

13. The range and complexity of issues facing Congress means that no one can be up to speed on all topics. When members have to vote on issues about which they know and care little, they often turn to colleagues and trade votes. This is called

    a. logrolling.
    b. cloture.
    c. pork barrel.
    d. delegation.

14. Since 1961, there has been a substantial increase in the use of one of Congress' functions. That is

    a. lawmaking.
    b. oversight.
    c. impeachment and removal.
    d. advise and consent.

15. The legislative veto was ruled unconstitutional by the Supreme Court in

   a. *Immigration and Naturalization Service v. Chadha.*
   b. *U.S. v. Nixon.*
   c. *Shaw v. Reno.*
   d. *Thornburg v. Gingles.*

TRUE/FALSE QUESTIONS

1. In 1929, the size of the House of Representatives was fixed at 435 by statute.

2. The House of Representatives has the authority to approve presidential appointments.

3. The Senate Rules Committee is very powerful and controls the flow of bills.

4. The advantages of incumbency include access to the media, pork barreling, and casework.

5. Voter frustration in the 1980s and 90s has led to term limits being placed on many members of Congress.

6. Every two years, a new Congress is seated.

7. The majority party in the House names the Speaker and all committee chairs.

8. The Framers designed Congress to work on the basis of the two-party system.

9. Any governmental official may introduce a bill for the consideration of Congress.

10. Members of Congress rely heavily on their staffs for information on pending legislation.

COMPARE AND CONTRAST

apportionment, redistricting, and gerrymandering

bill and law

impeachment and removal

differences in operation between the House and Senate

powers of House and Senate

officers of House and Senate

trustees, delegates, and politicos

> standing committees, ad hoc committees, joint committees, and conference committees
>
> rules in the House and the Senate on speaking about issues and bills
>
> general veto, line-item veto, and legislative veto
>
> CRS, GAO, and CBO

SHORT ANSWER AND ESSAY QUESTIONS

1. Discuss the roots of the legislative branch prior to the adoption of the U.S. Constitution.

2. What are apportionment and redistricting and their implications?

3. Discuss the incumbency advantage.

4. How representative is Congress? (Be sure to discuss the definition and theories of representation.)

5. Discuss the types of committees in Congress.

6. What are the constitutional powers of Congress?

7. How do the powers and functions of the House and Senate differ?

8. Discuss the role of leadership and party in the House and Senate.

9. What is the lawmaking function of Congress? Compare and contrast the two ways the text discusses about how a bill becomes a law. Be sure to specify all points at which a bill could die.

10. How do members of Congress make decisions?

ANSWERS TO STUDY EXERCISES

multiple choice answers

1.	c	p. 217
2.	a	p. 217
3.	b	p. 218
4.	d	p. 222
5.	b	p. 224
6.	d	p. 230
7.	c	p. 230

8.	a	p. 230
9.	a	p. 233
10.	c	p. 237
11.	d	p. 240
12.	d	p. 244
13.	a	p. 249
14.	b	p. 253
15.	a	p. 254

true/false answers

1.	T	p. 218
2.	F	p. 219
3.	F	p. 219
4.	T	p. 222
5.	F	p. 223
6.	T	p. 230
7.	T	p. 230
8.	F	p. 235
9.	F	p. 240
10.	T	p. 251

CHAPTER 8
THE PRESIDENCY

Chapter Goals and Learning Objectives

Ask a friend, "Who is your Congressman?" and you are likely to get a blank stare in return. Ask her, however, "Who is the president?" and she will respond instantly, "George Bush, of course!" Congress, constitutionally the first branch of government, has taken a back seat in American politics to the president, not only in public awareness but in raw power. The constitutional authority, statutory powers, and burdens of the modern presidency make it a powerful position and an awesome responsibility. Most of the men who have been president in the past two decades have done their best; yet, in the heightened expectations of the American electorate, most have come up short. Our awareness of the president in our public life is high, and our expectations of the man in that office are even higher. Not only did the Framers not envision such a powerful role for the president, they could not have foreseen the skepticism with which many presidential actions are now greeted in the press, on talk radio, and on the Internet. These expectations have also led presidents into policy areas never dreamed of by the Framers.

This chapter is designed to give you a basic understanding of the presidency as an institution as well as some information on the men who have occupied the office. The main topic headings of the chapter are:

- The Roots of the Office of President of the United States
- The Constitutional Powers of the President
- The Development of Presidential Power
- The Presidential Establishment
- The Role of the President in the Legislative Process: The President as Policy Maker
- The Presidency and Public Opinion

In each section you will find certain facts and ideas that you should work to understand. Many are in boldface type and appear in both the narrative and in the glossary at the end of the book. Other ideas, dates, facts, events, people, etc., are more difficult to find in the narrative. (Keep in mind that the process of reading and studying for objective [multiple choice, T/F] exams is different than for essay tests. See the Study Guide section on test taking for help with study skills.)

In general, after you finish reading and studying this chapter, you should understand the following:

- the roots of the office of president of the United States and how the Framers created the executive for a new nation
- Article II and the constitutional powers of the presidency
- the development of presidential power in response to events, crises, personalities, and other influences

- the increasing personalization of the presidency and how success has come to depend on the officeholder's personality, popularity, and leadership style
- how the presidency managed to become the central focus of power and action in the United States
- the growth of the presidential establishment of advisors, assistants, and departments
- the role of the president in the legislative process and how presidential agenda-setting has caused Congress to try to reassert their own powers in this area
- the role of public opinion and its impact on the American president as well as the effect the president has on public opinion
- the president's changing role and proposals for reforming the presidency
- the effect public opinion has on the American presidency and the role the president plays in molding public opinion

Chapter Outline and Key Points

In this section, you are provided with a basic outline of the chapter and any key words/points you should know. Use this outline, in your own notebook, to develop a complete outline of the material. This will help you study and remember the material in preparation for your tests, assignments, and papers.

The Roots of the Office of President of the United States

The Constitutional Convention

Qualifications for Office

Terms of Office

Removal

impeachment--

articles of impeachment--

Succession

Presidential Succession Act of 1947--

25th Amendment--

The Vice President

The Constitutional Powers of the President

Article II--

basis of the president's authority--

The Appointment Power

The Cabinet--

The Power to Convene Congress

The State of the Union--

The Power to Make Treaties

advise and consent of the Senate--

Wilson and the Treaty of Versailles--

executive agreement--

Veto Power

veto power--

The Line-Item Veto

line-item veto--

The Power to Preside Over the Military as Commander-in-Chief

The War Powers Act--

The Pardoning Power

pardon--

The Development of Presidential Power

The First Three Presidents

inherent powers--

Louisiana Purchase--

Congressional Triumph: 1804-1933

Jacksonian democracy--

Lincoln's "questionable acts"--

stewardship theory--

Taftian theory--

The Growth of the Modern Presidency

FDR and the New Deal--

FDR's "Fireside Chats"--

Modern presidency--

The Presidential Establishment

The Cabinet

The First Lady

The Executive Office of the President (EOP)

The Executive Office of the President--

National Security Council (NSC)--

White House Staff

Kitchen Cabinet--

size of president's White House staff--

The Role of the President in the Legislative Process: The President as Policymaker

presidentialist--

congressionalist—

president's most important power--

divided government --

Presidential Involvement in the Budgetary Process

FDR and the Bureau of the Budget--

OMB --

Gramm-Rudman Act--

Ruling Through Regulation

executive order --

President Bush and the Presidential Records Act--

Winning Support for Programs

Patronage and Party Ties

patronage--

Presidential Style

Presidential Leadership

examples of how "great crises make great presidents"--

The Power to Persuade

The President and Public Opinion

executive privilege --

US v. Nixon (1974) --

Going Public

bully pulpit--

going public--

Presidential Approval Ratings

Research Ideas and Possible Paper Topics

1. Examine the growth and impact of the modern presidency. Compare it to the role of the president through the first century-and-a-half of the history of the United States. What precipitated the development of the modern presidency and what fueled its tremendous development over the past 70 years? Discuss what you think James Madison and Alexander Hamilton might say about the modern status of the limited chief executive they helped create?

2. Do some research on the vice presidency of Dick Cheney. The book calls him the most active vice president in history. What types of activities has he been involved in and

why? Is it a function of his personal relationship with Bush or a permanent change in the office of the vice president? What role, if any, did 9/11 have in Cheney's role? Discuss.

3. We have experienced periods of "divided government" where the Congress is of one party and the presidency of another. The executive and legislative branches have also recently been controlled by one party. Do some research into public opinion on this issue. Which situation do Americans prefer? Why? Also research the impact divided government has had on the policy process versus the impact of single party control. Do more bills fail in a divided government? Are Congress and the president more confrontational due to partisan differences in a divided government? Which scenario works better for our democracy? Discuss.

4. Choose two presidents from history and write a paper discussing the impact they had on the office. Two interesting variants might be to choose one president who had a positive effect and one who had a negative effect, or to choose two extremely different personalities who seem equally successful and explain why.

5. Group Project: Do a media analysis of presidential coverage. For one month, watch a variety of network and cable news programs, read a variety of newspapers and weekly news magazines, listen to talk radio (be sure to get right and left wing programs), and check out Internet news sites. How is the president covered? What gets the attention of the media and why? Is the president "staging" or "spinning" any of the coverage or are the media in control? What implications do your findings have on how we perceive the president?

Websites

The official **White House** site for information on George W. Bush and the office of the president.
www.whitehouse.gov/WH/EOP/OP/html/OP_Home.html

The **National Archives and Records Administration** offers links to all presidential libraries.
www.nara.gov/nara/president/address.html

The **National Portrait Gallery's Hall of Presidents** has information on and portraits of American presidents.
www.npg.si.edu/col/pres/index.htm

The **University of North Carolina** site offers biographies of the presidents and first ladies, including links to presidential libraries.
metalab.unc.edu/lia/president/

Federal Web Locator has links to all government websites, including presidential ones.
www.infoctr.edu/fwl

The Atlantic Monthly offers a simulation of presidential decision-making. Several scenarios from 1996 to 2000 were offered in the magazine and are archived on their website. Advisory memos are presented by policy advisors. The reader is then asked to make a decision. After submitting a decision, readers could provide interactive feedback about the effects of the decision. Entertaining but useful tool to demonstrate the politics of decision-making and why the "best" decisions are not always the politic ones.
http://www.theatlantic.com/politics/decision/memos.htm

POTUS: Presidents of the United States is assembled by the Internet Public Library and provides background information, election results, cabinet members, notable events, and some points of interest on each of the presidents. Links to biographies, historical documents, audio and video files, and other presidential sites listed.
http://www.ipl.org/div/potus/

You can search the **Public Papers of the Presidents of the United States** online at this site provided by the Office of the Federal Registrar. Not all presidential papers are available currently online. Presidential photographs can be accessed as well.
http://www.access.gpo.gov/nara/pubpaps/srchpaps.html

Statistics, facts and biographies of U.S. Vice-Presidents are available at **Vice-Presidents.Com**.
http://www.vicepresidents.com/

Current events and video clips about the Bush Administration are available on the
C-SPAN website page devoted to the Executive Branch.
http://www.c-span.org/executive/

Practice Tests

MULTIPLE CHOICE QUESTIONS

1. In order to be president of the United States, according to the Constitution, a candidate must be

    a. male.
    b. at least 35 years old.
    c. a resident for over five years.
    d.) a natural-born citizen

2. The Constitution says the president

    a. may serve only two terms.
    b. is limited to a maximum of ten years in office.
    c.) serves for a four-year term.
    d. serves a six-year term.

3. The Presidential Succession Act of 1947 states that if the president should die and the vice president cannot succeed him, then the next in line is the

   a. speaker of the house.
   b. president pro tempore of the Senate.
   c. secretary of state.
   d. majority leader of the Senate.

4. The first president to assume that office after appointment, not election, to the office of the vice-presidency was

   a. William H. Harrison.
   b. Dwight D. Eisenhower.
   c. Gerald R. Ford.
   d. George Bush.

5. Which of the following offices is the president not constitutionally empowered to appoint?

   a. members of the U.S. Supreme Court
   b. U.S. ambassadors to foreign countries
   c. officers of the United States (such as cabinet officers)
   d. speakers of the house and president pro tempore of the Senate

6. An example of the Senate using its advise and consent power to reject a treaty signed by the president was when the Senate rejected the Treaty of Versailles which had been negotiated and signed by

   a. Theodore Roosevelt.
   b. Franklin Roosevelt.
   c. Woodrow Wilson.
   d. Dwight D. Eisenhower.

7. The president can enter into treaty-like relations with foreign countries for his term only without Senate approval on the basis of

   a. executive powers.
   b. executive privilege.
   c. executive orders.
   d. executive agreements.

8. In 1996, Congress voted to give the president line-item veto power. What is the status of that power now?

   a. President Clinton refused to use it, claiming that the Republican Congress was attempting to trick him.
   b. The Congress voted to repeal the line-item veto given to the president saying that the president was trying to trick them.
   c. In 1998, the U.S. Supreme Court struck down the line-item veto as unconstitutional.
   d. The president continues to use the line-item veto and has done so over twenty times during the past year.

9. Thomas Jefferson expanded the powers of the president through

   a. the Louisiana Purchase.
   b. the use of veto powers.
   c. the use of political parties to cement ties with Congress.
   d. the doctrine of enumerated powers.

10. The first president who behaved as a strong national leader was

    a. Thomas Jefferson.
    b. Andrew Jackson.
    c. James Monroe.
    d. Franklin D. Roosevelt.

11. The growth of the modern presidency began with

    a. Thomas Jefferson.
    b. Abraham Lincoln.
    c. Franklin Roosevelt.
    d. Ronald Reagan.

12. The last cabinet department established, approved by Congress in November, 2002, was the Department of

    a. Homeland Security
    b. Energy.
    c. Veteran's Affairs.
    d. Education.

13. The president most scholars consider to be the most effective in working with Congress was

   a. Lyndon B. Johnson.
   b. Richard M. Nixon.
   c. Gerald R. Ford.
   d. Bill Clinton.

14. According to Richard Neustadt, the most important presidential power is

   a. his constitutional power.
   b. the mandate power.
   c. the power to persuade.
   d. his commander-in-chief power.

15. The term "bully pulpit" was used first by what president to describe the power of the president to reach out to the American people to gain support for his programs?

   a. Theodore Roosevelt
   b. Woodrow Wilson
   c. Franklin Roosevelt
   d. John F. Kennedy

TRUE/FALSE QUESTIONS

1. Under the Articles of Confederation, no executive branch, and therefore no president, existed.

2. The president is limited to two terms in Article II of the Constitution.

3. In 1967, the Twenty-Fifth Amendment was added to the Constitution to allow a president to fill a vacancy in the office of vice president.

4. Vice presidents are chosen solely for their abilities to replace the president if he dies in office.

5. The president has no actual power to make Congress enact legislation he supports.

6. The president's power to make treaties is limited by the requirement of a vote of two-thirds of the Senate to ratify the treaty.

7. The president has the power to reject all or part of any bill passed by Congress.

8. While only the Congress has the power to declare war, the president has the power to make and wage war.

9. F Since the 1973 adoption of the War Powers Act by Congress, each president since Richard Nixon has scrupulously followed the dictates of that act limiting presidential war-making authority.

10. T Direct, personal appeals to the American people by the president, going over the heads of Congress via radio and television (called "going public") effectively empowers the president to influence Congress.

COMPARE AND CONTRAST

executive agreement and executive order

general and line-item veto

presidential and congressional war powers

stewardship and Taftian theory

the Cabinet and the EOP

presidentialist and congressionalist views

presidential and congressional roles in the budget-making process

the Article II presidency versus the modern presidency

ESSAY AND SHORT ANSWER QUESTIONS

1) What are the formal requirements for the presidency? Are there also informal requirements? What are they?

2) How is the vice president chosen and what are the duties of the office? Have they changed over time? Why?

3) How did the first three presidents affect the powers of the presidency?

4) Compare and contrast the nature and functions of the cabinet, the Executive Office of the President, and other advisors.

5) Discuss the nature of war powers. What are the presidential and congressional powers at issue and has this conflict been solved?

6) Discuss the roots of the office of president and the constitutional debate surrounding the office of the presidency, including a full discussion of the results: Article II.

7) How has presidential power developed? What makes for a powerful president?

8) Analyze the nature and functions of the "presidential establishment".

9) What is the role of the president in the legislative process? What makes a president most effective in this role?

10) Discuss why Americans are dissatisfied with the office of the presidency and whomever inhabits it. What proposals have been made to reform the presidency? Do they adequately reflect the problems and conflicts of the office? Can we "fix" the presidency so that the majority of Americans are satisfied? Discuss.

ANSWERS TO STUDY EXERCISES

multiple choice answers

1. d p. 272
2. c p. 272
3. a p. 275
4. c p. 275
5. d p. 278
6. c p. 280
7. d p. 280
8. c p. 283
9. a p. 287
10. b p. 287
11. c p. 286
12. a p. 291
13. a p. 302
14. c p. 302
15. a p. 305

true/false answers

1. T p. 271
2. F p. 273
3. T p. 275
4. F p. 226
5. T p. 278
6. T p. 280
7. F p. 283
8. T p. 283
9. F p. 284
10. T p. 305

CHAPTER 9
THE EXECUTIVE BRANCH AND FEDERAL BUREAUCRACY

Chapter Goals and Learning Objectives

Often called the "fourth branch of government" because of the power agencies and bureaus can exercise, the federal bureaucracy draws criticism from many sectors. Political conservatives charge that the bureaucracy is too liberal and that its functions constitute unnecessary government inference in the business sector. In contrast, liberals view the bureaucracy as too slow, too unimaginative to solve America's problems, and too zealous a guardian of the status quo. And while many Americans complain of the efficiency and impact of the government, most Americans regard the government services they receive through the bureaucracy important to their lives. Indeed, it is the executive branch organizations which deliver the myriad of services citizens have come to expect from their government. A basic knowledge of these organizations is important to you, a consumer of these services.

This chapter is designed to give you a better understanding of the executive branch and federal bureaucracy. The main topic headings of this chapter are:

- The Roots and Development of the Executive Branch and the Federal Bureaucracy
- The Modern Bureaucracy
- Policymaking
- Holding Agencies Accountable

In each section, there are certain facts and ideas that you should strive to understand. Many are in boldface type and appear in both the narrative and in the glossary at the end of the book. Other ideas, dates, facts, events, people, etc., are more difficult to pull out of the narrative. (Keep in mind that studying for objective-[multiple choice, T/] style tests is different than studying for essay tests. See the Study Guide section on test taking for hints on study skills.)

In general, after you finish reading and studying this chapter, you should understand the following:

- the historical roots of the executive branch and federal bureaucracy and its development
- how the modern bureaucracy is structured and how it works
- how policies are made and the impact of the bureaucracy on policymaking
- how agencies are held accountable

Chapter Outline and Key Points

In this section, you are provided with a basic outline of the chapter and any key words/points you should know. Use this outline, in your own notebook, to develop a complete outline of the material. This will help you study and remember the material in preparation for your tests, assignments, and papers.

The Roots and Development of the Federal Bureaucracy

bureaucracy--

characteristics of model bureaucracies--
1)
2)
3)
4)
5)
6)

The Civil War and Its Aftermath

Pension Office--

patronage--

From Spoils to Merit

spoils system--

Pendleton Act--

civil service system--

merit system--

National Efforts to Regulate the Economy

independent regulatory commissions--

Department of Commerce and Labor--

What Should Government Do?

laissez-faire--

The New Deal and Bigger Government

NIRA--

NLRB--

WWII and its Aftermath

GI Bill--

The Modern Bureaucracy

key to modern bureaucracy--

Who are Bureaucrats?

GS Grades--

federal workforce not covered by civil service commission--

how to fire a bureaucrat--

Formal Organization

The Cabinet Departments

department--

clientele agencies--

Government Corporations

government corporations--

Independent Executive Agencies

independent executive agencies--

Independent Regulatory Commissions

independent regulatory commission--

Politics and Government Workers

Hatch Act--

Federal Employees Political Activities Act--

Policymaking

implementation--

Iron Triangles and Issue Networks

iron triangles--

issue networks--

Administrative Discretion

administrative discretion--

rule-making--

regulations--

The Federal Register --

administrative adjudication--

Making Agencies Accountable

Executive Control

president has what authority? (Table 9.3)--

executive order--

Congressional Control

Congress has what authority? (Table 9.3)--

police patrol oversight--

fire alarm oversight--

investigatory powers--

power of the purse--

Judicial Control

injunctions--

specialized courts--

Research Ideas and Possible Paper Topics

1. Service Learning (learn by doing): Visit at least three federal offices in your area. Research each agency on the Internet prior to your visit. Watch what goes on. Ask questions. Investigate the functions and efficiencies of the procedures used. If possible, schedule interviews with managers and staff at these offices. Ask about misconceptions and problems with the bureaucracy. How does what you find compare with what you learned in the text?

2. One of the oldest bureaucratic departments is the Department of State. Research to determine how they have reorganized over the years to cope with new challenges and directives. How large is the DOS? What functions do they perform? What is their budget? How effective are they in carrying out their goals? In addition, analyze whether Secretary of State Colin Powell, the first African-American and former General to take this post, has managed to change the culture of the department and if so how.

3. The postal service has changed its relationship with the government and the American people over time. Research the history of the postal service, its past and present ties to the government, its effectiveness, and reputation. Many of us complain incessantly about the mail. Are we justified? How are rate increases determined? If we are truly unhappy, what avenues of complaint are open?

4. Service Learning (learn by doing): Write to or visit your local congressional office. Ask to speak with one of the caseworkers who deals with bureaucratic snafus and red tape. Find out how they intervene on behalf of constituents, how effective they are, how many constituents avail themselves of this service, and their impressions of the bureaucracy. Write a paper or discuss in class what you have learned.

5. How does the bureaucracy affect you? Consider the innumerable ways that government helps or hinders your life. Keep a journal for the semester and note in it ways you interact with bureaucracy and government. At the end of class, compare notes with friends and colleagues. Discuss whether, in total, your experiences with government are positive, negative, or neutral.

Websites

President Bush's Cabinet is a website hosted by the White House presenting photographs of cabinet officers, biographies, and links to their departments.
    www.whitehouse.gov/government/cabinet.html

Federal Web Locator provided by the Chicago-Kent College of Law has links to all government websites, including all governmental departments, agencies, corporations, and affiliates.
    www.infoctr.edu/fwl

FedWorld, hosted by the Department of Commerce, is a comprehensive index of federal government agencies, searchable by keyword. Access to thousands of U.S. Government web sites, more than a 1/2 million U.S. Government documents, databases and other information products with links to the FedWorld File Libraries and other sources.
www.fedworld.gov

The Departments of the Federal Government

Department of Agriculture
www.usda.gov

Department of Commerce
www.doc.gov

Department of Defense
www.defenselink.mil

Department of Education
www.ed.gov

Department of Energy
www.energy.gov

Department of Health and Human Services
www.os.dhhs.gov

Department of Housing and Urban Development
www.hud.gov

Department of Interior
www.doi.gov

Department of Justice
www.usdoj.gov

Department of Labor
www.dol.gov

Department of State
www.state.gov

Department of Transportation
www.dot.gov

Department of Treasury
www.ustreas.gov

Department of Veteran's Affairs
www.va.gov

Department of Homeland Security
www.whitehouse/homeland

Practice Tests

MULTIPLE CHOICE QUESTIONS

1. In 2001, the executive branch had approximately __ million civilian employees.

    a. 1.78
    b. 2.6
    c. 3.9
    d. 5

2. The reform measure that created the civil service is commonly referred to as the

    a. Anti-Patronage Act.
    b. Hatch Act.
    c. Pendleton Act.
    d. Garfield Act.

3. The first independent regulatory commission, established to regulate railroad rates after the Civil War, was called the

    a. Independent Transportation Commission.
    b. Federal Trade Commission.
    c. National Railroad Relations Board.
    d. Interstate Commerce Commission.

4. An agency created by Congress that is concerned with a specific economic activity or interest is called a(n)

    a. cabinet department.
    b. clientele agency.
    c. independent regulatory commission.
    d. government corporation.

5. Which of the following is *not* a reason why iron triangles no longer dominate most policy processes?

    a. a tremendous increase in the number of D.C.-based interest groups
    b. recent Supreme Court decisions undermining Congressional authority
    c. problems are increasingly more complex
    d. issues cut across several policy areas

6. Administrative discretion--the ability of bureaucrats to make choices concerning implementation of congressional intentions--is exercised through two formal administrative procedures:

    a. administrative adjudication and rule-making.
    b. rule-making and issue networking.
    c. sunset review and administrative oversight.
    d. congressional review and oversight.

7. There are currently _____ cabinet departments.

    a. 10
    b. 12
    c. 13
    d. 15

8. Executive departments directed by law to foster and promote the interests of a specific segment of group in the U.S. population is called a(n)

    a. cabinet department.
    b. clientele agency.
    c. government corporation.
    d. executive agency.

9. The Environmental Protection Agency (EPA) is an example of a(n)

    a. independent executive agency.
    b. government corporation.
    c. clientele agency.
    d. independent regulatory commission.

10. A law enacted in 1939 to protect civil servants from being forced to give money to or work on political campaigns by prohibiting them from becoming directly in involved in political campaigns is known as the

    a. Pendleton Act.
    b. Civil Service Reform Act.
    c. Hatch Act.
    d. Partisan Protection Act.

11. The relatively stable relationship and pattern of interaction that occur among an agency, interest groups, and congressional committees is called a(n)

   a. issue network.
   b. implementation network.
   c. policy circle.
   d. iron triangle.

12. The bureaucracy performs some quasi-judicial functions such as

   a. administrative discretion.
   b. administrative adjudication.
   c. regulation.
   d. rule-making.

13. The president has the power to hold agencies accountable through

   a. appointment and removal of agency heads.
   b. changing budget proposals.
   c. issuing executive orders.
   d. all of the above.

14. Congress can hold the bureaucracy accountable through

   a. rulings on bureaucratic compliance with the laws.
   b. appointment and removal of bureau heads.
   c. investigation and appropriations.
   d. all of the above.

15. The most commonly used and effective form of congressional oversight is

   a. staff communication with agency personnel.
   b. removal of agency heads.
   c. regulation.
   d. adjudication.

TRUE/FALSE

1. The bureaucracy consists of a set of complex, hierarchical departments, agencies, commissions, and their staffs that exist to help the president enforce the laws of the country.

2. The "spoils system" allowed each political party to "pack" the bureaucracy with their supporters when they won the presidency.

3. Less than half of the federal bureaucracy is covered by civil service laws.

4. Governments exist for the public good, not to make money and, therefore, cannot be run like a business.

5. The U.S. Postal Service is an example of an independent executive agency.

6. Bureaucrats make, as well as implement, policies.

7. The first president to tackle the issue of bureaucratic accountability was Thomas Jefferson.

8. The bureaucracy is accountable to no one except the president.

9. An executive order is a presidential directive to an agency that provides the basis for carrying out laws or for establishing new policies.

10. The most popular technique of congressional oversight of the bureaucracy is cutting agency funding.

SHORT ANSWER AND ESSAY QUESTIONS

1. Detail the development of the Department of Homeland Security which was created by Congress late in 2002. How effective has this, the most extensive governmental reorganization in almost half a century, been?

2. What was the spoils system and how did it lead to civil service reforms? What were those reforms?

3. What are iron triangles and why are they no longer as significant as they once were?

4. Does the bureaucracy make policy? Discuss two ways that it does or does not.

5. Discuss three methods by which the bureaucracy can be held accountable.

6. Discuss the roots and development of the federal bureaucracy.

7. What is the formal organization of the bureaucracy and what are the main functions of each agency, commission, or department? Give examples.

8. Discuss the nature of bureaucratic policymaking.

9. Discuss the checks and balances the president, Congress, and the judiciary have on the bureaucracy. Which techniques are used most often and which are most effective and why?

10. What problems plague bureaucratic politics and what reforms have been aimed at addressing them? How effective have these reform efforts been?

COMPARE AND CONTRAST

patronage, spoils system, and merit system

cabinet departments, government corporations, independent executive agencies, and independent regulatory commissions

iron triangles and issue networks

administrative discretion and administrative adjudication

executive versus congressional control of the bureaucracy

ANSWERS TO STUDY EXERCISES

multiple choice answers

1. a   p. 318
2. c   p. 320
3. d   p. 320
4. c   p. 330
5. b   p. 333
6. a   p. 336
7. d   p. 328
8. b   p. 328
9. a   p. 330
10. c   p. 331
11. d   p. 332
12. b   p. 337
13. d   p. 338
14. c   p. 338
15. a   p. 340

true/false answers

1. T   p. 316
2. T   p. 318
3. F   p. 320
4. T   p. 323
5. F   p. 330
6. T   p. 332
7. T   p. 338
8. F   p. 338
9. T   p. 340
10. F   p. 340

CHAPTER 10
THE JUDICIARY

Chapter Goals and Learning Objectives

Today, the role of the federal courts, particularly the U.S. Supreme Court, differs dramatically from its function early in the nation's history. The "least dangerous branch" gained prominence from the development of the doctrine of judicial review and, as well, from the growth in the size and reach of the federal government. The Framers never envisioned the authority and reach of the Supreme Court and lower federal courts; of course, the Framers never envisioned the incredible growth of the federal government and its laws, laws adjudicated by the federal courts. The Supreme Court today, as arbiter of the Constitution, can, in a single decision, dramatically reshape the social and political structure of the country as evidenced, for example, by *Roe v. Wade* and *Bush v. Gore*. As our social and political beliefs change in the country, so does the interpretations of our laws by judges and justices on the federal bench. Who sits on the Supreme Court and in the federal courts across the land truly matters. It is no wonder that many scholars believe the most lasting decision a president makes is who he appoints to the Supreme Court and the federal bench.

This chapter is designed to give you an overview of the federal judicial system. The main topic headings in the chapter are:

- The Constitution and the Creation of the National Judiciary
- The Judiciary Act of 1789 and the Creation of the Federal Judiciary
- The American Legal System
- The Federal Court System
- How Federal Court Judges are Selected
- The Supreme Court Today
- How the Justices Make Decisions and Vote
- Judicial Policymaking and Implementation

In each section, there are certain facts and ideas that you should strive to understand. Many are in boldface type and appear in both the narrative and in the glossary at the end of the book. Other ideas, dates, facts, events, people, etc., are more difficult to pull out of the narrative. (Keep in mind that studying for objective-[multiple choice, T/F] style tests is different than studying for essay tests. See the Study Guide section on test taking for hints on study skills.)

In general, after you finish reading and studying this chapter, you should understand the following:

- the creation of the national judiciary by Article III of the Constitution and congressional statute--the Judiciary Act of 1789
- the rules and structures of the American legal system
- the types and jurisdictions of the various federal courts
- how federal court judges are selected through the political process of presidential nomination and Senatorial review

- the operation and function of the Supreme Court today
- how Supreme Court justices make their decisions based on legal and extra-legal factors
- how judicial policies are made and implemented

Chapter Outline and Key Points

In this section, you are provided with a basic outline of the chapter and any key words/points you should know. Use this outline, in your own notebook, to develop a complete outline of the material. This will help you study and remember the material in preparation for your tests, assignments, and papers.

The Constitution and the National Judiciary

    Article III--

    judicial review--

    original jurisdiction of the Supreme Court--

    Marbury v. Madison (1803)--

    Martin v. Hunter's Lessee (1816)--

The Judiciary Act of 1789 and the Creation of the Federal Judicial System

    Judiciary Act of 1789--

    John Jay--

    Chisholm v. Georgia (1793)--

The Marshall Court (1801-1835)

    John Marshall--

    Fletcher v. Peck (1810)--

    McCulloch v. Maryland (1819)--

Asserting Judicial Review

    Marbury v. Madison (1803)--

    judicial review--

The American Legal System

    trial courts--

    appellate courts--

Jurisdiction

    jurisdiction--

    original jurisdiction--

    appellate jurisdiction--

Criminal and Civil Law

    criminal law --

    civil law --

    plaintiff --

    defendant --

The Federal Court System

    constitutional courts--

    legislative courts--

District Courts

    district court jurisdiction--
        1)
        2)
        3)

    U.S. Attorney--

The Courts of Appeal

    eleven numbered circuit courts--

    D.C. Court of Appeal--

    U.S. Court of Appeals for the Federal Circuit--

en banc--

jurisdiction over two categories of cases--

right to appeal--

purpose of appellate courts and procedures--

brief--

precedent--

stare decisis--

The Supreme Court

number of members--

role of Chief Justice--

assignment of majority opinion--

How Federal Court Judges are Selected

political process of selection--

Who are Federal Judges?

characteristics (Table 10.3)--

Appointments to the U.S. Supreme Court

constitutional requirements--

Ruth Bader Ginsburg--

importance to president--

Nomination Criteria

Competence

Ideological or Policy Preference

strict constructionist--

Rewards

Abe Fortas--

Pursuit of Political Support

Sandra Day O'Connor

Religion

"Jewish seat"--

Race and Gender

Thurgood Marshall--

The Supreme Court Confirmation Process

power of the Senate--

Investigation

ABA--

Senate Judiciary Committee--

Lobbying by Interest Groups

Robert Bork--

The Senate Committee Hearings and Senate Vote

first nominee to testify in detail--

simple majority in Senate--

The Supreme Court Today

"cult of the robe"--

Deciding to Hear a Case

petitions received and opinions issued in 2001-2002 term--

The Supreme Court's Jurisdiction

two types of jurisdiction--

substantial federal questions--

writ of certiorari--

in forma pauperis--

The Rule of Four

two requirement for *certiorari*--

Rule of Four --

The Role of Clerks

what do clerks do? (Table 10.7)--

How Does a Case Survive the Process?

criteria for Court accepting a case--

amicus curiae--

The Solicitor General

solicitor general --

Conflict Among the Circuits

what does the Court seek to do?--

Interest Group Participation

how justices use interest group participation--

Starting the Case

Oral Arguments

when do they take place?--

who participates?--

how do justices use oral arguments?--

The Conference and the Vote

role of conferences--

majority vote wins--

Writing Opinions

majority opinion --

concurring opinion --

plurality opinion --

dissenting opinion --

per curiam opinion --

How the Justices Vote

Legal Factors

Judicial Philosophy and Original Intent

judicial restraint--

judicial activism--

Precedent

role of precedent--

Extra-Legal Factors

Behavioral Characteristics

Ideology

The Attitudinal Model and Strategic Mode

attitudinal model--

strategic mode--

Public Opinion

how public perceives Court--

impact of public opinion on Court--

Judicial Policymaking and Implementation

Policymaking

political questions--

Implementing Court Decisions

judicial implementation--

three requirements for effective implementation--
1)
2)
3)

Research Ideas and Possible Paper Topics

1. Research the Court's current docket (see official Supreme Court website below). How many cases will it hear? How many came to the Court through *cert* and how many through *in forma pauperis*? What types of cases will the Court hear? What constitutional issues are at stake? Why do you think the Court has chosen to rule on these cases?

2. Research biographies on the current Supreme Court justices. What are their backgrounds? Why were they chosen for the Court and by whom? How are they perceived by court-watchers? (In other words, what do the experts think of them?) Is there a definite majority on the Court for any single set of constitutional issues? The Warren Court was characterized as very activist, particularly regarding due process rights. Can the Rehnquist Court be characterized? If so, how?

3. Choose two well-known Supreme Court cases. Research to determine interest group activity and attempts at public persuasion on the Court during the cases. Using those examples and the text, write a paper (or prepare a short talk) about the impact of public opinion and lobbying on the Supreme Court.

4. Shakespeare, loosely quoted, once said that to fix our problems, we should first kill all the lawyers. Of course, this was said by characters who sought a means to undermine society. In contemplating that scenario, what is the current state of our justice system? Research court filings, plea bargains, violent crime, white collar crime, and other issues. Is America more contentious or just more litigious? What are the effects of litigation on individuals, the body politic, and public opinion?

5. Constitutional law is taught textually. The language and nuance of what the Court says in its opinions is very important. Choose five cases and read the actual opinions. What types of language does the Court tend to use? Are rulings broad or narrow? Are precedents overturned? How does the Court use precedent generally? What did you learn about the Court from reading opinions?

Websites

The official website of the **Supreme Court of the United States** offers transcripts of oral arguments before the Court, recent case decisions, a history of the Court, the Court's docket, and other information.
www.supremecourtus.gov

Oyez-Oyez-Oyez is a comprehensive database of major constitutional cases including multimedia aspects such as audio.
http://oyez.nwu.edu

The site of the **Supreme Court History Society** covers the basic history of the Court and has a gift catalog.
www.supremecourthistory.org

Findlaw is a searchable database of S.C. decisions plus legal subjects, state courts, law schools, bar associations, and international law.
www.findlaw.com

Rominger Legal Services provides U.S. Supreme Court links, including history, pending cases, rules, bios, etc.
www.romingerlegal.com/supreme.htm

FLITE: Federal Legal Information Through Electronics offers a searchable database of Supreme Court decisions from 1937-1975.
www.fedworld.gov/supcourt/index.htm

U.S. Supreme Court Plus has decisions from the current term as well as legal research, bios, basic Supreme Court information, and more. Also offers a free email notification service of Supreme Court rulings.
www.usscplus.com

The Legal Information Institute offers Supreme Court opinions under the auspices of Project Hermes, the court's electronic-dissemination project. This archive contains (or will soon contain) all opinions of the court issued since May of 1990.
http://supct.law.cornell.edu/supct/

The **Federal Judiciary Homepage** offers a wide variety of information about the U.S. Federal Court system.
www.uscourts.gov

Practice Tests

MULTIPLE CHOICE QUESTIONS

1. Article III establishes

    a. the Supreme Court.
    b. inferior courts.
    c. ten-year terms for federal judges.
    d. all of the above.

2. The three-tiered structure of the federal court system was established by

    a. Article III.
    b. Article IV.
    c. the Judiciary Act of 1789.
    d. the Hamilton Act.

3. Judicial review comes from

    a. the Judiciary Act of 1789.
    b. Article III.
    c. *Chisholm v. Georgia.*
    d. *Marbury v. Madison.*

4. Before a federal or state court can hear a case, it must have

    a. standing.
    b. jurisdiction.
    c. review powers.
    d. precedent.

5. Federal district courts are courts of original jurisdiction, meaning that they hear

    a. cases only involving federal questions.
    b. appellate cases or trials.
    c. appellate cases.
    d. trial cases.

6. The court that handles most cases involving federal regulatory agencies is the

   a. First Circuit Court of Appeals.
   b. District Court.
   c. D.C. Court of Appeals.
   d. U.S. Court of Appeals for the Federal Circuit.

7. The reliance on past decisions to formulate decisions in new cases is based on the doctrine of

   a. *stare decisis.*
   b. *per curiam.*
   c. *amicus curiae.*
   d. *seriatim.*

8. The size of the Supreme Court is

   a. alterable only by constitutional amendment.
   b. set by Congress.
   c. set by the Constitution.
   d. all of the above.

9. Which of the following is not a criteria for nomination to the U.S. Supreme Court?

   a. must be over the age of 35
   b. must be a native-born citizen
   c. must have graduated from an accredited law school
   d. none of the above

10. The original jurisdiction of the Supreme Court

    a. involves disputes between states.
    b. includes cases affecting ambassadors, public ministers, or the State.
    c. includes territorial disputes among states.
    d. all of the above.

11. Nearly all Supreme Court cases arrive at the Court through

    a. *in forma pauperis* petitions.
    b. original jurisdiction cases.
    c. a writ of *certiorari.*
    d. federal district courts.

12. For the Court to grant a writ of *cert*, the case must

    a. involve a substantial federal question.
    b. come from a state court of last resort or the U.S. Court of Appeals.
    c. be approved by four justices of the Supreme Court for review.
    d. all of the above. ✓

13. The person responsible for handling appeals on behalf of the U.S. government to the Supreme Court is the

    a. solicitor general. ✓
    b. attorney general.
    c. procurator.
    d. U.S. prosecuting attorney.

14. When a justice disagrees with the ruling of a Court majority opinion, he/she may write a

    a. concurring opinion.
    b. dissenting opinion. ✓
    c. *per curiam* opinion.
    d. plurality opinion.

15. The idea that unelected judges should refrain from making policy is referred to as

    a. democratic theory.
    b. delegation.
    c. judicial restraint. ✓
    d. judicial activism.

TRUE/FALSE QUESTIONS

F 1. John Marshall was the first Chief Justice of the United States.

T 2. The opinion by John Marshall in *Marbury v. Madison* (1803) dramatically increased the power and importance of the Supreme Court.

F 3. In courts of original jurisdiction, judges are interested only in questions of law.

F 4. The federal court structure is established in Article III.

F 5. The Supreme Court has nine justices as stipulated in the Constitution.

F 6. President Eisenhower was pleased with the work on the Court of his appointee as Chief Justice, Earl Warren.

7. Politics permeates the selection process of federal court judges and Supreme Court Justices.

8. Nominees to the Supreme Court must be non-partisan lawyers with previous judicial experience.

9. The Chief Justice of the Supreme Court always assigns the writing of opinions.

10. The Supreme Court is in no way subject to public opinion or the lobbying of interest groups

COMPARE AND CONTRAST

original and appellate jurisdiction

Supreme Court's exercise of original jurisdiction in its early days versus today

criminal and civil law

federal and state court systems

constitutional and legislative courts

common law and statutory (legislative) law

selection of federal and state judges

writ of *certiorari* and *in forma pauperis*

opinions: *seriatim*, majority, concurring, plurality, dissenting, and *per curiam*

judicial restraint and judicial activism

SHORT ANSWER AND ESSAY QUESTIONS

1. Discuss the facts and ruling in *Marbury v. Madison* and the significance of the case to American jurisprudence. Does opposition to the doctrine of judicial review still exist today? Research this latter question.

2. What impact did John Marshall have on the Court and the nation?

3. Define and discuss the concepts of jurisdiction and precedent.

4. What are briefs and how do they affect the Supreme Court?

5. What kinds of opinions does the Supreme Court issue and what are their effects?

6. Explain the basics of the American judicial system. How was it created and what are its structures and rules?

7. How are federal judges and Supreme Court justices selected? Discuss fully the legal and political issues involved.

8. Discuss the jurisdictions of the Supreme Court and how cases reach that body.

9. What is the process by which the Supreme Court decides a case? Be sure to start at the process of getting on the docket and going through to the opinion stage.

10. What "extra-legal" factors shape judicial decision-making?

ANSWERS TO STUDY EXERCISES

multiple choice answers

1. a   p. 350
2. c   p. 351
3. d   p. 353
4. b   p. 355
5. d   p. 357
6. c   p. 359
7. a   p. 361
8. b   p. 361
9. d   p. 367
10. d   p. 373
11. c   p. 374
12. d   p. 374
13. a   p. 376
14. b   p. 380
15. c   p. 381

true/false answers

1. F   p. 352
2. T   p. 353
3. F   p. 355
4. F   p. 351
5. F   p. 361
6. F   p. 365
7. T   p. 365
8. F   p. 367
9. F   p. 380
10. F   p. 386

CHAPTER 11
PUBLIC OPINION AND SOCIALIZATION

Chapter Goals and Learning Objectives

Public opinion polls reveal that Americans are a diverse lot, but nonetheless, agree on many issues. Politicians and others who want to sway public opinion depend on public opinion polls to inform them of what Americans believe and want from their government and elected officials. This is nothing new. Politicians back in the time of the Framers did not have sophisticated public opinion polls to tell them what the citizens believe or wanted, nor did they have national news media to tell them the results of those polls, but they sought to mold public sentiment nevertheless. What are opinions? Why do they count to politicians? How are opinions and values formed and how are they changed? These are vital questions in a democracy. We all want our opinion and our beliefs to mean something to others. We want our voices heard. Do polls effectively reflect our values? Do they accurately predict the trends, directions, and decisions?

This chapter is designed to give you a better understanding of polling and the nature of public opinion. It is also designed to help you better understand from whence your own opinions, and the opinions of others, have come. The main topic headings of the chapter are:

- What is Public Opinion?
- Early Efforts to Influence and Measure Public Opinion
- Political Socialization and Other Factors That Influence Opinion Formation
- How We Form Political Opinions
- How We Measure Public Opinion
- How Polling and Public Opinion Affect Politicians, and How Politicians Affect Public Opinion

In each section, there are certain facts and ideas that you should strive to understand. Many are in boldface type and appear in both the narrative and in the glossary at the end of the book. Other ideas, dates, facts, events, people, etc., are more difficult to pull out of the narrative. (Keep in mind that studying for objective-[multiple choice, T/F] style tests is different than studying for essay tests. See the Study Guide section on test taking for hints on study skills.)

In general, after you finish reading and studying this chapter, you should understand the following:

- the definition of public opinion and its role in determining public perception of issues
- early efforts to influence and measure public opinion from *The Federalist Papers* on
- political socialization and other factors that lead us to form or change our opinions about political matters
- how Americans form opinions about political issues
- how public opinion is measured and problems with polling techniques
- how polling and public opinion affect politicians and vice versa

Chapter Outline and Key Points

In this section, you are provided with a basic outline of the chapter and any key words/points you should know. Use this outline, in your own notebook, to develop a complete outline of the material. This will help you study and remember the material in preparation for your tests, assignments, and papers.

What is Public Opinion?

    public opinion--

    public opinion polls--

    George Gallup--

Early Efforts to Influence and Measure Public Opinion

    The Federalist Papers--

    Common Sense--

    Uncle Tom's Cabin--

    Walter Lippmann--

    Office of Strategic Influence--

    Early Efforts to Measure Public Opinion

    Public Opinion (1922)--

        Early Election Forecasting

        Literary Digest--

        straw polls--

        What Went Wrong

        Polling Matures

        "Dewey Defeats Truman"--

Political Socialization and Other Factors That Influence Opinion Formation

    political socialization--

The American Voter--

National Election Study--

The Family

    family influence factors--

School and Peers

    elementary school influence--

    high school influence--

    peer influence--

The Mass Media

    impact of TV--

    time in front of TV--

    average time for sound bite--

    role of Internet--

Social Groups

    Religion

    Race and Ethnicity

    Gender

    Age

    Region

Impact of Events

    November 22, 1963--

    Nixon's resignation--

    America's collective memory (Table 11.1)--

    effects of 9/11/01--

Political Ideology and Public Opinion About Government

political ideology--

conservatives--

liberals--

How We Form Political Opinions

Personal Beliefs

"I"-centered--

Political Knowledge

Leno's "Jaywalking"--

V.O. Key--

Cues from Leaders

bully pulpit--

How We Measure Public Opinion

Traditional Public Opinion Polls

Determining the Content and Phrasing of the Questions

Selecting the Sample

random sampling--

Nonstratified Sampling

Stratified Sampling

stratified sampling--

Contacting Respondents

Telephone Polls

In-Person Polls

Political Polls

Push Polls

push polls--

Tracking Polls

tracking polls--

Exit Polls

exit polls--

TV networks in Florida, November 2000 election--

Shortcomings of Polling

VNS--

Sampling Error

sampling error--

Limited Respondent Options

Lack of Information

Intensity

How Polling and Public Opinion Affect Politicians, Politics, and Policy

"bandwagon" effect--

"underdog" effect--

Research Ideas and Possible Paper Topics

1. Use the library or Internet to find a number of polls. Bring them to class and in discussion groups, analyze the quality and reliability of those polls. Be sure to discuss sampling, error rates, question wording, how respondents are contacted, and other factors that affect the results.

2. Write a paper based on your own political ideology and opinions. How were they formed? Consider those who have influenced these opinions and political views. Is the text correct in asserting what the dominant factors of political socialization are? Compare your experiences with those of your classmates.

3. Most people's opinions are affected by what can be called a "formative political event." For some people, this event was the assassination of JFK, for others, it was Watergate or the Iranian hostage crisis, and for still others, it was the Persian Gulf War, the scandals of Bill Clinton, or 9/11. Think about your "formative political event" or first political memory. How did that event shape your political ideas and worldview? What about your parents and grandparents? Ask them what major events affected their political perceptions. Compare notes with your classmates.

4. As a class project, choose an issue of interest and formulate your own poll. Then administer it on campus. Discuss the process, the results, and problems of your poll and extrapolate that to polling in general.

5. Stage a debate in class. One side should argue that public opinion polling is inherently problematic and should not be used by government or politicians. The other side should argue that polling is a valid way to determine the will of the people. Each side should do research to flesh out their arguments.

Websites

The **Gallup Organization** is one of the best-known and most well-respected polling agencies. Their website offers access to reports, polling data, and more about a variety of issues.
www.gallup.com

The **National Election Study** at the University of Michigan offers regular polls on elections, voting behavior, and electoral issues.
www.umich.edu/~nes

The **National Opinion Research Center (NORC)**, a research arm of the University of Chicago, offers surveys of American attitudes and opinions.
www.norc.org

Roper Center for Public Opinion Research, located at the University of Connecticut, is the largest library of public opinion data in the world. The Center's mission focuses on data preservation and access, education, and research. Includes the GSS--General Social Survey.
www.ropercenter.uconn.edu/

The **Subject Guide to Political Socialization and Political Culture** is a website hosted by Appalachian State University.
www.library.appstate.edu/reference/polsoc.html

The **Washington Post Data Directory** is a guide to public opinion data published on the Internet by nonpartisan organizations.
www.washingtonpost.com/wp-srv/politics/polls/datadir.htm

The **Research Industry Coalition** is an organization promoting professionalism and quality in public opinion and marketing research. Site includes an interesting article on the problems with the proliferation of "call in" polls and 900 number polls.
www.researchindustry.org/index.html

The **American Association for Public Opinion Research** is a professional association that publishes *Public Opinion Quarterly* whose tables of contents are available at this site.
www.aapor.org

The **Virtual Reference Desk at Binghamton University** offers a site devoted to polling and public opinion, including information on bad polls and techniques; also offers links to some opinion sites.
//library.lib.binghamton.edu/vrd/polls.html

Practice Tests

MULTIPLE CHOICE QUESTIONS

1. The founder of modern-day polling is

   a. Louis Harris.
   b. George Gallup.
   c. Steve Roper.
   d. Walter Lippman.

2. An unscientific survey used to gauge public opinion on issues and policies is called a

   a. deliberative poll.
   b. exit poll.
   c. straw poll.
   d. public opinion poll.

3. The book that showed how class coalitions led to party affiliation and hence voting behavior was

   a. *Public Opinion.*
   b. *The Voice of the People.*
   c. *Public Opinion and American Democracy.*
   d. *The American Voter.*

4. The University of Michigan has a center for the study of public opinion that puts out a report on surveys focusing only on the political attitudes and behavior of the electorate titled

   a. *The National Election Studies* (NES).
   b. *The General Social Survey* (GSS).
   c. *The Roper Public Opinion Research Bulletin.*
   d. *The Gallup Polls.*

5. The influence of family on political socialization stems from

   a. communication.
   b. receptivity.
   c. time with parents.
   d. all of the above.

6. In the 2000 campaign, _____ percent of Americans got most of their information on the election from Letterman, Leno, *Saturday Night Live*, or other alternative news sources.

   a. 51
   b. 45
   c. 25
   d. 15

7. For _____ percent of Americans under 30, their main sources of political news are MTV, *Saturday Night Live*, and other alternative news sources.

   a. 90
   b. 79
   c. 51
   d. 25

8. During middle and high school, the most important political influences on kids are

   a. events.
   b. parents.
   c. peers.
   d. media.

9. In 2000, _____ percent of Americans reported that they belong to a church or synagogue.

   a. 67
   b. 78
   c. 81
   d. 90

10. In 2000, _____ percent of Americans reported they believe in God.

    a. 94
    b. 78
    c. 67
    d. 58

11. Most people--who are not ideologues--filter their ideas about politics through social group, party, and ideology. But they are also influenced by

    a. personal benefits.
    b. political knowledge.
    c. cues from leaders and opinion-makers.
    d. all of the above.

12. The political knowledge of Americans is quite low. In 1996, _____ percent of Americans could not identify the Chief Justice of the Supreme Court.

    a. 94
    b. 82
    c. 75
    d. 65

13. The use of more sophisticated analytical methods involving perceived issue distances between political candidates and votes reveals

    a. generally less issue voting than previously believed.
    b. generally more issue voting than previously believed.
    c. generally the same level of issue voting as before.
    d. issue voting of greater significance to politicians than to voters.

14. One reason that polls can be misleading is that

    a. most people lie on polls.
    b. slight differences in question wording or question placement in the interview occurs.
    c. pollsters are often bribed by politicians.
    d. computer technology currently makes it difficult to accurately process the raw data.

15. Most national surveys and commercial polls use samples of _____ to obtain fairly accurate polling results.

    a. 75 to 100
    b. 300 to 400
    c. 1,000 to 1,500
    d. 5,000

TRUE/FALSE QUESTIONS

1. Presidents as early as Woodrow Wilson recognized the power of public opinion and tried to control it.

2. Straw polls are scientifically based and relatively accurate.

3. The dominant force in presidential elections, according to *The American Voter*, is party affiliation based on class.

4. When George W. Bush went on TV talk shows such as *Oprah* and Letterman in the 2000 election, his poll ratings dropped significantly.

5. The Internet has not yet become a forum for swaying and informing voters.

6. Events can have a very strong effect on political attitudes and values.

7. The fastest-growing age group, and that most likely to vote, is citizens over 65.

8. Region has no effect on voter attitudes and political opinions.

9. Tracking polls are highly reliable indicators of political attitudes and voting behavior.

10. Polls clearly can distort the presidential election process, particularly in the early stages such as the New Hampshire primary, by creating a "bandwagon" effect.

COMPARE AND CONTRAST

agents of political socialization: family, mass media, school and peers, events, social groups, and political ideology

random sampling, non-stratified sampling, and stratified sampling

telephone polls and in-person polls

tracking polls, exit polls, straw polls, and deliberative polls

sampling error and margin of error

SHORT ANSWER AND ESSAY QUESTIONS

1. Discuss early efforts to measure public opinion.

2. What is political socialization?

3. What is political ideology?

4. Compare and contrast the various ways of sampling used in polls.

5. Discuss deliberative polling. What are the costs and benefits of this method of polling?

6. What is public opinion? How do we measure it and how accurate are those measurements?

7. Discuss the various processes of political socialization. What factors affect our opinion formation and how do these factors affect the broader political system?

8. How do we form political opinions and ideologies? What is the relationship between opinion and ideology?

9. How do we measure public opinion? Discuss methods of sampling, polling, and their shortcomings.

10. How do politicians and the media use polls? What are the implications of these uses?

ANSWERS TO STUDY EXERCISES

multiple choice answers

1. b p. 399
2. c p. 401
3. d p. 404
4. a p. 405
5. d p. 405
6. c p. 407
7. b p. 407
8. c p. 406
9. a p. 409
10. d p. 408
11. d p. 417
12. a p. 417
13. b p. 417
14. b p. 418
15. c p. 420

true/false answers

1. T p. 400
2. F p. 401
3. T p. 404
4. F p. 407

5. F p. 407
6. T p. 414
7. T p. 412
8. F p. 413
9. F p. 422
10. T p. 429

CHAPTER 12
POLITICAL PARTIES

Chapter Goals and Learning Objectives

Are you a Democrat? Are you a Republican? Or, perhaps, do you spurn party labels and vote for a candidate based upon his or her qualifications, record, platform or, even, how he or she looks on television rather than a party affiliation? To many Americans, party affiliation is not a significant factor in their political lives. Indeed, we have entered a new, more fluid era of party politics. Some maintain that our two-party system is likely to be replaced by a chaotic multiparty system or a system in which presidential hopefuls bypass party nominations altogether and compete on their own. However, it is important to note that the two major parties control the power structure in Congress and in all fifty states. And, therefore, since Democrats and Republicans write the laws, including the election laws across the country, the predicted demise of the two-party system in this county is, at best, premature. In one form or another, political parties have been staples of American political life since the late 1700s and they will continue to be. In essence, political parties are the engines which run the process of government. While you need not become a mechanic, you should look under the hood and develop an understanding of how these engines operate.

This chapter is designed to give you an overview of political parties and how they have changed over time. The main topic headings of the chapter are:

- What is a Political Party?
- The Evolution of American Party Democracy
- The Roles of the American Parties
- The Basic Structure of American Political Parties
- The Party in Government
- The Modern Transformation of Party Organization
- The Party-In-The-Electorate
- One-Partyism and Third-Partyism

In each section, there are certain facts and ideas that you should strive to understand. Many are in boldface type and appear in both the narrative and in the glossary at the end of the book. Other ideas, dates, facts, events, people, etc., are more difficult to pull out of the narrative. (Keep in mind that studying for objective-[multiple choice, T/F] style tests is different than studying for essay tests. See the Study Guide section on test taking for hints on study skills.)

In general, after you finish reading and studying this chapter, you should understand the following:

- the definition and importance of a political party
- the history and evolution of American political parties
- the roles of American parties in our political system
- the basic structure of the two major American political parties: the Democratic Party and the Republican Party

- the party in government, including the office holders and candidates who serve and run under their party's banners
- how parties have changed, particularly with the advent of modern technology and communication strategies
- the party in the electorate--parties' influence beyond the role of leaders and activists, including changing partisan alignments
- single-party dominance, or one-partyism, and the rise and fall of third parties

Chapter Outline and Key Points

In this section, you are provided with a basic outline of the chapter and any key words/points you should know. Use this outline, in your own notebook, to develop a complete outline of the material. This will help you study and remember the material in preparation for your tests, assignments, and papers.

What is a Political Party?

political party--

governmental party--

organizational party--

party-in-the-electorate --

The Evolution of American Party Democracy

George Washington's farewell warning--

Jefferson and political parties--

The Early Parties Fade

Era of Good Feelings--

Democrats and Andrew Jackson--

Republicans and Abraham Lincoln--

Democrats and Republicans: The Golden Age

GOP--
FDR's New Deal Coalition--

The Modern Era Versus the Golden Age

political machines--

Plunkitt and Tammany Hall--

Is the Party Over?

direct primary--

civil service laws--

patronage--

spoils system--

issue-oriented politics--

ticket-split--

political consultant--

The Parties Endure

1)
2)
3)
4)

The Roles of the American Parties

Mobilizing Support and Gathering Power

coalition--

A Force for Stability

segregation and the growth of the GOP in the South--

Unity, Linkage, Accountability

party-linkage function--

The Electioneering Function

elections in a democracy can only have meaning if what?

Party as a Voting and Issue Cue

party identification as filter for information--

Policy Formulation and Promotion

Huey Long--

national party platform--

"presidential candidate-centered platforms"--

The Basic Structure of American Political Parties

National Committees

Democratic National Committee (DNC)--

Republican National Committee (RNC)--

Leadership

who heads the national party?--

National Conventions

national convention--

television coverage of national conventions--

States and Localities

precinct--

state legislative campaign committee--

Informal Groups

think tanks --

Democratic Leadership Council (DLC) --

GOPAC --

The Party in Government

    The Congressional Party

        political parties most visible in Congress; why?--

        party discipline--

        Newt Gingrich--

    The Presidential Party

        pro-party presidents--

        coattail effect--

        non-partisan presidents--

        Bush and 108th Congress--

    The Parties and the Judiciary

        party affiliation as predictor of judicial decisions--

    The Parties and State Government

    Parties and Governors

        Governor's office as launching pad--

    Parties and State Legislatures

The Modern Transformation of Party Organization

    Republican Strengths

        Party Staff

        Voter Contact

        Polling

        Media Advertising

        Campaign Staff Training and Research

Democratic Party Gains

Democratic defeats in 1980s led to what?--

The Party-In-The-Electorate

party-in-the-electorate--

Party Identification

party identification--

Sources of Party Identification

what factors affect party loyalty?--

Declining Loyalty

voter-admitted partisanship--

Group Affiliations

Geographic Region

Race and Ethnicity

Age

Social and Economic Factors

Religion

Marital Status

Ideology

One-Partyism and Third-Partyism

one-partyism--

Minor Parties: Third-Partyism

Third-partyism--

Ralph Nader--

Jesse Ventura--

George Wallace--

Why Third Parties Tend to Remain Minor

proportional representation--

institutional and historical factors--

dualist theory--

Research Ideas and Possible Paper Topics

1) Using the Internet or the library, look up state party organizations in three different states (for example, a Southern state, a New England state, and a Western state). Compare the Democratic and Republican parties from those states on a variety of indicators, including issue positions, platforms, and organization. Are they different? How and why?

2) In 1998, Jesse Ventura--a former professional wrestler--won the governorship of Minnesota under the banner of the Reform Party. At the same time, the lower and upper houses of the state legislature were captured by different parties (one is Democratic, the other Republican). Discuss how this might affect policymaking and political parties in the state. In addition, Ventura has been the most successful candidate of the Reform Party. Did his success contribute to the Reform Party's current problems? Why or why not? Why did he not seek reelection in 2002? Was his decision to not seek reelection in any way related to his third-party status?

3) Go and visit, or invite to class, some local party activists. Ask them to talk to you about what they do in the party, why and how they got involved in politics, and the issues that they consider important. Does the information you learn ring true with what you have read in the text?

4) Congress currently has several independent members. Do some research to determine whether their independent status truly makes them different from the Democrats and Republicans. What kinds of compromises must an independent member of Congress make? How about independent governors? What can this tell us about the role of parties?

5) Find copies of the most recent national platforms for the two major parties. Compare them on a variety of issues. Then look at public opinion polls to see how the party positions correspond to those of average Americans. What do you find? Why do you think that is the case?

Websites

University of Michigan Documents Center offers links to political parties; includes national and state parties, as well as links to congressional party leadership and platforms.
www.lib.umich.edu/govdocs/psusp.htm/#party

Third Party Central offers links to third parties.
www.3pc.net/index.html

Politics 1 offers links to political parties, campaign information, candidate information, and more. They also offer a free email newsletter.
www.politics1.com/parties.htm

Major Parties

The **Democratic National Committee** site.
www.democrats.org

The **Republican National Committee** site.
www.gop.org

Third Parties

The **Reform Party**.
www.reformparty.org/

The **Libertarian Party**.
www.lp.org

The **Green Party.**
www.greenparty.org

Practice Tests

MULTIPLE CHOICE

1. Party politics was nearly non-existent on the national level during the

    a. Gilded Age.
    b. Era of Good Feelings.
    c. Populist Era.
    d. Progressive Era.

2. FDR's New Deal coalition of Democrats included

   a. Southerners and farmers.
   b. organized labor and minorities.
   c. big-city machines.
   d. all of the above.

3. The power of political parties has been undercut by a variety of factors, including

   a. civil service laws.
   b. direct primaries.
   c. issue-oriented politics.
   d. all of the above.

4. Virtually all governmental regulation of political parties is handled by

   a. the states.
   b. the Federal Election Commission.
   c. the Congress.
   d. the U.S. Constitution.

5. In Congress, parties perform a number of functions, including

   a. enforcing absolute party discipline through the use of sanctions.
   b. providing leadership and organization.
   c. decentralizing power in Congress.
   d. all of the above.

6. Political parties are most important in the

   a. legislative branch.
   b. executive branch.
   c. judiciary.
   d. state governments.

7. Among the most party-oriented, party-building presidents was

   a. Dwight Eisenhower.
   b. George Washington.
   c. Woodrow Wilson.
   d. Lyndon Johnson.

8. Among the most nonpartisan of presidents was

   a. Dwight Eisenhower.
   b. Gerald Ford.
   c. Franklin Roosevelt.
   d. George Bush.

9. One state, _____, has a nonpartisan legislature.

   a. Utah
   b. Nebraska
   c. Rhode Island
   d. Vermont

10. Republicans surpass Democrats in fundraising more than two to one. Most Republican fundraising comes from

    a. rich, private donors.
    b. wealthy corporations.
    c. direct mail solicitation.
    d. conservative interest groups.

11. Money that flows to the party or candidate who seems most likely to win is called

    a. soft money.
    b. hard money.
    c. pragmatic money.
    d. smart money.

12. The highest number of individuals who have ever declared themselves to be politically "independent" is ____ percent in the late 1970s.

    a. 19
    b. 38
    c. 45
    d. 50

13. Since 1831, _____ third-party candidates have won more than 10% of the vote in a presidential election.

    a. 3
    b. 5
    c. 8
    d. 11

14. The most successful third party in U.S. history was the

    a. American Independent Party.
    b. Free Soil Party.
    c. Bull Moose Party.
    d. Reform Party.

15. Third parties often find their roots in

   a. economic protest.
   b. sectionalism.
   c. issues and charismatic personalities.
   d. all of the above.

TRUE/FALSE

1. A political party is a group of office holders, candidates, activists, and voters who identify with a group label and seek to elect to public office individuals who run under that label.

2. George Washington advocated the formation of parties because they perform a useful organizational function in Congress.

3. Party affiliation loses its importance once a candidate has successfully won office.

4. Parties are a source of stability, unity, and linkage in our political system.

5. Few platform promises ever get implemented.

6. Third parties tend to remain minor due to ballot access laws, public funding of campaigns, news coverage, and efforts by the major parties.

7. The Democratic and Republican parties are based in Washington and are primarily national organizations.

8. Judges, in the American system, are nonpartisan.

9. There has been a drastic decline in party identification in recent years.

10. Young people today are tending to become more Democratic in party affiliation.

COMPARE AND CONTRAST

governmental party, organizational party, and party-in-electorate

modern era and Golden Age

civil service laws, patronage, and spoils system

one-partyism and third-partyism

proportional representation and single-member plurality electoral systems congressional party and presidential party

pro-party and nonpartisan presidents

parties and the judiciary versus parties and state governments

Republican strengths and Democratic strengths

Democratic platform and Republican platform

ESSAY AND SHORT ANSWER QUESTIONS

1) Discuss the political machines of the "golden age" of parties.

2) The significance of political party among the electorate has diminished over the past several decades, yet the significance of the two parties in operating the government remains strong. Discuss the factors that contributed to overall party loyalty among the electorate and why party affiliation remains important for most officeholders.

3) What is the role of the national platform and how is the platform treated by office holders, once elected?

4) What are one-partyism and third-partyism? Why are they important in our system?

5) Discuss the party-in-the-electorate.

6) What are the roles of political parties in the U.S. political and governmental system?

7) What is a third party and why do they tend to remain peripheral to the political system?

8) Discuss the basic structure of American political parties on the state and national level.

9) Discuss the meaning of the term "party-in-government".

10) Compare and contrast the strengths and strategies of the Republican and Democratic parties.

ANSWERS TO STUDY EXERCISES

multiple choice answers

1.	b	p. 438
2.	d	p. 440
3.	d	p. 441-443
4.	a	p. 451
5.	b	p. 453
6.	a	p. 453
7.	c	p. 457
8.	a	p. 460
9.	b	p. 464
10.	c	p. 465
11.	d	p. 469
12.	b	p. 471
13.	c	p. 477
14.	c	p. 477
15.	d	p. 477

true/false answers

1.	T	p. 437
2.	F	p. 438
3.	F	p. 445
4.	T	p. 446
5.	F	p. 447
6.	F	p. 451
7.	F	p. 462
8.	F	p. 472
9.	T	p. 475
10.	T	p. 480

CHAPTER 13
VOTING AND ELECTIONS

Chapter Goals and Learning Objectives

Do you vote? Do your friends and family vote? Probably, you know people who consider their vote meaningless. Or they consider the process of voting too cumbersome for so little impact. Of course, ask Al Gore if a handful of votes matter. A few more people showing up at the polls in Florida in November of 2000 and the presidential election would not have produced such a questionable and controversial outcome.

Elections in America allow a peaceful and legitimate transfer of power. The United States has more elections more often than any other country in the world. We also have the lowest turnout of the industrialized countries--fewer than half of our eligible voters vote on a regular basis. There are a wide variety of explanations for non-voting. There are even those who claim that having a low voter turnout is a good thing and increases stability in the political system. Others argue that reform is necessary to increase voter turnout. After the 2000 presidential election, where, some argue, the votes of five Republican members of the U.S. Supreme Court rather than the votes of the people of Florida were the final arbiter of who would be president, calls for reform of the electoral college system were widespread. This chapter will look at those arguments and others related to voting and elections.

This chapter is designed to give you an overview of voting and elections in the United States. The main topic headings of the chapter are:

- The Purposes Served by Elections
- Different Kinds of Elections
- Presidential Elections
- Congressional Elections
- Voting Behavior
- Reforming the Electoral Process

In each section, there are certain facts and ideas that you should strive to understand. Many are in boldface type and appear in both the narrative and in the glossary at the end of the book. Other ideas, dates, facts, events, people, etc., are more difficult to pull out of the narrative. (Keep in mind that studying for objective-[multiple choice, T/F] style tests is different than studying for essay tests. See the Study Guide section on test taking for hints on study skills.)

In general, after you finish reading and studying this chapter, you should understand the following:

- the purposes served by elections, particularly their importance in legitimizing the political system
- different kinds of elections, from primaries and caucuses to congressional and presidential elections

- how presidential elections work from the primaries through the national conventions
- how congressional elections work and how they differ from presidential elections
- how voters behave in the election cycle
- arguments for reforming the electoral process for the presidency

Chapter Outline and Key Points

In this section, you are provided with a basic outline of the chapter and any key words/points you should know. Use this outline, in your own notebook, to develop a complete outline of the material. This will help you study and remember the material in preparation for your tests, assignments, and papers.

The Purposes Served by Elections

    electorate--

    mandate--

    retrospective judgement--

    prospective judgment--

Different Kinds of Elections

Primary Elections

    primary elections--

    closed primary--

    open primary--

    crossover voting--

    raiding--

    blanket primary--

    runoff primary--

    nonpartisan primary--

General Elections

> general election--

Initiative, Referendum, and Recall

> initiative--
>
> referendum--
>
> recall--

Presidential Elections

winner-take-all primary--

proportional representation primary--

proportional representation with bonus delegates primary; beauty contest with separate delegate selection; delegate selection with no beauty contest--

caucus--

Primaries versus Caucuses

> regional primary--
> earliest open primary--
>
> front-loading--

The Party Conventions

> uncommitted delegates--
>
> three ways national party conventions are different today--
>
> **Delegate Selection**
>
> > unit rule--
> >
> > superdelegates--
>
> **National Candidates and Issues**
>
> **The News Media**
>
> > gavel-to-gavel coverage--

Who are the Delegates?

> contrast between Democrats and Republicans--

The Electoral College: How Presidents Are Elected

> electoral college--
>
> electors--
>
> number of electors--
>
> what Framers devised the electoral college for--

Electoral College in the Nineteenth Century

> 12th Amendment (1804) --
>
> 1876 race between Hayes and Tilden--

The Electoral College in the 20th and 21st Centuries

> 2000 Presidential election--
>
> implications of reapportionment after 2000 census--
>
> winner-take-all system--
>
> **Abolition**
>
> **Congressional District Plan**
>
> **Keep the College, Abolish the Electors**

Patterns of Presidential Elections

> **Party Realignments**
>
> > party realignments--
> >
> > critical elections--
> >
> > last confirmed major realignment--
> >
> > realignments accomplished in two main ways--

Secular Realignment

secular realignment--

Congressional Elections

The Incumbency Advantage

incumbency--

congressional reelection rates--

"scare off" effect--

Redistricting, Scandals, and Coattails

census--

redistricting--

gerrymandering--

Midterm Congressional Elections

midterm election--

The 2002 Midterm Elections

first time since 1934 a first-term president did what?--

party control of Congress--

Voting Behavior

Patterns in Voter Turnout

turnout--

Education

Income

Age

Race and Ethnicity

Voting Rights Act of 1965

Interest in Politics

Why is Voter Turnout So Low?

Too Busy

Difficulty of Registration

Difficulty of Absentee Voting

Number of Elections

Voter Attitudes

Weak Political Parties

How Can the United States Improve Voter Turnout?

Easier Registration and Absentee Voting

Motor Voter Law--

Make Election Day a Holiday

Strengthen Parties

Other Suggestions

Does Low Voter Turnout Matter?

Patterns in Vote Choice

Race and Ethnicity

Gender

Income

Ideology

Issues and Campaign-Specific Developments

Ticket-Splitting

ticket-splitting--

Reforming the Electoral Process

McCain-Feingold Bipartisan Campaign Finance Reform Act of 2002--

Research Ideas and Possible Paper Topics

1) Many reform proposals argue that the U.S. should adopt proportional representation. In this method of election, voters choose a party list as opposed to an individual candidate. This method strengthens parties and tends to increase voter turnout and the number of parties in the political system. Among those countries that use PR are: Holland, Poland, and others. Research the nature of PR and how it might work, or why it would not work, in the United States.

2) Run a party convention in class. Nominate candidates, write a platform, and deal with media coverage of the event. Compare various methods of running a party convention and discuss which ones work best.

3) Many scholars argue that low voter turnout is due to electoral rules, frequency of elections, apathy, etc. Discuss how you would change these impediments to voting and discuss the impact increased voter turnout would have on the electoral process.

4) Look at several sources discussing the electoral. What reforms have been proposed? How useful is the electoral college now? Would you advocate a different approach? What do you think would happen if some candidate won the electoral college but not the popular vote today? Hold a debate in class on the merits of the various routes to reform.

5) The governor of California moved the California primary earlier in the process of nominating a president and many have argued that the first elections of the nomination process--the New Hampshire primary and the Iowa caucuses--have too much influence and these states are not highly representative of the country. How would you change the primary system? Consider the issue of campaign finance (shorter primary seasons cost less), the ideal of democracy (competition is good and everyone should have a fair chance to win), the way the media tend to cover elections, and other issues.

Websites

Project Vote-Smart is a non-partisan information service funded by members and non-partisan foundations. It offers "a wealth of facts on your political leaders, including biographies and addresses, issue positions, voting records, campaign finances, evaluations by special interests." It also offers "CongressTrack," a way for citizens to track the status of legislation, members and committees, sponsors, voting records, clear descriptions, full text, and weekly floor schedules, as well as access to information on elections, federal and state governments, the issues, and politics. Includes thousands of links to the most important sites on the Internet.
        www.vote-smart.org/

The **National Election Studies** are a key source of data on voting behavior.
www.umich.edu/~nes

Campaigns and Elections magazine's website is oriented toward campaign professionals but is also useful to teachers and students. It offers articles, their table of contents from the print version, job opportunities, and more.
www.campaignline.com

The **Federal Election Commission (FEC)** website offers campaign finance information, a citizens' guide to political contributions, news and information about elections and voting. Includes data about state regulations on voting (registration and residency rules, etc.) as well as elections data from a variety of elections.
www.fec.gov

Rock-the-Vote is an organization dedicated to getting young people involved in politics.
www.rockthevote.org/

The **League of Women Voters** provides information to voters across the country on state, federal, and local elections and works to encourage election reform and campaign finance reform. Their website offers an interactive section on election information.
www.lwv.org

The **Office of the Federal Register** coordinates the functions of the Electoral College on behalf of the Archivist of the United States, the States, the Congress and the American people. This site assembles a variety of information and statistics on the Electoral College, past and present.
wwww.archives.gov/register/electoral_college/electoral_college.html

The **Census Bureau** has information on voter registration and turnout statistics.
www.census.gov/population/www/socdemo/voting.html

Practice Tests

MULTIPLE CHOICE

1. Elections serve a number of functions, including

    a. legitimizing change.
    b. filling public offices.
    c. an organization function.
    d. all of the above.

2. An election that is held to choose a party's candidate and that allows only registered party members to vote for the general election is called a

   a. primary.
   b. closed primary.
   c. blanket primary.
   d. open primary.

3. In 1996, _____ percent of U.S. House members who ran for reelection won.

   a. 94
   b. 85
   c. 73
   d. 68

4. Many people favor the use of caucuses to select party nominees because

   a. caucus participants tend to be knowledgeable party stalwarts.
   b. caucuses reduce the influence of the media.
   c. the quality of participation in caucuses is higher than in primaries.
   d. all of the above.

5. The electoral college encountered problems in the election of 1800. In order to remedy the problem of selecting a president of one party and a vice president of another, Congress passed the

   a. Law on Presidential Elections.
   b. Law on the Electoral College.
   c. Twelfth Amendment.
   d. Eleventh Amendment.

6. If there is no majority in the electoral college for a candidate, the election is decided by the

   a. popular vote.
   b. House of Representatives.
   c. Senate.
   d. Congress as a whole.

7. The current era of party orientation is characterized by

   a. party loyalty, straight ticket voting, and low voter turnout.
   b. a clear majority for the Republican party, indicating an obvious realignment of party balance.
   c. ticket-splitting, independence, and voter volatility.
   d. all of the above.

8. If an incumbent member of Congress loses a reelection bid, the cause is likely to be

   a. redistricting.
   b. a high-spending challenger.
   c. advertising by well-financed interest groups.
   d. all of the above.

9. About _____ percent of eligible adults vote regularly.

   a. 65
   b. 55
   c. 40
   d. 30

10. In 1971, the voting age was lowered to eighteen by the _____ Amendment.

    a. Nineteenth
    b. Twenty-Second
    c. Twenty-Fourth
    d. Twenty-Sixth

11. Women gained the right to vote in 1920 through the _____ Amendment.

    a. Seventeenth
    b. Nineteenth
    c. Twenty-First
    d. Twenty-Fifth

12. In general, women tend to favor the Democratic party by about _____ percent.

    a. 6
    b. 15
    c. 25
    d. 31

13. Voter turnout in this country is low due to the

    a. difficulty of registration.
    b. difficulty of absentee voting.
    c. frequency of elections.
    d. all of the above.

14. In 1993, Congress and President Clinton passed a law designed to increase voter turnout called the

   a. Election Law of 1993.
   b. Law on Participation.
   c. Motor Voter Law.
   d. Election Act.

15. Since 1968, the percentage of people who vote a split ticket in presidential election years is

   a. 75%.
   b. 60%.
   c. 48%.
   d. 35%.

TRUE/FALSE

1. Regular elections are a mechanism to keep office holders accountable.

2. Primaries are elections in which only the party faithful may vote.

3. Caucuses are more democratic than primaries.

4. The first national party convention was held in 1800.

5. Delegates to the national convention tend to be more extreme in their views than average voters.

6. Incumbency advantage in congressional elections is quite high due to name recognition, media access, opportunities to help constituents, and free mailing privileges.

7. In midterm or off-year elections, members of the president's party tend to gain a significant number of seats.

8. Today, about 65% of eligible Americans vote in presidential elections.

9. Less than half of eligible citizens ages eighteen to twenty-four are even registered to vote.

10. Most people who don't vote say that they didn't vote due to problems getting to the polls.

COMPARE AND CONTRAST

electorate and mandate

retrospective and prospective judgement

primary elections: open, closed, blanket, runoff

primary and general elections

initiative, referendum, and recall

primaries vs. caucuses

presidential and congressional elections

Democratic convention delegates and Republican convention delegates

Democratic and Republican platforms

party realignment and critical election

incumbency advantage, redistricting, scandals, and coattails

presidential year and off year/midterm elections

participation: turnout, income, age, gender, race, interest

ticket-splitting and straight ticket voting

ESSAY AND SHORT ANSWER QUESTIONS

1) Explain the various types of primary. How are they similar, how are they different and why would a state choose one variant over another?

2) Discuss initiative, referendum, and recall. Why and where do we have them? How pervasive are they? And what are some examples of recent uses of each?

3) What impact could regional primaries and front loading have on the process of nominating a president?

4) What is the electoral college? Why is it often the subject of reform proposals? What problems did it present in the 2000 election?

5) What is incumbency advantage for Congress and what events serve to lessen it?

6) Compare and contrast the nature of primary and general elections for both congressional and presidential candidates.

7) Discuss the changing nature of the party conventions and how the Republican and Democratic conventions are similar and different.

8) Discuss the role of party in presidential elections and the nature of party alignments.

9) Analyze the nature of congressional elections from 1994 to 1998.

10) Discuss voting behavior and voter turnout. Who votes and why? What voting patterns exist? Why is voter turnout so low? Does low turnout matter?

ANSWERS TO STUDY EXERCISES

multiple choice answers

1.	d	p. 490
2.	b	p. 494
3.	a	p. 510
4.	d	p. 497
5.	c	p. 505
6.	b	p. 505
7.	c	p. 531
8.	a	p. 510
9.	c	p. 519
10.	d	p. 520
11.	b	p. 529
12.	a	p. 530
13.	d	p. 523
14.	c	p. 527
15.	b	p. 531

true/false answers

1.	T	p. 491
2.	F	p. 494
3.	F	p. 497
4.	F	p. 499
5.	T	p. 500
6.	T	p. 510
7.	T	p. 515
8.	F	p. 523
9.	T	p. 523
10.	F	p. 523

CHAPTER 14
THE CAMPAIGN PROCESS

Chapter Goals and Learning Objectives

You come home from school or work, flop down on the sofa, click on the TV to relax and what do you see? Those annoying political commercials. They seem to go on and on for months before an election. And usually it's one guy trashing another. Irritating, right? But for most Americans, the TV ad is where they get most of their information about political candidates running for office. Isn't there a better way of doing this?

American political campaigns are long and expensive. We have more elections than most other countries and they last longer, too. Our campaigns also seem to turn a large number of voters off the process entirely. People say they hate negative campaigning, but negative campaign ads work. Many Americans believe that wealthy donors and political action committees have a disproportionate influence on the process. Do candidates sell themselves on TV like advertisers sell toothpaste or soap, processed and packaged like products for sale? Indeed, the art of electioneering has seemingly merged with the science of marketing and advertising. Yet the goals of campaigning remain the same: Get voters' attention and get their votes. How candidates pursue these goals is the subject of this chapter.

This chapter is designed to give you a basic understanding of the campaign process from how candidates are chosen to who wins and loses. The main topic headings of the chapter are:

- The Structure of a Campaign
- The Candidate or the Campaign: Which Do We Vote For?
- The Campaign and the News Media
- Campaign Finance
- The 2000 Presidential Campaign and Election

In each section, there are certain facts and ideas that you should strive to understand. Many are in boldface type and appear in both the narrative and in the glossary at the end of the book. Other ideas, dates, facts, events, people, etc., are more difficult to pull out of the narrative. (Keep in mind that studying for objective-[multiple choice, T/F] style tests is different than studying for essay tests. See the Study Guide section on test taking for hints on study skills.)

In general, after you finish reading and studying this chapter, you should understand the following:

- the structure of the campaign: nomination, general election, personal, organization and media campaigns
- do we vote for the candidate or the campaign? What has the greater influence--a sophisticated campaign or a candidate's abilities and qualifications?
- how campaigns meet the challenges and seize the opportunities afforded by the modern media

- the evolution of the campaign finance system since the Federal Election Campaign Act of 1971, with special emphasis on the 2002 Bipartisan Campaign Finance Reform Act
- the controversial 2000 presidential campaign and election

Chapter Outline and Key Points

In this section, you are provided with a basic outline of the chapter and any key words/points you should know. Use this outline, in your own notebook, to develop a complete outline of the material. This will help you study and remember the material in preparation for your tests, assignments, and papers.

The Structure of a Campaign

nomination campaign--

general election campaign--

personal campaign--

organizational campaign--

media campaign--

British elections and campaigns--

The Nomination Campaign

bandwagon effect--

diehard activists--

The General Election Campaign

which special interest groups generally support Democrats and which support Republicans in the general election campaign--

campaign slogans--

The Personal Campaign

value of personal campaigning--

typical campaign day for candidate for high office--

The Organizational Campaign

    campaign manager--

    political consultant--

    media consultant--

    pollster--

    direct mailer--

    finance chair--

    voter canvass--

    get-out-the-vote (GOTV)--

The Media Campaign

    paid media--

    free media--

    positive ad--

    negative ad--

    negative attacks on Jefferson--

    contrast ad--

    spot ad--

    inoculation ad--

    debate over impact of negative ads--

The Candidate or the Campaign: Which Do We Vote For?

    role of campaign techniques--

    candidate-centered view of politics--

    assertions by political scientists regarding effect of economy on election results--

    failure of political science models in predicting 2000 presidential election--

The Campaign and the News Media

three ways campaigns try to manipulate press coverage--

1)

2)

3)

sound bites--

spin--

candidate debates--

Televised Debates

Kennedy-Nixon, 1960--

Carter-Ford, 1976--

Reagan-Carter, 1980--

Bush-Gore, 2000--

effects of presidential debates--

Can the Press be Handled?

candidates appearing on talk shows--

horserace aspect of media coverage of campaigns--

effect of tone of media coverage--

Campaign Financing

Campaign Finance, 1971-2002

Federal Election Campaign Act of 1971--

Individual Contributions

maximum allowable for individual presidential and congressional campaigns--

aggregate individual limit for each calendar year--

Political Action Committee (PAC) Contributions

political action committee (PAC)--

who benefits most from PACs, incumbents or challengers--

Political Party Contributions

effect on party discipline--

Member-to-Candidate Contributions

leadership PACs--

limits on members' contributions--

Candidates' Personal Contributions

Buckley v. Valeo (1976) --

Public Funds

public funds--

matching funds--

Independent Expenditures

Colorado Republican Federal Campaign Committee v. Federal Election Commission (1996)--

hard money--

Soft Money/Issue Advocacy Advertisements

soft money--

express advocacy--

issue advocacy--

A Summary of Contributions and Expenses, 2002

typical U.S. Senate candidate's contributions--

greatest single campaign outlay--

Are PACs Good or Bad for the Process?

how do PAC contributions affect members of Congress--

citizen-based PACs vs. PACS with wealthy parent organization--

small group of PACs conduct bulk of total PAC activity (percentages)--

James Madison and "factions"--

Campaign Finance Reform and Beyond

Bipartisan Campaign Finance Reform Act of 2002--

John McCain--

Major Provisions of the Bipartisan Campaign Finance Reform Act

three major ways 2002 Campaign Finance Reform Act amends FECA--

1)

2)

3)

Potential Implications of Campaign Finance Reform

Senator Mitch McConnell's opposition--

The Internet and Campaign Finance

self-directed medium--

Bringing It Together: The 2000 Presidential Campaign and Election

closest election in modern U.S. history--

The Party Nomination Battle

Bill Bradley and John McCain--

The Third Force

Ralph Nader--

The Party Conventions

Republican Convention

Democratic Convention

The Presidential Debates

third party participation--

expectations and performance for Bush and Gore--

The Fall Campaign and General Election

Election Results

Katherine Harris--

Bush v. Gore (2000)--

Research Ideas and Possible Paper Topics

1. Write a campaign plan. Call your local political parties and ask for copies of their grassroots electioneering materials or candidate training course materials. Using those materials, write up a campaign plan for a candidate for the House or Senate. Be sure you can explain why you chose your tactics and strategies.

2. Choose which candidate you like for president in the 2004 election. Consider yourself his or her campaign consultant. Have a plan for media, fundraising, scheduling and travel, get out the vote, and other aspects of the campaign. Write up your campaign plan.

3. Write an essay designed to prepare your candidate for an upcoming presidential debate. Choose a strategy and a message for your campaign. What tactics, etc. will help you win the debate?

4. Go to the library or Internet and find a cache of campaign commercials and free media coverage of one of the last few elections. Compare tactics, strategies, and content of the ads. How would you classify them? How effective is each ad? To whom are they targeted? Discuss what these ads tell you about the political process and the candidates.

5. Research the current campaign finance laws and the reform measures recently passed by Congress. Once you understand the nature of the laws and their purpose, devise a reform plan of your own. And consider how you would sell it to the people, the incumbents in the House and Senate, the president, and other interested parties.

Websites

Project Vote-Smart is a non-partisan information service funded by members and non-partisan foundations. It offers "a wealth of facts on your political leaders, including biographies and addresses, issue positions, voting records, campaign finances, evaluations by special interests." It also offers "CongressTrack" a way for citizens to track the status of legislation, members & committees, sponsors, voting records, clear descriptions, full text, and weekly floor schedules, as well as access to information on elections, federal & state governments, the issues, and politics. Includes thousands of links to the most important sites on the Internet.
    www.vote-smart.org/

The **Democracy Project of PBS** offers a website called "**Dissect the Ad**" that features a changing set of campaign ads that visitors are asked to criticize, dissect, and discuss. The point is to determine how the message is constructed--what images, tones, music, etc. and how it is designed to sway us. There are numerous current and past ads on which to practice from all ends of the political spectrum. You can read the content of the ads or, by downloading a player, you can view them. Following each ad are commentaries on both sides discussing the ad and you get the chance to post your comments, if you are so inclined, and read the comments of others.
    www.pbs.org/democracy/readbetweenthelines/index.html

The **30-Second Candidate** PBS website provides information about campaign television ads including historical timelines, "from idea to ad," questions and answers and a transcript of the 1999 Emmy Award winning program.
    www.pbs.org/30secondcandidate/

Campaigns and Elections magazine's website is oriented toward campaign professionals but is also useful to teachers and students. It offers articles, their table of contents from the print version, job opportunities, and more.
    www.campaignline.com

Democratic Congressional Campaign Committee - DCCC
    www.dccc.org/

Democratic Senatorial Campaign Committee-DSCC
    www.dscc.org

National Republican Congressional Committee-NRCC
    www.nrcc.org/

National Republican Senatorial Committee-NRSC
    www.nrsc.org

Federal Election Commission website on campaign finance laws.
    www.fec.gov/finance_law.html

The **Alliance for Better Campaigns** advocates more "candidate-centered discourse" on national TV in the month preceding the general election. The website examines television as a medium for election news and details the weight that ad dollars have in campaigns. Be sure to click on "Greedy TV."
www.bettercampaigns.org

The **Washington Post OnPolitics** webpage reports on campaigns and elections.
www.washingtonpost.com/wp-dyn/politics/elections

The **New York Times** maintains an archive of articles analyzing political ads from recent campaigns from across the country. Links to some videos are available.
www.nytimes.com/library/politics/camp/ads-index.htm

Brookings Institution's Campaign Finance Web Page
www.brookings.org/dybdocroot/gs/cf/cf_hp.htm

Common Cause offers information on soft money donations, PAC contributions, and voting records on campaign finance issues as well as other information.
www.commoncause.org

The Public Campaign offers articles on campaign finance reform at the state and national levels as well as numerous links.
www.publicampaign.org

Open Secrets, the website for The Center for Responsive Politics, documents the money raised and spent by congressional candidates, individual donors, and PACs. It includes information on large soft money donations and the financial disclosure reports of members of Congress.
www.opensecrets.org

The **American Association of Political Consultants** provides information for and about political campaign consultants.
www.theaapc.org

Practice Tests

MULTIPLE CHOICE QUESTIONS

1. The public part of the campaign in which the candidate makes appearances and meets voters, in part to stimulate local activists, is called the

    a. general election campaign.
    b. nomination campaign.
    c. personal campaign.
    d. media campaign.

2. The danger for a candidate in the nomination campaign is

   a. extremism.
   b. shifting strategy.
   c. lack of organization.
   d. all of the above.

3. The best-known consultants for any campaign are usually

   a. campaign managers.
   b. media consultants and pollsters.
   c. the organizational campaign.
   d. the financial people.

4. Advertising that attempts to counteract an anticipated attack from the opposition before the attack is launched is called an _____ advertisement.

   a. attack
   b. assault
   c. inoculation
   d. immunization

5. In most cases, a candidate wins or loses a campaign according to

   a. how much money she is able to raise and spend.
   b. who she hires as her political and media consultants.
   c. her abilities, qualifications, communication skills, issues and weaknesses.
   d. the amount of TV time she can buy.

6. In the first televised presidential debate in 1960 between Richard Nixon and John F. Kennedy, people who heard the debate on radio rather than seeing it on television thought

   a. Kennedy had won, just as those who saw it on TV did.
   b. Nixon had won, unlike those who saw it on TV who considered Kennedy the winner.
   c. Kennedy had won, unlike those who saw it on TV who considered Nixon the winner.
   d. it was a tie between the two.

7. In a political campaign covered extensively by the news media, such as a presidential race, which of the following would the news media most likely emphasize in its coverage?

   a. an announcement by the candidate of his proposed economic stimulus package for the country
   b. a speech by the candidate before a group of veterans concerning his proposal to tie veterans' benefits to the cost of living index .
   c. new poll results showing significant slippage in the candidate's lead
   d. a major announcement by the campaign concerning the candidate's position on Social Security benefits

8. Individuals are allowed to contribute _____ to a single candidate in each of the primary and general elections.

   a. $5,000
   b. $3,000
   c. $2,500
   d. $1,000

9. In 1976, the Supreme Court ruled that no limit could be placed on a candidate's personal spending in his or her own election campaign due to free speech guarantees in the case of

   a. *U.S. v. Nixon.*
   b. *Rockefeller v. U.S.*
   c. *Buckley v. Valeo.*
   d. *Perot v. Mitchell.*

10. There are approximately ____ PACs in the U.S.

    a. 6,500
    b. 4,000
    c. 2,400
    d. 1,500

11. Political parties supply about _____ percent of campaign expenditures for presidential candidates.

    a. 65
    b. 50
    c. 25
    d. 15

12. Presidential candidate George W. Bush refused to accept federal matching funds during the 2000 primary season because

    a. he felt it inappropriate for taxpayer dollars to go toward a political campaign.
    b. to accept the public funds would have limited the amount of his own personal wealth he could spend on his own campaign.
    c. to forego the public funds allowed him to freely raise and spend unlimited sums of money in his campaign.
    d. he believed he has raised sufficient funds to defeat his opponents and did not wish to appear greedy to potential voters.

13. The 2002 Bipartisan Campaign Finance Reform Act calls for

    a. banning soft-money contributions.
    b. increasing the amount of hard money individuals may donate.
    c. imposing new restrictions on political advertising close to elections.
    d. all of the above

14. Among the third party candidates who ran in the 2000 presidential elections was (were)

    a. Ross Perot.
    b. Jesse Ventura.
    c. Ralph Nader.
    d. all of the above.

15. In the 2000 presidential election, George W. Bush lost the popular vote of the American people by

    a. less than ten thousand votes.
    b. approximately 100,000 votes.
    c. by just under a quarter million votes.
    d. by over half a million votes.

TRUE/FALSE QUESTIONS

1. Negative advertising is a new phenomenon.

2. Media and organizational techniques advocated by consultants often fail.

3. Candidate debates are entirely staged and scripted.

4. Knowing they cannot be successful in doing so, modern candidates rarely attempt to manipulate press coverage.

5. Political action committees can give unlimited amounts of money to candidates.

6. Candidates can spend as much of their own money as they wish on their own campaigns.

7. Soft money is spent independently of campaigns and candidates but is highly regulated by the Federal Election Commission.

8. PACs are the primary source of election funding and threaten to destroy the legitimacy of the election process.

9. In 2000, Bill Bradley's campaign seriously challenged Al Gore's in the primaries.

10. In 2000, third party candidates were barred from participating in the presidential candidate debates.

COMPARE AND CONTRAST

the types of campaign: nomination, general election, personal, organizational, and media

free and paid media

positive, negative, contrast, and spot ads

campaign finance: individual vs. member vs. party vs. PAC contributions

public funds, matching funds, personal funds, voluntary contributions

soft money and hard money

express advocacy and issue advocacy advertisements

campaign finance reform and the First Amendment

ESSAY AND SHORT ANSWER QUESTIONS

1) What are the personal and organizational aspects of a campaign?

2) What are the pressures and hazards of the nomination campaign?

3) What are independent expenditures? What are the constitutional issues and concerns surrounding them?

4) Discuss candidate debates. How effective are they? Are they truly debates? How might they be changed to make them more effective and useful?

5) Can the press be manipulated by candidates? Does spin work? How do the media cover political campaigns?

6) Discuss the structure of a political campaign and the personnel involved.

7) Discuss the types of media and advertising a candidate may choose to use.

8) What are the rules regarding campaign finance for presidential elections? Do they work? Why or why not?

9) What are PACs and how do they affect the election process?

10) Discuss the 2000 presidential campaign and election.

ANSWERS TO STUDY EXERCISES

multiple choice answers

1.	c	p. 543
2.	a	p. 541
3.	b	p. 544
4.	c	p. 545
5.	c	p. 548
6.	b	p. 550
7.	c	p. 552
8.	d	p. 553
9.	c	p. 555
10.	b	p. 554
11.	d	p. 554
12.	c	p. 555
13.	d	p. 562
14.	c	p. 567
15.	d	p. 576

true/false answers

1.	F	p. 545
2.	T	p. 548
3.	F	p. 550
4.	F	p. 549
5.	F	p. 554
6.	T	p. 555
7.	F	p. 556
8.	F	p. 558
9.	F	p. 566
10.	T	p. 568

CHAPTER 15
THE NEWS MEDIA

Chapter Goals and Learning Objectives

Have you ever sat down with George Bush or Colin Powell over coffee to talk about the threat of terrorism and what to do about it? When did you last sit in on a Congressional hearing to learn how the proposed new federal budget will effect your student loans? Probably never. You're busy at home working and going to school and don't have the time or resources to go to Washington and learn first hand about what's happening with your government.

That's why the news media is so important in our democracy. An essential function of the press is to report to the American people on what your elected representatives are doing in Washington. That is why the news business is the only private business protected directly by the U.S. Constitution. The First Amendment protects the freedom of the press to report on the activities of our government. The manner in which they do it and how effectively they do it is another matter entirely.

The news media--the aggregate of electronic and print journalism--has the potential to exert enormous influence over Americans. The news media is crucial in facilitating public awareness of and discourse on politics necessary for the maintenance of a free country. The First Amendment grants the media broad rights. But is there a corresponding responsibility? Do citizens get the information from the news media we need to make educated decisions about elections? Does the news media provide complete, objective, issue-based coverage of politicians and public policy or does it focus on the trivial, entertaining and sensational? In this chapter, we look at these questions as well as the historical development and evolving nature of the journalism in America.

This chapter is designed to give you a basic understanding of the opportunities, challenges, and problems posed by the news media today as well as the effects of our (the citizenry's) unthinking consumption of the media's messages. The main topic headings of the chapter are:

- The American Press of Yesteryear
- The Contemporary Media Scene
- How the Media Cover Politicians and Government
- The Media's Influence on the Public
- The Public's Perception of the Media
- How Politicians Use the Media
- Government Regulation of the Electronic Media

In each section, there are certain facts and ideas that you should strive to understand. Many are in boldface type and appear in both the narrative and in the glossary at the end of the book. Other ideas, dates, facts, events, people, etc., are more difficult to pull out of the narrative. (Keep in mind that studying for objective-[multiple choice, T/F] style tests is different than studying for essay tests. See the Study Guide section on test taking for hints on study skills.)

In general, after you finish reading and studying this chapter, you should understand the following:

- the evolution of the press from the partisan newspapers of the 1790s through the yellow journalism of the 1890s to today's news media: the press, radio, television, and the Internet
- the current structure and role of the news media
- how politicians and government are covered by the news media, the trend away from Watergate-era investigative journalism to trivial coverage of personality, horserace issues and personal scandal
- the media's influence on the public and what sway the news media has over public opinion
- public perception of the news media's integrity, effectiveness and biases
- how politicians and the government attempt to manipulate media coverage toward their own political ends.

Chapter Outline and Key Points

In this section, you are provided with a basic outline of the chapter and any key words/points you should know. Use this outline, in your own notebook, to develop a complete outline of the material. This will help you study and remember the material in preparation for your tests, assignments, and papers.

The American Press of Yesteryear

journalism--

landmarks of the American news media (table 15.1)--

Anti-Federalists and the press--

fourth branch of government--

early partisan press--

Washington and Jefferson and the press--

penny press--

rise of mass circulation press--

William Randolph Hearst--

Joseph Pulitzer--

yellow journalism--

muckraking--

role of corporate profit--

The Contemporary Media Scene

print press--

electronic media--

decline of newspaper circulation--

newspaper chains--

role of television news--

print elite--

TV vs. print--

role of cable television--

substance of local news--

two effects of media mergers--

networks--

affiliates--

wire service-

newsmagazines--

political websites--

impact of Internet on news coverage--

How the Media Cover Politicians and Government

Covering the Presidency

president is first among equals in coverage--

Franklin D. Roosevelt and the bully pulpit--

press release --

press briefing --

press conference --

presidential press secretary

Ari Fleischer--

Covering Congress

why it is difficult for news media to survey Congress--

news media focuses on three groups in covering Congress--

investigative committee hearings--

McCarthy--

Watergate--

Iran-Contra--

Whitewater--

Enron and WorldCom--

C-SPAN

Covering the Courts

why scant coverage of courts--

Bush v. Gore (2000)--

Kenneth Starr investigation--

Watergate and the Era of Investigative Journalism

Watergate--

Woodward and Bernstein--

investigative journalism--

The Post-Watergate Era

post-Watergate press--

The Character Issue in Media Coverage of Politicians

Carter's 1976 campaign--

Edward Kennedy--

Bill Clinton--

George W. Bush campaign--

news journalism--

behind-the-scenes books--

Barber's *Presidential Character*--

shift from print to TV coverage (Roderick Hart theory)--

three assumptions regarding coverage of character--

Loosening of the Libel Law

libel--

New York Times v. Sullivan (1964)--

public figures--

actual malice--

The Question of Ideological Bias

why does bias exist--

liberal and conservative press bias--

Other Sources of Bias

getting the story first--

horserace coverage--

celebrity status and wealth of journalists--

Pat Buchanan--

The Media's Influence on the Public

effect of media on public--

media effects--

effect on uncommitted--

topics far removed from lives and experience of public--

news media determines agenda--

2000 presidential election coverage--

Public's Perception of the Media

low public confidence in news media--

credibility ratings for national news media--

credibility of TV vs. print media--

How Politicians Use the Media

focus groups

role of local news and talk shows--

Bill Clinton, media master--

"Wag the Dog"--

"Buddy" and the media--

John McCain and media--

on background--

deep background--

off-the-record--

on-the-record--

Government Regulation of the Electronic Media

two reasons for unequal treatment of print and broadcast media--

FCC

1996 Telecommunications Act--

2002 FCC ruling on cable internet service--

regulation of private ownership

Content Regulation

content regulation--

equal time rule--

right-of-rebuttal rule--

fairness doctrine--

Censorship

prior restraint--

Pentagon Papers--

New York Times v. U.S. (1971)

Gulf War and "Vietnam Syndrome--

role of media in 1991 coup against Mikhail Gorbachev--

Research Ideas and Possible Paper Topics

1. For several days, tape each of the major network's newscasts (ABC, CBS, NBC) and the two largest non-networks' (FOX and CNN). View at least two days of each broadcast. Pay attention to the order and length of each story, the tone of the report, and the graphics/images used. How are these broadcasts similar or different? Which reports seem most objective and why? What kinds of information are they offering? Is it the type of information you need to make educated decisions about politics and world affairs? Why or why not?

2. Choose a current event and compare the coverage in local press, national press, network news, and cable news. How and why do the ways each of these types of media cover the issues differ? How are they similar? What media outlets do you find most useful?

3. Find three or four news sites on the Internet. What types of information are you finding there? Does it differ from more traditional types of media? How and why?

4. Using a major national newspaper (*The New York Times, The Washington Post*, or *The Wall Street Journal*), analyze the way in which the current president is treated. Is he treated well or poorly? Why? Is there an obvious bias? What is it? Is he treated similarly or differently than other major political figures? Why?

5. Choose a political event such as an election, a scandal, a Supreme Court ruling, or some other public policy issue. Discuss the nature of the coverage it receives from a variety of media sources and discuss why that coverage may differ or be similar.

Websites

Fairness and Accuracy in Reporting (FAIR) is a liberal watchdog group looking for media bias. In their own words: " FAIR believes that independent, aggressive and critical media are essential to an informed democracy. But mainstream media are increasingly cozy with the economic and political powers they should be reporting on critically. Mergers in the news industry have accelerated, further limiting the spectrum of viewpoints that have access to mass media. With U.S. media outlets overwhelmingly owned by for-profit conglomerates and supported by corporate advertisers, independent journalism is compromised." The website offers examples of bias and more.
www.fair.org

Media Research Center is a conservative group that claims the media have a liberal bias. Offers links to conservative media and political sites.
www.mediaresearch.org/

The Pew Center for People and the Press is an independent opinion research group that studies attitudes toward the press, politics, and public policy issues. Its website offers the results of numerous surveys including those of public attitudes toward the media's coverage of politics and offers information trends in values and fundamental political and social attitudes.
www.people-press.org

The **Annenberg Public Policy Center** at the University of Pennsylvania conducts content analysis on TV coverage of politics.
www.appcpenn.org

The Pew Center for Civic Journalism works to encourage 'good journalism'. The institute is trying to battle cynicism and re-engage citizens in the political process.
www.pewcenter.org

The Project for Excellence in Journalism is sponsored by Pew, Columbia School of Journalism, and the Committee of Concerned Journalists. They are trying to raise the standards of journalism and are running several projects, including one on local TV news and the state of newspapers in America. This and more are available through their website.
    www.journalism.org/

Center for Media and Public Affairs conducts studies of new news media and politics.
    www.cmpa.com

The Center for Media Literacy encourages critical thinking about the news media including media values.
    www.medialit.org

Freedom Forum is an organization which champions freedom of the press under the First Amendment. This website provides a significant amount of full-text information (journal articles, press releases, study reports) about press freedom issues.
    www.freedomforum.org

J-Lab, a site hosted by the Institute for Interactive Journalism at the University of Maryland, uses new technologies to engage visitors in critical public policy issues covered by the press.
    www.j-lab.org/index.html

Journalism.org, sponsored by the Project for Excellence in Journalism of the Columbia School of Journalism, studies issues concerning the press and publishes a daily digest of news about the media.
    www.journalism.org

Practice Tests

MULTIPLE CHOICE QUESTIONS

1. Inclusion of a provision to protect the freedom of the press in the final version of the Constitution was demanded by

    a. George Washington.
    b. the Anti-Federalists.
    c. the Federalists.
    d. Thomas Jefferson.

2. Press coverage of the sexual proclivities of presidential candidates did not begin with Bill Clinton as evidenced by the fact that an early American newspaper printed rumors of illegitimate children fathered by

   a. George Washington.
   b. John Adams.
   c. Thomas Jefferson.
   d. James Madison.

3. Approximately _____ percent of adult Americans read a daily newspaper.

   a. 30
   b. 40
   c. 50
   d. 60

4. Most newspapers today are owned by chains, which

   a. reduces the diversity of editorial opinion available.
   b. results in the homogenization of the news.
   c. makes newspapers across the country very similar to one another.
   d. all of the above.

5. The results of the recent wave of media mergers have been that

   a. the bottom line has become much more important.
   b. news is being censored, especially anything that reflects badly on the parent companies' products or services.
   c. news is getting sleazier to expand the audience.
   d. all of the above.

6. The first president to use press conferences and a bully pulpit enhanced by broadcasting to shape public opinion and explain his actions was

   a. Franklin D. Roosevelt.
   b. Harry S Truman.
   c. Dwight D. Eisenhower.
   d. John F. Kennedy.

7. The first president to have a press secretary was

   a. Woodrow Wilson.
   b. Herbert Hoover.
   c. Franklin Delano Roosevelt.
   d. John F. Kennedy.

8. The branch of the federal government receiving the least coverage by the news media is the

   a. judiciary.
   b. Congress.
   c. presidency
   d. bureaucracy.

9. Which event had the most profound impact on the manner and substance of the press's conduct in the modern era of journalism?

   a. The Persian Gulf War.
   b. World War II.
   c. Watergate.
   d. Iran-Contra.

10. In what 1964 case did the Supreme Court rule that for public figures to claim libel, there must not only be a defamatory falsehood but also actual malice, making it much harder for public figures to prove libel?

    a. *Burnett v. National Enquirer.*
    b. *New York Times v. Sullivan.*
    c. *Hamilton v. Graber.*
    d. *Newman v. The Globe.*

11. The inception of the actual malice proof requirement in libel cases involving public figures had the effect of

    a. reducing the deterrent effect of libel litigation on the press, giving mass media greater latitude to publish information about public figures, thus enhancing First Amendment press protection.
    b. reducing the expense of defending libel claims.
    c. allowing editors and reporters to expend less time and energy on libel claims.
    d. increasing the number of libel suits filed.

12. Journalists, being people, reflect bias. The bias(es) most commonly exhibited by the news media is/are

    a. personal biases against or for individuals.
    b. fear of missing a good story.
    c. liberal.
    d. all of the above.

13. If you want to talk to a reporter and not be quoted or used as a source but you want the reporter to use the material you give her, you need to tell the reporter that you are talking

    a. off the record.
    b. on deep background.
    c. on background.
    d. on the record.

14. The fairness doctrine required broadcasters to cover events and present contrasting views on important government issues. It

    a. is still in effect.
    b. is also called the right of rebuttal.
    c. was in effect from 1949-1985.
    d. has been proposed by Congress but never passed.

15. In the 1971 case of *New York Times v. United States*, the U.S. Supreme Court held that prior restraint

    a. could not be imposed by the government upon the press.
    b. could be applied against broadcast media but not the print media.
    c. could be imposed on the publication of the Pentagon Papers.
    d. could not be imposed by the government except under extremely rare and confined circumstances.

TRUE/FALSE QUESTIONS

1. The first U.S. president to publicly condemn the press for its coverage of his presidency was Franklin D. Roosevelt.

2. The first presidential television advertisements were aired in 1960.

3. William Randolph Hearst and Joseph Pulitzer were known for championing sensationalized, oversimplified news coverage.

4. The modern press is less partisan and more concerned with corporate profit than the press in the eighteenth and nineteenth centuries.

5. Television is the most popular source for news today.

6. The news media gives less attention to scandals and investigations since Watergate.

7. According to your textbook, the news media, in general, does not have a large impact on public opinion.

8. The news media affects the public more by what events it chooses to cover as opposed to how it covers events.

9. Politicians have found that they have little ability to influence or manipulate the news media.

10. The U.S. Constitution prohibits all regulation of the news media.

COMPARE AND CONTRAST

yellow journalism and muckraking

American, Canadian, and Mexican approaches to the mass media

print press and electronic media

networks, affiliates, and wire services

media coverage of the president, Congress, and judiciary

on background, deep background, off-the-record, and on-the-record statements

equal time rule, right-of-rebuttal rule, and the fairness doctrine

ESSAY AND SHORT ANSWER QUESTIONS

1) Discuss the functioning of the U.S. press from its establishment in 1690 through the nineteenth century.

2) Discuss the impact of media mergers on the amount and types of information available to American citizens.

3) When covering Congress, which figures do the media tend to cover and why?

4) How did Watergate affect the media?

5) What kind of influence do the media have on the public's attitudes and opinions?

6) The media today consists of a number of types of media. What are they and how do they differ? How are they similar? What incentives do they operate under and how do they decide what to use and what not to use?

7) Compare and contrast the ways in which the media cover the three branches of government.

8) Are the media biased? How? Discuss fully and give examples.

9) Discuss the ways in which government regulates and censors the media.

10) How have the media changed in the last two decades? What have been the impacts of these changes?

ANSWERS TO STUDY EXERCISES

multiple choice answers

1.	b	p. 585
2.	c	p. 585
3.	c	p. 587
4.	d	p. 588
5.	d	p. 590
6.	a	p. 592
7.	b	p. 592
8.	a	p. 595
9.	c	p. 596
10.	b	p. 599
11.	a	p. 599
12.	d	p. 599
13.	b	p. 606
14.	c	p. 608
15.	d	p. 609

true/false answers

1.	F	p. 585
2.	F	p. 585
3.	T	p. 586
4.	T	p. 587
5.	T	p. 589
6.	F	p. 596
7.	T	p. 601
8.	T	p. 602
9.	F	p. 605
10.	F	p. 607

CHAPTER 16
INTEREST GROUPS

Chapter Goals and Learning Objectives

James Madison in the *Federalist Papers* warned against "a number of citizens, whether amounting to a majority or minority of the whole, who are united and actuated by some common impulse of passion, or of interest, adverse to the rights of other citizens or to the permanent and aggregate interest of the community." Madison called these groups "factions." Today we might call them interest groups.

Thomas Hobbes and other political philosophers discussed the designs of self-interest among men in society--beasts in competition. Some Americans today fault interest groups as "selfish interest groups," seeking benefits for the few at the expense of the many. Yet, as society that has its roots in the concept of individual freedom, do we not want individuals and groups to seek support for their unique, individual interests? What are the role of interest groups in American government? Participation in the political process is necessary for a democracy to flourish. Is it necessary and beneficial that individuals and groups pressure policymakers at all levels of government? What are interest groups today? What do they seek and how do they operate? Do they supplement and complement political parties? Do they enhance representation? Or are they vehicles for powerful and wealthy interests to take over policymaking? Do you have interests that could be served by participating in an interest group? This chapter addresses these questions and others about the nature of interest groups and participation in America.

This chapter is designed to give you some ideas about the nature and desirability of interest groups. The main topic headings of the chapter are:

- What are Interest Groups?
- The Roots and Development of American Interest Groups
- What Do Interest Groups Do?
- What Makes Interest Groups Successful?

In each section, there are certain facts and ideas that you should strive to understand. Many are in boldface type and appear in both the narrative and in the glossary at the end of the book. Other ideas, dates, facts, events, people, etc., are more difficult to pull out of the narrative. (Keep in mind that studying for objective-[multiple choice, T/F] style tests is different than studying for essay tests. See the Study Guide section on test taking for hints on study skills.)

In general, after you finish reading and studying this chapter, you should understand the following:

- definitions and characteristics of interest groups
- the historical roots and development of interest groups in America, from the days of James Madison and the Federalists to today's groups such as the AARP and NRA

- strategies and tactics used by interest groups to further their agenda and how much influence they actually have
- the factors that contribute to interest group success

Chapter Outline and Key Points

In this section, you are provided with a basic outline of the chapter and any key words/points you should know. Use this outline, in your own notebook, to develop a complete outline of the material. This will help you study and remember the material in preparation for your tests, assignments, and papers.

What Are Interest Groups?

operational definitions of interest groups--

disturbance theory--

interest group--

Multi-Issue Versus Single-Issue Interest Groups

single-issue interest groups--

multi-interest groups--

NOW--

NARAL--

NRA

Kinds of Organized Interests

Economic Interest Groups

economic interest group--

"big three" economic interest groups--

Public Interest Groups

public interest group--

Governmental Units

The Roots and Development of American Interest Groups

James Madison and factions

Federalists--

National Groups Emerge (1830-80)

Women's Christian Temperance Union--

lobbyist--

Progressive Era (1890-1920)

Progressive movement--

Organized Labor

American Federation of Labor--

open shop laws

1914 Clayton Act--

Business Groups and Trade Associations

National Association of Manufacturers--

U.S. Chamber of Commerce--

trade associations--

The Rise of the Interest Group State

ACLU--

AARP--

Common Cause--

Ralph Nader--

Unsafe at Any Speed--

Conservative Backlash: Religious and Ideological Groups

    Moral Majority--

    Christian Coalition--

Business Groups, Trade, and Professional Associations

    Business Roundtable--

    Kyoto Protocol--

    contributions by large corporations--

    Wendy Gramm and Enron--

    Rock the Vote--

Organized Labor

    AFL-CIO--

    declining union membership--

What Do Interest Groups Do?

    Center for Public Integrity

    to whom are legislators more inclined to listen--

    downside to interest groups--

Lobbying

    lobbying--

    providing information--

    lobbying techniques (table 16.3)--

Lobbying Congress

    types of lobbying efforts on Congress--

    former members and staff as lobbyists--

iron triangle--

on what does lobbyist's effectiveness depend--

Attempts to Reform Congressional Lobbying

1995 Lobbying Disclosure Act—

Lobbying the Executive Branch

on what does lobbyist's effectiveness depend--

Title IX--

Ethics in Government Act--

Lobbying the Courts

litigation as lobbying tool--

amicus curiae brief--

influencing nominations to federal courts--

Grassroots Lobbying

grassroots lobbying--

flash campaigns--

Protest Activities

Boston tea party--

Martin Luther King, Jr.--

Election Activities

Endorsements

EMILY's List--

Rating the Candidates or Office Holders

scoring voting records--

Creating Political Parties

Reform Party--

Green Party--

Interest Groups and Political Action Committees

political action committee (PAC)--

research on impact of PACs on legislative voting--

2002 McCain-Feingold campaign finance reform bill and PACs--

What Makes an Interest Group Successful?

pressure politics--

shaping the public agenda--

Leaders and Patrons

patron--

of what must potential members of the groups be convinced--

Funding

direct mail marketing--

Members

three kinds of group members--

upper-class bias--

collective good--

free rider problem--

Research Ideas and Possible Paper Topics

1. Find polling data about the reliability of interest groups and the attitudes of the public towards them (try Gallup Polls, Roper Polls, and Congressional Quarterly sources among others). Do the public attitudes you find correlate with what you have learned about interest groups in this chapter? Why or why not?

2. Call, write, or visit the Websites of a number of interest groups. What are they doing? What are their key issues and tactics? Who are their members? How many members do they have? How does this information correlate with what you have learned in this chapter?

3. Interview your member of Congress or their staff members about their views of interest groups and lobbyists (or have your professor invite them to class to discuss the issue). What do they say? How much access do lobbyists actually have? How much influence? What kinds of tactics work best with Congress?

4. Interview several lobbyists (or ask your professor to invite several lobbyists to talk to your class). Discuss how they see their job and what tactics work and which ones don't. What issues do they deal with and what do they offer to politicians? How do they define a successful lobbyist? After talking with the professional lobbyists, what do you think about lobbying now? Does it seem less "unsavory"? Do the media do lobbyists justice in their coverage?

5. As a class project, form an interest group. Decide what issue(s) you will promote and how you would promote them. What strategies and tactics would you use? How would you attract members? How would you ensure the success of your group?

Websites

Open Secrets, sponsored by the Center for Responsive Politics, maintains a searchable Washington lobbyist database.
 www.opensecrets.org/lobbyists/index.asp

Public Citizen, a non-profit, non-partisan consumer advocacy group, maintains a special interests reports page listed by industry group.
 www.citizen.org/congress/special_intr/index.cfm

American Association of Retired Persons (AARP) is an interest and advocacy group devoted to the interests of those over 50.
 www.aarp.org

American Civil Liberties Union (ACLU) offers information on the entire Bill of Rights, including racial profiling, women's rights, privacy issues, prisons, drugs, etc. Includes links to other sites dealing with the same issues.
www.aclu.org

AFL-CIO is the largest trade union organization in America. Their website offers policy statements, news, workplace issues, and labor strategies.
www.aflcio.org

The United States **Chamber of Commerce** is a business-oriented interest group whose website offers articles of interest, policy information, and membership info.
www.uschamber.org

The **American Trial Lawyers Association** is an interest group for trial lawyers who support access for citizens to civil courts and which opposed business groups working to limit these rights. The website offers news and information for the reporters and citizens.
www.atla.org

Common Cause, founded by Ralph Nader, was one of the first public interest groups. They promote responsible government.
www.commoncause.org

Mexican American Legal Defense and Education Fund (MALDEF) website offers information on Census 2000, scholarships, job opportunities, legal programs, regional offices information, and more.
www.maldef.org

Native American Rights Fund (NARF) website offers profiles of issues, an archive, resources, a tribal directory, and treaty information, as well as a lot of other information.
www.narf.org

The **National Association for the Advancement of Colored People** (NAACP) website offers information about the organization, membership, and issues of interest to proponents of civil rights. Has sections on the Supreme Court, Census 2000, the Education Summit and includes links to other websites.
www.naacp.org

The **National Rifle Association (NRA)** offers information on gun ownership, gun laws, and coverage of legislation on associated issues.
www.nra.org

National Organization of Women (NOW) website offers information on the organization and its issues/activities including women in the military, economic equity, reproductive rights, and so on. They offer an email action list and the ability to join NOW on-line. Also has links to related sites.
www.now.org

Public Interest Research Group (PIRG) is a public interest group that promotes issues such as the environment, anti-tobacco, and so on.

www.pirg.org

Practice Tests

MULTIPLE CHOICE QUESTIONS

1. Political scientist David Truman argues that interest groups form to counteract other groups that already exist. This theory is called

    a. patron theory.
    b. disturbance theory.
    c. potential group theory.
    d. group formation

2. An example of a multi-issue group is the

    a. Christian Coalition.
    b. NAACP.
    c. NOW.
    d. all of the above.

3. Groups such as Common Cause are often categorized as a

    a. public interest group.
    b. single issue group.
    c. economic issue group.
    d. all of the above.

4. During the 1960s and 70s, interest groups often formed around issues important to groups, such as

    a. religious groups and economic organizations.
    b. minorities, the elderly, the poor, and consumers.
    c. elites, activists, and party regulars.
    d. economic, foreign policy advocates, and conservatives.

5. The largest interest group in the United States is the

    a. AFL-CIO.
    b. American Civil Liberties Union (ACLU).
    c. American Association of Retired Persons (AARP).
    d. Christian Coalition.

6. Labor unions were formed beginning in the 1900s. In 2000, approximately _____ percent of workers were unionized.

    a. 50
    b. 35
    c. 25
    d. 14

7. The vast majority of lobbyists and interest groups primarily use _____ as lobbying techniques.

    a. testimony at legislative hearings and personal contacts
    b. the endorsement of candidates and working on elections
    c. favors and monetary contributions
    d. protest and demonstrations

8. In order to be successful, a lobbyist must

    a. strongly advocate their side of the issue.
    b. provide accurate information.
    c. work to change the minds of legislators who do not agree with them.
    d. all of the above.

9. The Ethics in Government Act requires that executive branch employees must

    a. disclose the source and amount of their income.
    b. reveal any positions held in business, labor, or nonprofit groups.
    c. not represent anyone before their agency for one year after leaving office.
    d. all of the above.

10. Interest groups have a particularly strong link and strong influence with

    a. Congress.
    b. the president.
    c. regulatory agencies.
    d. the courts.

11. Today's grassroots campaigns by interest groups are

    a. more high-tech, using faxes, email, and the Internet.
    b. using telemarketers.
    c. causing Congress to be afraid and to look for simple, easy answers.
    d. all of the above.

12. A federally registered group that raises funds to donate to the political process is known as a(n)

    a. political action committee.
    b. interest group.
    c. political party.
    d. special interest.

13. Organizations generally have several types of members, including

    a. leaders.
    b. active members.
    c. rank and file.
    d. all of the above.

14. Many people belong to more than one group. This overlapping membership can have the effect of

    a. increasing member activity in both groups.
    b. increasing the cohesiveness of the groups.
    c. reducing the cohesiveness of the groups.
    d. enhance the activity level of members.

15. Something of value, such as a clean environment, that cannot be withheld from a non-interest group member can reduce the number of paying members an interest group can attract. This is known as

    a. a collective good.
    b. the potential membership problem.
    c. the overlapping interest problem.
    d. cost of membership.

TRUE/FALSE QUESTIONS

1. *The Federalist Papers* were one of the first, and most successful, examples of interest group activity in the United States.

2. The AFL-CIO is the largest and most influential interest group in America.

3. The growth and success of conservative groups ultimately led to a liberal backlash and a large amount of group formation for liberal causes in the 1980s.

4. Lobbying is the process by which interest groups attempt to influence public policy.

5. The term 'iron triangle' refers to the relationship between political parties, interest groups, and the executive branch.

6. Interest groups often lobby the courts by filing briefs in court cases.

7. Many interest groups claim to be nonpartisan.

8. Interest groups do not want to shape the public agenda.

9. The United States is a nation of joiners.

10. The National Organization of Women (NOW) has some 140 million potential members but only about 150,000 actual members.

COMPARE AND CONTRAST

potential vs. actual group membership

collective goods and free riders

multi-issue and single issue groups

kinds of interest groups: economic, public, governmental

business groups, trade, and professional organizations

election activities of interest groups: endorsements, ratings, creating parties, PACs

ESSAY AND SHORT ANSWER QUESTIONS

1) Define interest groups and discuss their functions.

2) Why do interest groups form? Discuss a number of theories and their rationales for group formation.

3) Compare and contrast potential vs. actual interest group membership.

4) What is lobbying and why is it important? Is it "good" or "bad" or neither?

5) How do interest groups lobby the courts?

6) What are interest groups? How were they formed and what are their roots?

7) Discuss the rise of the "interest group state".

8) Discuss the changes in the nature and outlook of interest groups from the 1950s and 60s to the 1970s and 80s.

9) What do interest groups do?

10) Discuss the various reforms attempted in lobbying practices.

ANSWERS TO STUDY EXERCISES

multiple choice answers

1. b   p. 622
2. d   p. 622
3. a   p. 624
4. b   p. 627
5. c   p. 627
6. d   p. 631
7. a   p. 635
8. b   p. 635
9. d   p. 641
10. c   p. 640
11. d   p. 641
12. a   p. 646
13. d   p. 649
14. c   p. 649
15. a   p. 649

true/false answers

1. T   p. 625
2. F   p. 631
3. F   p. 628
4. T   p. 634
5. F   p. 637
6. T   p. 641
7. T   p. 644
8. F   p. 647
9. T   p. 649
10. T   p. 649

CHAPTER 17
SOCIAL POLICY

Chapter Goals and Learning Objectives

Social welfare policy involves a broad and varied range of government programs designed to provide people with protection against want and deprivation, to improve their health and physical well-being, to provide educational and employment opportunities, and otherwise to enable them to lead more satisfactory, productive, and meaningful lives. These social policies are meant to benefit all members of society, but especially the less fortunate. Social welfare policy focuses on issues such as public education, income security, medical care, sanitation and disease prevention, public housing, employment training, children's protective services, and improvements in human nutrition. The idea behind these policies is that these services are so worthy to society as a whole that they should be provided by the government regardless of the ability of the recipients to pay. The question of where the line should be drawn between government and individual responsibility for these services and goods is the essence and scope of social welfare policy development.

This chapter is designed to give you a basic understanding of the broad range of programs called social welfare. The main topic headings of the chapter are:

- The Roots of Social Welfare Policy
- The Policy-Making Process
- Social Welfare Policies Today

In each section, there are certain facts and ideas that you should strive to understand. Many are in boldface type and appear in both the narrative and in the glossary at the end of the book. Other ideas, dates, facts, events, people, etc., are more difficult to pull out of the narrative. (Keep in mind that studying for objective-[multiple choice, T/F] style tests is different than studying for essay tests. See the Study Guide section on test taking for hints on study skills.)

In general, after you finish reading and studying this chapter, you should understand the following:

- the history of social welfare policy, income security, and health care and public education
- how public policy is made, including a model of the process
- the current state of welfare policy, including income security, health care and public education policies

Chapter Outline and Key Points

In this section, you are provided with a basic outline of the chapter and any key words/points you should know. Use this outline, in your own notebook, to develop a complete outline of the material. This will help you study and remember the material in preparation for your tests, assignments, and papers.

The Roots of Social Welfare Policy

social welfare policy--

Income Security

Great Depression--

Social Security Act (1935)--

"creeping socialism"--

Aid to Dependent Children--

Health Care

Medicare and Medicaid--

Public Education

G.I. Bill--

historical responsibility for public education--

The Policy-Making Process

public policy--

elite theory--

stages of the policy-making process--

Problem Recognition and Definition

Voting Rights Act of 1965--

Agenda Setting

Defining Agendas

agenda--

systemic agenda--

governmental or institutional agenda--

Getting on the Congressional Agenda

agenda setting--

agenda setting as a competitive process--

Policy Formulation

routine formulation--

analogous formulation--

creative formulation--

Policy Adoption

policy adoption--

congressional policy adoption consequences--

unilateral presidential decision-making--

Budgeting

policy and program review--

Policy Implementation

policy implementation--

authoritative techniques--

incentive techniques--

capacity techniques--

hortatory techniques--

Policy Evaluation

    policy evaluation--

    possible players in policy evaluation--

Social Welfare Policies Today

    greater control by states--

Income Security

    social insurance programs--

    non-means-based programs--

    means-tested programs--

    Social Insurance: Non-Means-Based Programs

        Old Age, Survivors, and Disability Insurance

            Social Security Trust Fund--

            retirement age--

            COLAs--

            recommendations of George W. Bush's Commission to Strengthen Social Security--

        Unemployment Insurance

            how financed--

    Social Insurance: Means-Tested Programs

        means tested programs--

    Supplementary Security Income

        SSI--

        TANF--

Family and Child Support Act

    Family and Child Support Act of 1988--

    workfare provision--

Personal Responsibility and Work Opportunity Reconciliation Act

    PRWORA of 1996--

    Charles Murray, *Losing Ground*--

    seven significant features of PRWORA of 1996--

Earned Income Tax Credit Program (EITC)

    earned income tax credit--

    objectives of EITC program--

Food Stamp Program

    food stamps--

Effectiveness of Income Security Programs

    entitlement programs--

Health Care

    Veterans' health care--

    National Institution of Health (NIH)--

    how much spent for public health in U.S. versus other countries--

    quality of health care in U.S. versus other countries--

Medicare

    Medicare--

    Part A and Part B--

    1988 Catastrophic Health Care Act--

Medicaid

Medicaid--

to whom does most of the benefits paid out go--

funding--

AIDS Funding

Bragdon v. Abbott (1998)--

New Health Initiatives

effect of 1997 Balanced Budget Act--

Health Insurance Portability and Accountability Act--

right to sue HMOs--

The Cost of Health Care

percentage of budget and GDP for health programs in U.S.--

factors in rising costs of health care--

Public Education

traditional function of state and local government--

public school financing--

Federal Aid to Education

Goals 2000--

Disabilities Education Act of 1975--

student loans--

Inequality in Spending Among School Districts

right to education--

property taxes--

Voucher Plans and Charter Schools

Milwaukee voucher program--

charter schools--

Research Ideas and Possible Paper Topics

1. Go to the Website of the House of Representatives or call your local representative's office. Find out what social welfare laws are on the agenda for this session of Congress. Choose one and follow it over the course of the semester. Pay attention to partisan issues, which interest groups get involved and how, which members of Congress sponsor the bill, and how this bill fits the policy process you have learned about in this chapter.

2. Go to the library or the Internet and find out what the official poverty level is in your country and the demographics of poor people and folks who receive federal assistance (one possible source is Meredith Bagby's *The Actual State of the Nation*). How was it determined and how appropriate is this figure today? Can a family of four really live on it? In addition, do some additional research about the policies designed to help the poor. Discuss what the country is doing for the poor. Is it enough? Why or why not?

3. Do some research on the failed national health care plan which had been proposed by President Clinton during his administration. What mistakes were made, according to what you learned about the policy process? What tactics and strategies could have been used to promote this policy?

4. Over the past several years, many of the responsibilities for social welfare policies have been delegated to the states. Choose three states and find out what they are doing regarding social welfare. Are the states different or similar in their approach? Why?

5. Interview your grandparents or older people in your neighborhood about the impact of the GI Bill on their lives and education. Find out whether their parents ever went to college and whether they think they would have been able to go without the GI Bill. You may also want to ask them about what they learned in high school and college, including asking them if they still have their old textbooks. Use that information to evaluate the current state of education in the country. Do they have different ideas than you do? Why do you think that might be?

Websites

The Social Security Administration (SSA) website has information rules, regulations, and policies of the federal government on social security, both active and proposed. It offers information for citizens, scholars, and recipients. The website also offers historical perspectives on social security and its funding.
   www.ssa.gov

The **U.S. Department of Education** "mission is to ensure equal access to education and to promote educational excellence for all Americans." The Education Department's web site provides information about its offices, programs, information and assistance services, as well as funding opportunities, education statistics and publications.
   www.ed.gov

GPO Access offers the full text of many Government Printing Office publications on the web, including the economic indicators prepared for the Joint Economic Committee by the Council of Economic Advisors; updated monthly. Among the growing list of titles available are the Federal Register, the Congressional Record, Congressional Bills, United States Code, Economic Indicators and GAO Reports.
   www.access.gpo.gov/su_docs/index.html

The **Concord Coalition** is a nonpartisan, grassroots organization dedicated to eliminating federal budget deficits and ensuring Social Security, Medicare, and Medicaid are secure for all generations; founded by Senators Paul Tsongas (D) and Warren Rudman (R). The Coalition Website offers information about the debt and deficit as well as some social policy issues. It also offers email newsletters, grassroots initiatives, statistics, and more.
   http://www.concordcoalition.org/

The **Cato Institute** is a libertarian think tank promoting free market ideas. Their website offers a variety of articles and links.
   www.cato.org

The **American Enterprise Institute** is a conservative think tank that addresses a variety of issues. Their website offers information on their calendar of events, a variety of articles, and links.
   www.aei.org

The **Brookings Institution** is the oldest think tank in America and has the reputation of being fairly moderate. Their website offers policy briefings, articles, books, *The Brookings Review*, discussion groups, and links.
   www.brook.edu

The **Children's Defense Fund** website has many articles and links of interest to advocates for issues affecting children and families. They offer a listserv and publications.
   www.childrensdefense.org/

The **Institution for Research on Poverty** of the University of Wisconsin studies social inequity and poverty. The IRP develops and tests social policy alternatives. Reports are available on this website.
    www.ssc.wisc.edu/irp/

The **Center on Budget and Policy Priorities** is a non-profit research and policy institute devoted to studying governmental policies and programs, particularly those affecting low- and moderate-income people.
    www.cbpp.org

Practice Tests

MULTIPLE CHOICE QUESTIONS

1. All public issues that are viewed as requiring governmental attention are referred to as the

    a. systemic agenda.
    b. governmental agenda.
    c. institutional agenda.
    d. defining agenda.

2. Among those who set the agenda for Congress are

    a. interest groups.
    b. political changes or events.
    c. the president.
    d. all of the above.

3. The crafting of appropriate and acceptable proposed courses of action to ameliorate or resolve public problems is called

    a. agenda setting.
    b. policy formulation.
    c. policy implementation.
    d. problem resolution.

4. In order for a policy to be adopted, it must

    a. be the subject of negotiation, bargaining, and compromise.
    b. clear the House Rules Committee.
    c. win a series of majority votes in subcommittees, committees, and both Houses of Congress.
    d. all of the above.

5. Providing people with information, education, resources, and training as a technique of policy implementation is called a(n) _____ technique.

   a. hortatory
   b. incentive
   c. capacity
   d. authoritative

6. The process of determining whether a course of action is achieving its intended goals is called

   a. policy evaluation.
   b. problem recognition.
   c. policy implementation.
   d. policy adoption.

7. Social insurance programs that provide cash assistance to qualified beneficiaries are called

   a. security assistance.
   b. supplemental benefits.
   c. non-means-based programs.
   d. means based programs.

8. The poverty line for an urban family of four in 2001 was _____ per year.

   a. $8,920
   b. $18,267
   c. $24,649
   d. $35,136

9. Expenditures for Social Security have greatly increased in the last few years due to

   a. longer life expectancies.
   b. a rise in the number of elderly people in society due to Baby Boomers retiring.
   c. lower fertility rates.
   d. all of the above.

10. Unemployment insurance is funded through a

    a. payroll tax paid by individuals.
    b. payroll tax paid by employers.
    c. general revenue funds.
    d. state tax on employers.

11. The Earned Income Tax Credit was designed to help

    a. the middle class.
    b. very poor families without work.
    c. working poor people.
    d. all of the above.

12. The average food stamp recipient receives approximately _____ of food stamps per month.

    a. $250
    b. $190
    c. $118
    d. $73

13. In 1996, approximately _____ million Americans received Medicaid.

    a. 36
    b. 32
    c. 21
    d. 14

14. In 2001, the federal government provided _____ percent of public school funding.

    a. 7
    b. 17
    c. 37
    d. 47

15. Most school revenues come from

    a. the federal budget.
    b. the Department of Education.
    c. property taxes.
    d. income taxes.

TRUE/FALSE QUESTIONS

1. The national government has provided health care for some citizens since 1798.

2. All disturbing conditions become problems that can be addressed by public policy.

3. A governmental agenda is the changing lists of issues to which governments believe they should address themselves.

4. Only members of Congress are involved in congressional agenda setting.

5. Power is diffuse in Congress and the legislative process comprises a number of roadblocks and obstacles that a bill must successfully navigate before becoming a law.

6. A lack of funding can kill a policy even after it has been adopted.

7. Food stamps are a non-means tested program.

8. Social Security provides benefits only to senior citizens.

9. Most education funding comes from the national government.

10. Since most schools are funded by property taxes, there is substantial inequality in funding among school districts.

COMPARE AND CONTRAST

the phases of policy formation: problem recognition, agenda setting, formulation, policy adoption, budgeting, policy implementation, policy evaluation

systemic agenda, government agenda, and congressional agenda

means tested and non-means tested programs

Social Security and Supplemental Security Income (SSI)

entitlement programs and regular budget items

Medicare and Medicaid

vouchers and charter schools

ESSAY AND SHORT ANSWER QUESTIONS

1) What are public policy and social welfare policy?

2) What is a policy problem and how do they get identified?

3) What is an entitlement program? Give examples.

4) What is the historical role of the national government in education policy?

5) Compare and contrast voucher plans and charter schools. How does each proposal affect public schools?

6) Fully explain the stages of the policy process.

7) What are the techniques of policy implementation? Discuss how each one works using examples.

8) Discuss policies designed to increase income security.

9) What policies has the U.S. followed regarding health care? Which ones have been enacted and which ones have been defeated and why?

10) What is the national government's role in education? Be sure to discuss the various reform proposals on this issue.

ANSWERS TO STUDY EXERCISES

multiple choice answers

1.	a	p. 666
2.	d	p. 667
3.	b	p. 668
4.	d	p. 669
5.	c	p. 671
6.	a	p. 672
7.	c	p. 673
8.	b	p. 673
9.	d	p. 674
10.	b	p. 675
11.	c	p. 680
12.	d	p. 684
13.	a	p. 687
14.	a	p. 691
15.	c	p. 692

true/false answers

1.	T	p. 659
2.	F	p. 665
3.	T	p. 666
4.	F	p. 667
5.	T	p. 669
6.	T	p. 670
7.	F	p. 673
8.	F	p. 674
9.	F	p. 690
10.	T	p. 692

CHAPTER 18
ECONOMIC POLICY

Chapter Goals and Learning Objectives

"It's the economy, stupid!" That slogan was Bill Clinton's mantra during his successful 1992 campaign to oust President George Bush from the White House. Just the year before, Bush had earned phenomenal ratings in the approval polls following the Gulf War and seemed invincible in his reelection campaign. But a sour economy turned voters away from Bush to the Arkansas Governor running for president promising an economic turn around.

Americans tend to measure their quality of life by their relative economic well-being, and woe betide any politician who overlooks that fact. People vote their pocketbooks because they intrinsically know that politics and economics are two sides of the same coin.

The government and economy are, indeed, closely intertwined. The government defines and protects property rights, provides a common monetary system, grants corporate charters, issues patents and copyrights, handles bankruptcies, maintains law and order, and protects the environment, as well as many other economic tasks. In the early years of the republic, the federal government did little to regulate the economy. Following the era of large trusts and monopolies, the government substantially regulated business. Since the 1970s, deregulation has become the dominant buzzword of economic policy. This chapter will cover these historical processes and help you come to an understanding of why the role of government in the economy changes over time, where we are now, and where we might be going.

This chapter is designed to give you a basic understanding of the economic policies of the United States. The main topic headings of the chapter are:

- Roots of Government Intervention in the Economy
- Stabilizing the Economy
- The Economics of Regulating Environmental Activity

In each section, there are certain facts and ideas that you should strive to understand. Many are in boldface type and appear in both the narrative and in the glossary at the end of the book. Other ideas, dates, facts, events, people, etc., are more difficult to pull out of the narrative. (Keep in mind that studying for objective-[multiple choice, T/F] style tests is different than studying for essay tests. See the Study Guide section on test taking for hints on study skills.)

In general, after you finish reading and studying this chapter, you should understand the following:

- the history of government intervention in the economy, the kind of interventions feared by the Anti-Federalists
- the government's role in stabilizing the economy, otherwise known as macroeconomic regulation

- the economics of government regulation of environmental activity, which is an important area of microeconomic regulation

Chapter Outline and Key Points

In this section, you are provided with a basic outline of the chapter and any key words/points you should know. Use this outline, in your own notebook, to develop a complete outline of the material. This will help you study and remember the material in preparation for your tests, assignments, and papers.

Roots of Government Intervention in the Economy

The Nineteenth Century

mixed free-enterprise economic system--

state regulation and promotion of economy--

business cycles--

Adam Smith's *The Wealth of Nations*--

laissez-faire--

Interstate Commerce Act of 1887--

Sherman Antitrust Act of 1890--

Morrill Land Grant Act --

The Progressive Era (1901-1917)

Progressive Movement--

Upton Sinclair's *The Jungle*--

consumer protection acts--

Clayton Act of 1914--

Sixteenth Amendment--

The Great Depression and the New Deal

Great Depression--

New Deal--

interventionist state--

Financial Reforms

    Roosevelt's banking holiday--

    Glass-Steagall Act of 1933--

    FDIC--

    Banking Act of 1935--

    Federal Reserve Board--

    Securities Exchange Act of 1934--

    SEC--

    stocks bought on margin--

Agriculture

    Agricultural Adjustment Act of 1933 and 1938--

    crop subsidies--

    price support--

    political reasons Bush signed the 2002 Farm Bill of $100 billion--

Labor

    National Labor Relations Act of 1935--

    Fair Labor Standards Act of 1938--

    Minimum Wage laws--

Industry Regulations

    Federal Communications Commission--

    Civil Aeronautics Board--

Consumer Protection

the Pure Food, Drug, and Cosmetic Act--

The Post-World War II Era

The Employment Act

fiscal policy

Murray Act and Employment Act of 1946

Council of Economic Advisors--

The Taft-Hartley Act

1947 Taft-Hartley Act--

closed shop and open shop--

The Social Regulation Era

economic regulation--

social regulation--

Employee Retirement Income Security Act of 1974--

four factors involved in social regulation surge--

Deregulation

deregulation--

Airline Deregulation Act of 1978--

savings and loan deregulation during Reagan administration--

Enron and WorldCom bankruptcies--

Stabilizing the Economy

Harding, Hoover and Roosevelt and depression--

John Maynard Keynes--

economic stability--

inflation--

recession--

Monetary Policy: Regulating Money Supply

monetary policy--

money--

The Federal Reserve System

Federal Reserve Board--

Federal Reserve Banks--

Federal Open Market Committee--

Alan Greenspan--

reserve requirements--

discount rate--

open market operations--

"moral suasion"--

The President and the FRB

"power to persuade"--

Fiscal Policy: Taxing and Spending

fiscal policy--

discretionary fiscal policy--

Revenue Act of 1964--

tax system and the economy--

The Effects of Globalization

free trade and globalization--

labor unions and free trade--

protectionist view--

1999 real after-tax income of middle-Americans--

six explanations for declining economic fortunes of the middle class versus the tremendous growth of wealth for the upper class--

minimum wage--

The Budgetary Process

Congressional budget consideration

Legislation and the Budget Process

OMB--

fiscal year--

two largest spending categories in 2001--

Budget and Impoundment Control Act of 1974--

Congressional Budget Office (CBO)--

Major Budget Conflicts

Clinton 1993 budget reduction plan--

government shutdown--

Budget Initiatives of the George W. Bush Administration

2001 Economic Growth and Tax Relief Reconciliation Act--

2002 supplemental request of $27.1 billion for Defense and Homeland Security--

The Deficit and the Debt

national debt--

gross domestic product (GDP)--

national debt tripled in 1980s (Reagan Administration)--

1993 Omnibus Budget Reconciliation Act (Clinton Administration)--

deficits and impact on economy—

Deficit Reduction Legislation

three components of Gramm-Rudman-Hollings Act--

1997 Budget Reduction Act--

Budget Compromises and the 1997 Balanced Budget Act

compromise between Clinton and Gingrich--

Budget Surplus and Renewed Deficits

Reagan legacy of huge deficits; Clinton legacy of budget surplus--

deficits under George W. Bush--

The Economics of Regulating Environmental Pollution

federal involvement in environmental controls until the late 1960s--

pollution and human use--

Environmental Policy Making

externality or social cost of industrial activity--

economic disadvantage of business cleaning up pollutants without government requirement--

Sierra Club--

Nature Conservancy--

Clean Air Act of 1970 and 1990--

major environmental laws since 1970--

The Environmental Protection Agency

EPA--

three major eras in life of EPA--

George W. Bush and Artic National Wildlife Refuge--

Hazardous and Toxic Wastes

    Love Canal--

    Superfund--

    George W. Bush undercutting Superfund cleanups--

Acid Rain

    Clinton Administration crack-down--

    G.W. Bush easing up on enforcement against acid rain--

    Kyoto Protocol--

    Clean Air Act Amendments of 1990--

Congressional Action and Environmental Protection

    Congress controlled by Republicans undercut environmental regulation--

    Rep. Tom DeLay (now House Majority Leader) called EPA what?--

    Christine Todd Whitman--

Research Ideas and Possible Paper Topics

1. The United States is a mixed free enterprise system. How many other countries of the world have similar economies? Are they as successful as that of the United States? Do some research to determine the answers to these questions. What other types of systems exist? Are any of them "successful"? Why or why not?

2. The Chairman of the Federal Reserve Bank is often described as the most powerful man in America. Do some research to determine why he is so powerful, who he is, and what his policies are. Compare our Fed to the Central Bank of another country. Do they have similar powers?

3. There is a huge debate in this country over the pros and cons of a constitutional amendment requiring a balanced budget. Do some research on this topic. Be prepared to give the arguments of all sides in the discussion. Be sure to look at the 27 amendments we currently have. Does a balanced budget amendment fit in with the others? If passed and ratified, what would happen? Who decides what to cut if the president and Congress can't propose a balanced budget regularly? Would the current Bush Administration support a balanced budget amendment, do you believe, considering the massive deficits created under G. W. Bush?

4. A major concern of the nineteenth century was the business cycle. Monetary and fiscal policies have minimized these swings to some extent. Test the truth of these statements by looking at historical economic trends.

5. The Environmental Protection Agency is the largest regulatory agency in the U.S. government. It has also been attacked for a variety of reasons by Republicans and Democrats. Using the information in this chapter as a starting point, do some research about the EPA. How effective is it? What does it do? What impact does it have on business? What effect has the rejection of the Kyoto Protocols by George W. Bush had on environmental policy in this country and the world and Americans' confidence in this Administration's protestations of environmental concern versus their record?

Websites

Federal Reserve Board website has basic information about the FRB, its structure, and purpose. Also has publications, announcements, lists of related websites, biographies of members, reports, and statistics.
   www.federalreserve.gov

Office of Management and Budget (OMB) website offers budget information, reports, testimony, regulatory policies, and more from the perspective of the administration.
   www.whitehouse.gov/OMB/

Congressional Budget Office (CBO) website offers Congress' opinions on budget matters including statistics, reports, budget reviews, testimony, and more.
   www.cbo.gov/

The **Council of Economic Advisors** website offers the Economic Report of the President and CEA publications as well as basic information about the CEA and its members.
   www.whitehouse.gov/cea/

The **National Debt Clock** offers a running account of the public debt and offers links to a variety of groups and organizations interested in the debt and/or deficit.
   www.brillig.com/debt_clock

GPO Access offers the full text of many Government Printing Office publications on the web, including the economic indicators prepared for the Joint Economic Committee by the Council of Economic Advisors; updated monthly. Among the growing list of titles available are the Federal Register, the Congressional Record, Congressional Bills, United States Code, Economic Indicators and GAO Reports.
   www.access.gpo.gov/su_docs/index.html

The **Concord Coalition** is a nonpartisan, grassroots organization dedicated to eliminating federal budget deficits and ensuring Social Security, Medicare, and Medicaid are secure for all generations; founded by Paul Tsongas (D) and Warren Rudman (R). The Coalition Website

offers lots of information about the debt and deficit as well as some social policy issues. They offer email newsletters, grassroots initiatives, statistics, and more.
www.concordcoalition.org/

The **Economic Policy Institute (EPI)** is a nonpartisan think tank devoted to economic issues. This website offers a variety of reports on economic issues and a monthly newsletter delivered by email. Despite their self classification as nonpartisan, their board of directors is predominantly left-leaning (liberal).
www.epinet.org/

The **Cato Institute** is a libertarian think tank promoting free market ideas. Their website offers a variety of articles and links.
www.cato.org

The **American Enterprise Institute** is a conservative think tank that addresses a variety of issues. Their website offers information on their calendar of events, a variety of articles, and links.
www.aei.org

Moving Ideas hosts policy, politics and news from progressive and liberal research organizations and advocacy groups.
www.movingideas.org

The **Brookings Institution** is the oldest think tank in America and has the reputation of being fairly moderate. Their website offers policy briefings, articles, books, *The Brookings Review*, discussion groups, and links.
www.brook.edu

Practice Tests

MULTIPLE CHOICE QUESTIONS

1. The doctrine of *laissez-faire* is based on the theories of

    a. Adam Smith.
    b. Alexander Hamilton.
    c. John Maynard Keynes.
    d. Milton Friedman.

2. State agricultural and mechanical arts colleges were established by the

    a. Homestead Act.
    b. Morrill Land Grant Act.
    c. Clayton Act.
    d. Wagner Act.

3. Congress passed the Federal Reserve Act in

   a. 1961.
   b. 1948.
   c. 1935.
   d. 1913.

4. The income tax was made possible by the

   a. Clayton Act.
   b. Congress that passed a law on income taxes.
   c. Sixteenth Amendment.
   d. Hatch Act.

5. The New Deal government program that created jobs building roads, bridges, parks, and public facilities was called the

   a. Civilian Conservation Corps.
   b. Works Progress Administration.
   c. National Parks Service.
   d. Federal Transportation and Public Works Administration.

6. The first acts of the New Deal were directed at

   a. banking.
   b. agriculture.
   c. labor.
   d. poverty.

7. Workers' rights to organize and bargain collectively through unions of their own choosing were codified in the

   a. Taft-Hartley Act.
   b. Glass-Steagall Act.
   c. Taylor Act.
   d. Wagner Act.

8. The radio, telephone, and telegraph industries became subject in 1934 to federal regulatory controls by the

   a. Federal Communications Act.
   b. Federal Communications Commission.
   c. Telecommunications Act.
   d. Multimedia Act.

9. In order to advise the president on economic matters, the _____ was created in the 1940s.

   a. Department of Commerce
   b. Federal Reserve
   c. Joint Economic Committee
   d. Council of Economic Advisors

10. Several new regulatory agencies were established in the 1960s and 70s to implement new social regulations, including

    a. Consumer Product Safety Commission.
    b. Occupational Safety and Health Administration.
    c. Environmental Protection Agency.
    d. all of the above.

11. The idea that government spending could offset a decline in private spending and thus help maintain high levels of spending, production, and employment was advocated by

    a. David Ricardo.
    b. John Maynard Keynes.
    c. Herbert Hoover.
    d. Franklin Roosevelt.

12. The seven members of the Federal Reserve Board are appointed for overlapping terms of _____ years.

    a. 14
    b. 10
    c. 7
    d. 4

13. Federal government policies on taxes, spending, and debt management are referred to as

    a. aggregate policy.
    b. economic policy.
    c. fiscal policy.
    d. monetary policy.

14. The president began preparing and submitting a budget to Congress under the authority given him by Congress in the Budget and Accounting Act of

    a. 1948.
    b. 1921.
    c. 1865.
    d. 1781.

15. Interest payments alone on the national debt in 1999 account for _____ percent of the national budget.

   a. 11
   b. 21
   c. 31
   d. 41

TRUE/FALSE QUESTIONS

1. The Progressive Movement sought to bring corporate power under the control of the government.

2. Taft-Hartley increased the power of labor unions.

3. Congressional Republicans have diligently sought deregulation of federal environmental laws in recent years.

4. The Federal Reserve Chairman is designated by the president from the sitting Federal Reserve Board for a term of 4 years.

5. The government's fiscal year begins on October 1.

6. The Congressional Budget Office is a bipartisan professional staff of technical experts.

7. The balanced budget was achieved largely due to the impact of the Gramm-Rudman-Hollings Act.

8. The EPA is now confronting issues of environmental civil rights because many polluting industries are located in poor black neighborhoods.

9. Acid rain has been an important environmental problem for over half a century.

10. House Republican Leader Tom DeLay opposes federal environmental protection measures, once calling the EPA "the Gestapo."

COMPARE AND CONTRAST

laissez-faire vs. interventionist state

Wagner Act, the Fair Labor Standards Act, and Taft-Hartley

economic regulation, social regulation, and deregulation

economic stability and inflation

recession and depression

reserve requirements, discount rate, and open market operations

monetary and fiscal policies

OMB and CBO

budget deficit and national debt

ESSAY AND SHORT ANSWER QUESTIONS

1) Discuss the American economic system, its roots and its interaction with political forces within the country.

2) Discuss the Interstate Commerce Act and the Sherman Anti-Trust Act.

3) What is the Taft-Hartley Act and what was its significance to American labor?

4) Compare and contrast economic and social legislation.

5) Briefly explain the Federal Reserve System.

6) Explain the process that America went through in its evolution from a *laissez-faire* state to an interventionist state.

7) Discuss the nature of economic and social regulation in the post WWII years.

8) How does the government use fiscal and monetary policy to stabilize the economy?

9) Discuss the economics of regulating environmental pollution.

10) The huge national debt has led many people to suggest a number of reforms in economic policy. Discuss the problem of the debt and deficit as well as the reforms that have been proposed. Discuss the positions Democrats and Republicans have taken, and flip-flopped over in recent years.

ANSWERS TO STUDY EXERCISES

multiple choice answers

1.	a	p. 704
2.	b	p. 704
3.	d	p. 706
4.	c	p. 706
5.	b	p. 707
6.	a	p. 707
7.	d	p. 709
8.	b	p. 710
9.	d	p. 711
10.	d	p. 712
11.	b	p. 716
12.	a	p. 717
13.	c	p. 720
14.	b	p. 724
15.	a	p. 724

true/false answers

1.	T	p. 705
2.	F	p. 711
3.	T	p. 715
4.	T	p. 717
5.	T	p. 724
6.	T	p. 726
7.	F	p. 731
8.	T	p. 739
9.	F	p. 741
10.	T	p. 743

CHAPTER 19
FOREIGN AND MILITARY POLICY

Chapter Goals and Learning Objectives

Americans who grew up during the height of the Cold War lived under the threat of nuclear annihilation every day. They understood that the Soviet Union had enough nuclear weapons to destroy the United States many times over. And Americans understood that we could destroy all life in the U.S.S.R. several times over as well. Americans lived "eyeball-to-eyeball" with the Soviets in a game of nuclear chicken for decades, holding each other's entire populations as hostages in a mad game called "mutually assured destruction," or MAD.

When the Cold War came to an end in 1991 after over four decades of constant, non-belligerent conflict between the U.S. and U.S.S.R., the foreign and military policy of the United States suddenly, stunningly and completely changed. For years it was us vs. them, two gigantic titans in the ring struggling for world domination. Yet in a matter of weeks, only one titan remained standing. The United States found itself as the world's remaining superpower with a new and ill defined mission in the world. Foreign and military policy had to undergo drastic introspection and changes. Many Americans put foreign and military affairs on a back-burner and turned to domestic matters--butter rather than guns.

Until September 11, 2001, when Americans found themselves confronting the rest of the world following the first attack on American soil by a foreign power since the War of 1812. America took stock of its foreign and military policy in a new and chilling light. Afghanistan, international terrorism, Iraq, an "axis of evil" and a new concern for our place in the world became apparent to a new generation of Americans.

While most Americans pay scant attention to foreign policy except in times of crisis, our lives are intertwined as citizens of this nation with our policies in dealing with the world. We do a substantial amount of foreign trade, we have a substantial military force and substantial military commitments overseas, and--as the Asian crisis of late 1998 shows, the oil crises surrounding the turbulent Middle East, and the volatility in the stock markets that resulted for each--we are interdependent on other economies in the world for our prosperity. Since the main purpose of government is to protect us and maintain our prosperity, it is incumbent upon Americans to understand and involve ourselves in our commitments and policies with the rest of the world.

This chapter is designed to give you a basic overview of U.S. foreign and military policy. The main topic headings of the chapter are:

- The Roots of U.S. Foreign and Military Policy
- The United States as a World Power
- The Executive Branch and Foreign Policy Making

- Other Factors in Foreign Policy
- 21st Century Challenges
- Building a Grand Strategy

In each section, there are certain facts and ideas that you should strive to understand. Many are in boldface type and appear in both the narrative and in the glossary at the end of the book. Other ideas, dates, facts, events, people, etc., are more difficult to pull out of the narrative. (Keep in mind that studying for objective-[multiple choice, T/F] style tests is different than studying for essay tests. See the Study Guide section on test taking for hints on study skills.)

In general, after you finish reading and studying this chapter, you should understand the following:

- the roots of modern U.S. foreign and military policy and how these policies evolved before America became a world power
- the expanding global role of the United States and the policies followed by the U.S. during and after the Cold War, the years the U.S. became a superpower
- the role the president and executive branch play in developing and executing foreign and military policy
- how Congress, the military-industrial complex, the media and the public influence and mold military and foreign policy
- crucial foreign and military policy challenges for the United States, including U.S. policy in the war on terrorism
- U.S. grand strategy for foreign and military policy in the 21st century

Chapter Outline and Key Points

In this section, you are provided with a basic outline of the chapter and any key words/points you should know. Use this outline, in your own notebook, to develop a complete outline of the material. This will help you study and remember the material in preparation for your tests, assignments, and papers.

isolationism--

unilateralism--

moralism--

pragmatism--

The Roots of U.S. Foreign and Military Policy

The Pre-Constitutional Era

John Adams' *Plan of Treaties*--

1778 military alliance with France--

The Constitution

foreign policy denied to the states--

The Insular Cases--

constitutional role of president in foreign and military policy--

constitutional role of Congress in foreign and military policy--

The Early History of U.S. Military and Foreign Policy

Jay's Treaty--

Washington's Farewell Address--

Barbary Wars--

War of 1812--

impressment--

Embargo Act--

1814 Treaty of Ghent--

The Monroe Doctrine

Monroe Doctrine--

The United States as an Emerging Power

I) Trade Policy and Commerce

Alexander Hamilton's *Report on Manufacturers*--

most favored nation status (MFN)--

reciprocity--

        tariffs--

        first protectionist tariff passed by Congress--

        "American system" of trade protection--

II)   Continental Expansion and Manifest Destiny

        manifest destiny--

        American colonialism--

III)   Interests Beyond the Western Hemisphere

        Commodore Perry--

        Spanish American War and U.S. colonial acquisitions--

        1899 Filipino revolt against U.S. colonialism--

The Early 20th Century

        Roosevelt Corollary to the Monroe Doctrine--

World War I

        "he kept us out of war"--

        the *Lusitania*--

        collective security--

        League of Nations--

IV)   The Inter-War Years

        1930 Smoot-Hawley Tariff--

        isolationism--

The United States Becomes a World Power

        Germany invades Poland, 1 September 1939

        Pearl Harbor--

World War II and its Aftermath

    Lend Lease Program--

    Big Three--

    Hiroshima and Nagasaki--

    United Nations--

    international governmental organization (IGO)--

    Bretton Woods Agreement--

    International Monetary Fund (IMF)--

    World Bank--

    General Agreement on Tariffs and Trade (GATT)--

    multilateralism--

The Cold War and Containment: 1947-1960

    Truman Doctrine--

    Marshall Plan--

    containment--

    North Atlantic Treaty Organization (NATO)--

    Korean War--

    deterrence--

    mutual assured destruction (MAD)--

V)   Containment, Cuba, and Vietnam: 1961-1969

    Cuban Missile Crisis--

    hot line--

    Vietnam War--

Détente, Human Rights, and Renewed Containment: 1969-1981

détente--

Nixon Doctrine--

Strategic Arms Limitation Treaty--

human rights--

Iranian hostage crisis--

Carter Doctrine--

Containment Revisited and Renewed: 1981-1989

Reagan arms build-up

Contras--

Reagan Doctrine--

Mikhail Gorbachev--

Searching for a New International Order: 1989-2001

fall of communism--

Tienanmin Square--

Operation Desert Storm--

1991 attempted Moscow coup--

engagement--

enlargement--

North American Free Trade Agreement (NAFTA)--

World Trade Organization (WTO)--

A New Order for the Twenty-First Century?

Vladimir Putin--

Bush and the 1972 Anti-Ballistic Missile Treaty--

al-Qaeda--

Office of Homeland Security (now Department)--

Taliban--

"axis of evil"--

war on terrorism--

2002 Strategic Offensive Arms Reduction Treaty--

Israeli-Palestinian conflict--

Saddam Hussein and Iraq--

The Executive Branch and Foreign Policy-Making

John Jay and *Federalist no. 8*--

U.S. v. Curtiss Wright Export Corporation (1936)--

National Security Acts of 1947 and 1949--

VI) The President

Teddy Roosevelt and "the Great White Fleet"--

presidents ordering troops overseas to fight without seeking approval from others--

exclusive sources of information for the president--

willingness of people to listen to the president alone on foreign and military policy--

The State and Defense Departments

Department of State--

Department of Defense--

post-Cold War cuts and tasks of Defense Department--

The Central Intelligence Agency and National Security Council

CIA--

NSC (role and membership)--

Department of Homeland Security--

Department of Homeland Security--

largest government reorganization since when?--

Tom Ridge--

Other Factors in Foreign Policy

Congress

Congressional Leadership

Congress has power to develop and implement policy--

Sputnik--

NASA--

Congressional Oversight

oversight powers of Congress--

Treaties and Executive Agreements

Senate power to approve or reject treaties--

fast-track legislation--

executive agreements--

Appointments

Senate advise and consent power--

1997 William Weld nomination--

Appropriations

power to appropriate funds belongs solely to whom?--

Congress, Reagan and funding for Contras--

The War Powers Act

Gulf of Tonkin Resolution--

War Powers Act of 1973--

constitutionality of War Powers Act--

The Military Industrial Complex

Eisenhower's farewell address of 1961--

military-industrial complex--

five ways military-industrial complex acquires power--

The News Media

Investigation

press in Vietnam--

press in Gulf War--

potential danger to military--

military uses news media for its own ends--

Agenda Setting

which issues get attention, which issues do not--

Influencing Public Opinion

effect of media coverage of Vietnam--

The Public

militarism/nonmilitarism and isolationism/internationalism--

rise in presidential popularity in foreign/military crisis--

Elections

>Eisenhower and Korea

>Nixon's "secret plan"--

>LBJ and Vietnam--

Public Opinion

>public more interested in domestic or foreign affairs?--

>Reagan and El Salvador--

Public Action

>protests and Vietnam--

>Elian Gonzalez--

>NGOs--

21st Century Challenges

>9/11/01 attack magnified two challenges--

Identifying Policies to Pursue in the National Interest

>post-Cold War challenges--

>need for containments after Cold War?--

Balancing Foreign and Domestic Affairs

>Americans believe U.S. should concentrate on what, generally?--

Meeting Threats from Weapons of Mass Destruction and Information Warfare

>weapons of mass destruction--

>information warfare--

>electronic Pearl Harbor--

Addressing Drug and Environmental Problems

>three tactics used by U.S. against drugs--

Chernobyl--

Kyoto Conference--

Deciding When to Intervene Overseas

preemptive defense--

Choosing Between Unilateralism and Multilateralism

Building a Grand Strategy

grand strategy--

three elements of building a grand strategy--

Donald Rumsfeld--

Colin Powell--

Research Ideas and Possible Paper Topics

1. Choose a foreign policy crisis (either contemporary or historical). Conduct research to determine what issues were at hand, what actors were making the decisions, and what the outcome was. Did public opinion matter? Was the president the strongest actor in the crisis? How did the various interests play themselves out?

2. American news, be it press or broadcast media, tends to skimp on international news. The argument is that Americans are not interested. Is that true? Find public opinion polling data, ask friends and colleagues, etc. about their interest in international relations. Next test the hypothesis that the media ignores foreign affairs. Watch several different types of media (network TV, newspapers, cable TV, news magazines) and determine if that is true. Now that you know more about U.S. foreign policy, are you more interested in such news? Discuss these issues or structure a debate about them.

3. As a class, discuss what the grand strategy of the U.S. ought to be after the post-Cold War is over. What are U.S. national interests? Should we intervene in Bosnia, Somalia, Rwanda, etc., and why or why not? What about Iraq? The war ended a decade ago and we are still enforcing sanctions. What is our national interest in that case? Trade and aid policy--with whom should we trade and to whom should we give aid? Are there limits to U.S. generosity? What are they?

4. Research the history and development of international terrorism. Has there been attacks on U.S. interests before the 9/11/01 attack on New York and Washington? What was U.S.

policy toward international terrorism before 9/11 and after? What is the future of U.S. anti-terrorism on the homefront and internationally?

5. Do some research on businesses in your area that are involved in international trade. Use the Internet or library to find out what kinds of businesses are doing business where and why. Are there more international ties in your area than you thought? What kinds of impacts does this trade have on you, your town/city, the country?

Websites

The **U.S. State Department** maintains a permanent electronic archive of foreign policy history including documents and photographs which can be searched and accessed on-line.
www.state.gov/www/about_state/history/frus.html

Official site of the **Pentagon** and **Department of Defense**.
www.defenselink.mil/pubs/pentagon/

Official site of the **Air Force**.
www.af.mil

Official site of the **Marine Corps**.
www.hqmc.usmc.mil

Official site of the **Army**.
www.army.mil

Official site of the **Navy**.
www.ncts.navy.mil

Official site of the **Joint Chiefs of Staff**.
www.dtic.mil/jcs/

The **Arms Control and Disarmament Agency**.
www.acda.gov

National Center for Policy Analysis is a nonprofit public policy research institute from a conservative perspective.
www.ncpa.org

Center for Defense Information is a nonprofit public policy center with a somewhat liberal perspective. "Founded in 1972 as an independent monitor of the military, the Center for Defense Information is a private, nongovernmental, research organization. Its directors and staff believe that strong social, economic, political, and military components and a healthy environment contribute equally to the nation's security. CDI seeks realistic and cost effective military spending without excess expenditures for weapons and policies that increase the danger of war.

CDI supports adequate defense by evaluating our defense needs and how best to meet them without wasteful spending or compromising our national security."
    www.cdi.org

Foreign Policy in Focus is a nonprofit foreign policy study group which examines such issues from a progressive perspective.
    www.fpif.org

Foreign Affairs Magazine is a monthly journal published by the Council on Foreign Relations and has long been considered one of the most prestigious publications on the issue of foreign policy. A selection of articles are on-line from the current issue.
    www.foreignaffairs.org

The **Council on Foreign Relations** also maintains a website with a broad range of available information.
    www.cfr.org/index.php

Cold War Hot Links is a website maintained by a professor at St. Martin's College in Washington State. This site offers links to a myriad of sites dealing with the Cold War and U.S. foreign and military policy during that period following the end of WWII until 1991.
    www.stmartin.edu/~dprice/cold.war.html

The website for the **Technical Support Work Group**, a multi-agency federal governmental study group, follows U.S. anti-terrorism developments.
    www.tswg.gov/tswg/home.htm

The **Office of Trade and Economic Analysis** does research and analysis of international trade issues and publishes data and statistics which are available at this site to the public.
    www.ita.doc.gov/td/industry/otea

Practice Tests

MULTIPLE CHOICE QUESTIONS

1.   The U.S. gained overseas colonies in the Spanish American War of 1898. In _____, the U.S. Supreme Court ruled that the national government had the power to acquire new territories and provide governments for them.

    a.   *U.S. v. Curtiss Wright Export Company.*
    b.   *Spain v. McKinley.*
    c.   *The Insular Cases.*
    d.   *Cortez v. Jay.*

2. The first important treaty signed by the U.S. was

   a. the Treaty of Ghent.
   b. Jay's Treaty.
   c. the U.S.-France Friendship Pact.
   d. the Treaty of London.

3. The roots of the War of 1812 lie in

   a. the British policy of impressment.
   b. French trading policies that conflicted with those of the United States.
   c. seizure of the Spanish fleet in the Philippines.
   d. border problems with French Canada.

4. The pledge that the United States would oppose attempts by European states to extend political control over the western hemisphere was called the

   a. containment policy.
   b. policy of Manifest Destiny.
   c. Truman Doctrine.
   d. Monroe Doctrine.

5. The theory that the United States was fated to be a continental power stretching to the Pacific Ocean was called

   a. western hegemony.
   b. colonialism.
   c. a *fait accompli*.
   d. manifest destiny.

6. During WWI, _____ American men served in the armed forces.

   a. 5 million
   b. 1.9 million
   c. 750,000
   d. 500,000

7. After WWI, America followed a policy of

   a. multilateralism.
   b. interventionism.
   c. high tariffs and isolationism.
   d. low tariffs and involvement in the League of Nations.

8. The policy adopted in 1947 to contain Soviet expansion, initially into Greece and Turkey, was called the

   a. Roosevelt Doctrine.
   b. Truman Doctrine.
   c. Churchill Doctrine.
   d. Marshall Plan.

9. The first peacetime military alliance joined by the United States was

   a. NATO.
   b. ASEAN.
   c. the League of Nations.
   d. the Organization of American States.

10. During the late 1960s and 1970s, the relaxation of tensions between the Soviet Union and the United States was called

    a. a thaw.
    b. a respite.
    c. détente.
    d. containment.

11. The policy that the United States would provide arms and military equipment to countries but not do the fighting for them was called the _____ Doctrine.

    a. Carter
    b. Brezhnev
    c. Ford
    d. Nixon

12. The National Security Acts of 1947 and 1949 established the

    a. CIA.
    b. Department of Defense.
    c. National Security Council.
    d. all of the above

13. One of the greatest foreign policy advantages the president has over Congress is

    a. war powers.
    b. greater access to and control over information.
    c. treaty power.
    d. all of the above

14. The president has the power to make treaties

    a. unilaterally.
    b. with the consent of the House.
    c. with the consent of the Senate.
    d. with the consent of both houses of Congress.

15. A U.S. government-to-foreign government accord binding only the current administration and not requiring Senate approval is called a(n)

    a. executive order.
    b. treaty.
    c. tariff.
    d. executive agreement.

TRUE/FALSE QUESTIONS

1. Manifest Destiny impelled the U.S. to prevent any European power from getting involved in our sphere of influence in Latin America.

2. The European Recovery Act or the Marshall Plan provided a massive transfer of aid to Western Europe after WWII in order to rebuild the basis for strong economies.

3. Mutual Assured Destruction (MAD) deterred the United States and the Soviet Union from attacking the other during the Cold War.

4. The easing of tensions between the superpowers under détente was evident in the number of summits between the leaders.

5. Jimmy Carter emphasized traditional power politics during his administration.

6. The collapse of communism in Eastern Europe was unexpected.

7. Congress rarely plays a significant role in foreign policy.

8. The media can put issues on the foreign policy agenda.

9. Direct action by the public can lead to a change in foreign policy.

10. There is substantial consensus on what the balance of foreign and military policies ought to be today.

COMPARE AND CONTRAST

treaty and executive agreement

Monroe Doctrine and Manifest Destiny

League of Nations and the United Nations

isolationism and interventionism

unilateralism and multilateralism

International Monetary Fund, World Bank, and the General Agreement on Tariffs and Trade

Cold War, Truman Doctrine, containment, NATO, and the Marshall Plan

National Security Council, National Economic Council, and the Central Intelligence Agency

Department of State and Defense

presidential vs. congressional powers in foreign affairs

media vs. public role in foreign policy

ESSAY AND SHORT ANSWER QUESTIONS

1) What were the views of the Framers on foreign affairs?

2) What is an executive agreement and why is it important?

3) What is isolationism? When and why did the U.S. adopt this policy?

4) Discuss the Truman Doctrine, the Marshall Plan, and NATO.

5) What is MAD?

6) Discuss the early history of U.S. military and foreign policy from the pre-Constitutional era through WWI.

7) Explain how the U.S. became a world leader in WWII and the role it played in the Cold War. What was the Cold War and why is it so significant historically and in our present development of foreign and military policy?

8) Discuss the role of the executive branch in foreign policy making.

10) Discuss executive-legislative conflict in the realm of foreign and defense policies. What other actors also vie for influence in these decisions and how effective are they?

ANSWERS TO STUDY EXERCISES

multiple choice answers

1. c p. 752
2. b p. 752
3. a. p. 753
4. d p. 753
5. d p. 754
6. a p. 756
7. c p. 756
8. b p. 759
9. a p. 759
10. c p. 762
11. d p. 763
12. d p. 769
13. b p. 769
14. c p. 775
15. d p. 775

true/false answers

1. F p. 753
2. T p. 759
3. T p. 761
4. T p. 763
5. F p. 763
6. T p. 764
7. F p. 774
8. T p. 781
9. T p. 783
10. F p. 785

Chapters 20-26 are to accompany *American Government,*

Texas Edition, Second Edition

CHAPTER 20
THE CONTEXT FOR TEXAS POLITICS AND GOVERNMENT

Chapter Goals and Learning Objectives

Texas history, geography, and mythology provide the social, cultural, ideological, and economic context for Texas politics and government. The Texas image competes with the reality of Texas. Texas has been an expansive land of opportunity and wealth for many. Many Texans have a pride in their state unmatched by any other state in the nation. Texas pride about the attempts to carve a civilization out of a wilderness can, however, also create a culture of denial about the very real lack of civilization experienced by some Texans. Texas can be a hostile, uncivilized environment for children, the elderly, the poor and the laborer. A political candidate who simply states "just the facts" about life in Texas can endure the wrath of the media elite who usually depend on their mythic as political and social watchdogs. Politicians who deny the problems facing modern Texas while paying homage to the historic and mythical Texas are rewarded.

To gain a better understanding of the power of the mythical Texas, students may want to watch such motion pictures such as *Giant*, *The Alamo*, or *The Last Picture Show* or such television programs as *Dallas*, *Lonesome Dove*, or *Walker, Texas Ranger*.

This chapter consists of five sections. The first section offers a brief account of the geographic size of Texas and its landforms, both of which affected the type of government and society early Texas settlers created. The second section addresses the racial and ethnic composition of Texas' population and the contributions that each racial and ethnic group made to Texas' historical development. The third section compares two ideologies, the Texan Creed and the American Creed, and links differences in these creeds to forces unique to Texas history, like a frontier era that lasted four decades. The fourth section discusses the components of the Texas economy and important shifts in the economy. The final section identifies key patterns in the distribution of income in Texas and how these patterns relate to the ethnic and racial groups discussed in the second section of the chapter.

After reading this chapter, you should be able to

- list the key features of Texas geography and understand the size of Texas relative to other states.
- identify the various racial and ethnic groups comprising Texas' population and the contributions that each group made to Texas' historical development.
- discuss the components of the Texan Creed and the American Creed, and understand how and why the two creeds differ.
- list the components of the Texas economy and discuss important shifts in the economy.
- discuss the distribution of income in Texas and how this distribution affects the racial and ethnic groups that compromise Texas' population.

Chapter Outline and Key Points

This section provides you with a basic outline of the chapter. The outline is composed of key concepts and terms.

    2000 presidential campaign and Texas--

    Texas Monthly's Proud of Texas Committee--

    Texan for Public Justice report on Texas--

    John Steinbeck's view on Texas--

VII) The Roots of Texas Politics and Government

    size of Texas--

    variety of landforms in Texas--

VIII) The Peoples of Texas: Past and Present

    Texas population--

    U.S. and Texas ethnic percentages--

Native Americans

    Caddoes--

    Tayshas--

    Comanches--

    Native America population in Texas today--

    gambling on reservations in Texas--

Hispanics

    four institutions of Spanish colonization--

    Mexican independence from Spain--
    Hispanics in Texas politics--

African Americans

    bulk of African-American settlement in Texas--

sharecropper system--

African American officer holders in Texas--

Asian Americans

first permanent resident Asian Americans in Texas--

Vietnamese immigrants--

Asian-American population in Texas in 2000--

Asian American officer holders in Texas--

Anglos

non-Hispanic whites--

empresario program--

increase in Anglo immigration from Texas' independence to Civil War--

post-Civil War Anglo immigration--

Anglo domination of Texas politics--

The Contemporary Population of Texas

2000 and 1990 Census reports on Texas--

Texas population compared to other states--

metropolitan growth accounts for Texas' population growth in 1990s--

change in ethnic demographics in Texas in 1990s--

impact of Hispanic population growth in Texas--

the politics of redistricting (p. 804)--

IX) The Ideological Context

I) The Texas Creed

five ideas of the Texas Creed--

Individualism

    landowners' ethos--

    frontier era--

    Texas Rangers--

    cowboy--

Liberty

    liberty--

    Texas Independence--

    Alamo--

    Tejanos--

Constitutionalism and Democracy

    constitutionalism--

    Jeffersonian democracy--

Equality

    Texas idea of equality--

    Fehrenbach description of African American slavery in Texas--

    Anglo response to Hispanics--

    American Creed--

    political ideology--

Political Ideologies in Texas

    the Texas Creed and ideas about government--

Libertarians

libertarianism--

Libertarian Party in Texas--

Populists

populists--

People's Party in Texas--

Farmer's Alliance--

Conservatives

American conservatism--

conservatives in contemporary Texas--

Liberals

liberalism--

modern liberalism in Texas--

two reasons ideologies in Texas are important--

X) The Economy of Texas

Cotton

Cattle

Petroleum

Spindletop--

OPEC--

The Contemporary Economy

gross state product since 1980s--

globalization of Texas economy--

technology and biotechnology--

NAFTA--

XI) Wealth and Poverty in Texas

share of income in Texas (chart, p. 819)--

Texas ranks third and fourth in income inequality--

Texas has fourth lower percentage of high school graduates--

poverty more pronounced in Texas than in nation as a whole--

ethnic breakdown of poverty in Texas--

extreme poverty for young children in Texas significantly higher than U.S. average--

Houston's "8-F Crowd"--

George Brown--

George Bush--

Bill Clements--

Clayton Williams--

other wealthy Texas businessmen in politics--

the "Texas Mystique"--

Research Ideas and Possible Paper Topics

1. Select a state and compare Texas to that state according to economic structure, political ideologies, and population.

2. Discuss what you think might be important demographic and economic changes in Texas during the next 40 years. How might these changes affect partisan politics and political issues in Texas?

3. Select five key historical events in Texas history and explain how these events contributed to the development of the Texan Creed.

4. Do research into the history of the Texas Rangers examining the view of the heroic law enforcement cowboys in Texas Anglo mythology versus the view of vigilant justice in the eyes of many minority groups in Texas.

5. Examine the mythology of Texas and how it ignores the state's dismal record of poverty and treatment of minorities.

Websites

Every ten years, the **U.S. Census** conducts a count and study of the U.S. population. The 2000 census contains a wealth of information about the nation's population as well as individual state population, including Texas.
www.census.gov

Lone Star Junction is a non-profit organization chartered by the state of Texas. The organization provides facts and details about Texas history, giving particular attention to Texas' early history.
www.lsjunction.com

The Institute of Texan Cultures is an educational center established and maintained by the University of Texas at San Antonio. The center's primary objective is to provide the public with information about the history of the diverse cultures of Texas. The center's website includes photographs of Texas settlers, primary and secondary documents on Texas history, and other material helpful to understanding Texas' diverse cultures.
www.texancultures.utsa.edu/public/index.htm

Texas Historical Commission is a state agency, created by the Texas Legislature to preserve Texas' historic cultural sites and inform the public about Texas history.
www.thc.state.tx.us/aboutus/abtdefault.html

The **Daughters of the Republic of Texas Library** is supported and maintained by the Daughters of the Republic of Texas. The library assists researchers interested in the history of the Alamo, San Antonio and Texas.
www.drtl.org

The **Center for Public Policy** is a Texas non-profit, non-partisan research organization studying policy issues involving low- and moderate-income Texas. Its website features a wide-range of information about poverty in Texas including **Texas Poverty: An Overview** which examines the demographics and characteristics of poverty in the state.
www.cppp.org/products/poverty101.htm

Practice Tests

MULTIPLE CHOICE QUESTIONS

1. The largest minority ethnic group in Texas is

    a. African-Americans.
    b. Asian-Americans.
    c. Native-Americans.
    d. Hispanics.

2. Texas politics and government have been dominated since independence from Mexico in 1836 by what ethnic population?

    a. African-Americans
    b. Hispanics
    c. Anglos
    d. Native-Americans

3. The majority of Texans have lived in urban areas since the

    a. 1920s.
    b. 1940s.
    c. 1880s.
    d. 1860s.

4. Which of the following historical events was important to the development of the Texan Creed concept of individualism?

    a. the American revolution
    b. World War II
    c. the frontier era
    d. the presidential election of Lyndon B. Johnson

5. The historical concept of equality which developed in Texas in the nineteenth century reflected a society based on land ownership and afforded equality to

    a. male and female Anglos only.
    b. all ethnic groups.
    c. Hispanics and Anglos.
    d. male Anglos only.

6. In contemporary Texas, conservatives are prominent in

    a. both of the major political parties.
    b. only the Democratic Party.
    c. the Republican Party.
    d. the Populist Party

7. Liberals favor a government that

    a. promotes an ordered liberty.
    b. regulates individual behavior.
    c. promotes extreme individualism.
    d. promotes equality.

8. Which of the following sectors of the Texas economy began a serious decline in the 1980s?

    a. cotton
    b. cattle
    c. computer
    d. petroleum

9. In Texas, _____ of children under eighteen years of age live in poverty.

    a. 60 percent
    b. 50 percent
    c. 22 percent
    d. eight percent

10. According to the Anglo myth of Texas, dependence on government to solve problems is
    a. a reflection of the pioneer spirit.
    b. a sign of weakness and the failure of individual initiative.
    c. which has improved the Texas economy.
    d. what led to the oil crisis of the 1980s.

TRUE/FALSE QUESTIONS

1. Texas is the second largest state in population and in territory.

2. By 2001, Hispanics had considerable political clout in Texas.

3. Texas' minority populations have increased much less rapidly than the Anglo population.

4. The frontier era in Texas proved important to the development of equality.

5. Cotton, cattle, and petroleum were important sectors of Texas' early economy.

COMPARE AND CONTRAST:

the Texan Creed and the American Creed.

liberalism and conservatism.

the early Texas economy and the contemporary Texas economy.

wealth and poverty in Texas and wealth and poverty in the nation.

Hispanics, African-Americans, and Anglos.

ESSAY AND SHORT ANSWER QUESTIONS

1. What are the major landforms in Texas and where are they found in Texas?

2. What important demographic changes have occurred in Texas between 1990 and 2000?

3. Why was The Alamo important to many Texans' concept of liberty?

4. How had the Texas economic history of dependence upon cattle, cotton and oil changed in the late 20th Century?

5. How are Texas' minority ethnic groups affected by poverty?

ANSWERS TO STUDY EXERCISES

multiple choice answers

1. d   p. 800
2. c   p. 803
3. b   p. 804
4. c   p. 808
5. d   p. 812
6. a   p. 815
7. d   p. 815
8. d   p. 817
9. c   p. 819
10. b   p. 821

true/false answers

1. T p. 797
2. T p. 800
3. F p. 805
4. F p. 808
5. T p. 816

CHAPTER 21
THE TEXAS CONSTITUTION

Chapter Goals and Learning Objectives

Like many states, particularly those located in the South, Texas has drafted several constitutions. Constitutions are social contracts which create governments, outline civil rights and liberties as a means of protecting citizens from their governments, and institute procedures for peaceful change in the form of the process of constitutional amendments. Like all constitutions, Texas' constitutions reflect specific historical circumstances of the periods in which these documents were written. Texas' current constitution is a reaction to Reconstruction, yet the amendments to the Texas Constitution reflect the impact of modern living on a structural foundation laid in a post Civil War political and social environment. As is the case with many state constitutions, particularly in the South and Southwest, Texas' current constitution, the Texas Constitution of 1876, is long, confusing, poorly structured and hindered by an over-reliance on amendments which undermine the very nature of a constitution--a set of basic laws for governing.

This chapter offers a broad overview of Texas' constitutions, giving particular attention to historical circumstances which shaped the writing of the documents. The chapter examines the current Texas constitution and the oft-used process of constitutional revision in Texas.

After reading this chapter you should be able to

- understand the historical roots of Texas' constitutions.
- discuss the strengths and weaknesses of the current Texas Constitution.
- understand constitutional revision in Texas and identify factors that have contributed to the failure of the 1974 Constitutional Convention.

Chapter Outline and Key Points

This section provides you with a basic outline of the chapter. The outline is composed of key concepts and terms.

The Roots of the Texas Constitution

definition of a constitution--

The 1836 Constitution

Republic of Texas--

Washington-on-the-Brazos--

Spanish Mexican law influence on 1836 Constitution--

The 1845 Constitution

annexation--

simple, straight-forward form of 1845 Constitution--

General Provisions--

The 1861 Constitution

secession--

emancipation in 1861 Constitution--

The 1866 Constitution

Presidential Reconstruction--

The 1869 Constitution

Congressional Reconstruction--

Fourteenth Amendment to the U.S. Constitution--

E.J. Davis (p. 829)--

The Current Texas Constitution

Governor Richard Coke--

Texas Constitutional Convention of 1875--

Reasons for 1876 Constitution

reaction to Reconstruction--

E.J. Davis Administration--

Enabling Act--

Militia Bill--

compulsory education--

"retrenchment and reform"--

Provisions of the 1876 Constitution

    liberal constitution--

    statutory constitution--

    Texas Bill of Rights (Article 1)--

    separation of powers (Article 2)--

    legislative branch (Article 3)--

    executive branch (Article 4)--

    judicial branch (Article 5)--

    amendment process (Article 17)--

    Texas Sodomy Law (p. 834)--

    by December 2002, Texas Constitution amendment how many times?--

Criticisms of the 1876 Constitution

    too many amendments--

    plural executive--

    part-time legislature--

    structure of judiciary and election of judges--

    restrictions on local government--

Constitutional Revision

    piecemeal revision--

    comprehensive revision--

Piecemeal Revision Efforts

    addition of amendments--

    Citizens' Advisory Committee--

    efforts by Governor John Connally--

Representative Anna Mowery--

Comprehensive Revision Efforts

1917 legislative resolution and Governor Jim Ferguson--

efforts by Governor Beauford Jester--

The 1974 Constitutional Convention

Constitutional Revision Commission--

Legislature meets as constitutional convention--

right-to-work--

Speaker Price Daniel, Jr.--

cockroach & revisionist--

1975 Constitutional Amendments

eight proposed amendments--

Sharpstown scandal--

Governor Dolph Briscoe--

1999 Constitutional Revision Effort

Representatives Rob Junnell and Senator Bill Ratliff--

Research Ideas and Possible Paper Topics

1. Scholarly dispute exists regarding the level of political experience and training of delegates to the Constitutional Convention of 1875. Research the lives of three of the delegates and evaluate whether they did or did not have the political experience and training necessary to draft an impressive constitution.

2. The current Texas Constitution has been criticized for its failure to provide an adequate foundation for governing in the twenty-first century. If you were a member of the Constitutional Revision Commission, which provisions of the Constitution would you change and why?

3. Imagine you have been elected governor of the state of Texas. Would you support a reform that would allow you to have appointment power over key offices in the executive branch? Is so, why? If not, why not?

4. Students at Angelo State University developed a proposal for a new state constitution. What were its provisions? Who carried the proposed constitution to the Legislature and why? What were the results?

5. Examine the reactions of Texans to Reconstruction. Why did Texans react so vigorously against it and what where the problems they say in the administration of Governor E.J. Davis? Were their objections sound in your opinion?

Websites

The website maintained by the **Texas Legislature** offers a copy of the entire Texas Constitution and features that allow users to search the Constitution according to concept or exact wording.
> www.capitol.state.tx.us/txconst/toc.html

In 1969, the Texas legislature created **The Legislative Reference Library**. The Library's primary purpose is to serve as a research and reference center for the legislature and its staff. The Library's website allows users to review past and current constitutional amendments by session/year, or by subject, by clicking on "Amendments to the Texas Constitution" and "Proposed Amendments to the Constitution".
> www.lrl.state.tx.us

The Texas Constitutions' Digitization Project is presented by the Tarlton Law Library of the University of Texas at Austin. The project makes digital versions of Texas' constitutions available online and provides explanatory texts. The project also offers an excellent list of links to other websites related to Texas constitutional history.
> www.law.utexas.edu/constitutions

Texas Reform Net, which describes itself as "a gateway to reform efforts and groups throughout the State of Texas," hosts a website titled "A Revised Texas Constitution," featuring a proposed Texas reformed constitution, an annotated 1975 constitutional proposal, and other related links.
> www.constitution.org/reform/us/tx/const/rev_con.htm

Practice Tests

MULTIPLE CHOICE QUESTIONS

1. _____ led to the drafting of the 1861 constitution.

    a. Secession
    b. Presidential reconstruction
    c. Congressional reconstruction
    d. Independence

2. The current Texas Constitution is best described as

    a. a liberal constitution.
    b. an organic, restrictive constitution.
    c. a populist constitution.
    d. an anti-populist constitution.

3. One of the reasons the 1974 Constitutional Convention failed was because of

    a. extreme partisan bickering.
    b. the lack of legislators present at the Convention.
    c. the presence of cockroaches and revisionists at the Convention.
    d. all of the above

4. Reconstruction is one of the reasons that the Texas Constitution is

    a. similar to the U.S. Constitution.
    b. different from previous Texas constitutions.
    c. similar to previous Texas constitutions.
    d. similar to the Confederate Constitution.

5. Texas has the _____ longest constitution in the United States.

    a. tenth
    b. twentieth
    c. second
    d. thirtieth

6. Most constitution revision efforts have been

    a. comprehensive revision efforts.
    b. referendum revision efforts.
    c. selective incorporation revision efforts.
    d. piecemeal revision efforts.

7. Part of Governor E. J. Davis's power under the 1869 constitution included control over the

    a. state police.
    b. legislature.
    c. courts.
    d. all of the above

8. The current Texas Constitution establishes a

    a. bill of rights.
    b. separation of powers.
    c. judicial branch.
    d. all of the above

9. In November of 1974, voters rejected eight constitutional amendments in part because of the

    a. Sharpstown scandal.
    b. cockroach scandal.
    c. Governor Davis scandal.
    d. revisionist scandal.

10. Constitutional amendments to the current Texas Constitution have

    a. dramatically changed the basic structure of Texas government.
    b. not fundamentally changed the basic structure of Texas government.
    c. changed the basic structure of the judicial branch.
    d. changed the basic structure of the executive branch.

TRUE/FALSE QUESTIONS

1. The Texas Constitution is identical to the U.S. Constitution.

2. Constitutional revision has never targeted the sections of the Texas Constitution that address the judicial branch of government.

3. The two-thirds rule was a source of dispute at the 1974 Constitutional Convention.

4. The Texas Bill of Rights includes an amendment for equal rights for women.

5. Texas is different from most other states in that it has drafted several constitutions.

COMPARE AND CONTRAST:

- The current Texas Constitution with the U.S. Constitution.
- The Texas Constitution with the U.S. Constitution.
- The Texas Bill of Rights with the U.S. Bill of Rights.
- Cockroaches and revisionists.
- Liberal constitutions and restrictive constitutions.

ESSAY AND SHORT ANSWER QUESTIONS

1. Select one of Texas' six constitutions and explain the historical circumstances that gave rise to and helped shape that constitution.
2. Why did Texans choose to adopt a restrictive constitution in 1876?
3. What are some of the weaknesses of the current Texas Constitution?
4. Discuss constitutional revision aimed at the executive branch.
5. Why did the 1974 Constitutional Convention fail?

ANSWERS TO STUDY QUESTIONS

multiple choice answers

1. a   p. 828
2. b   p. 832
3. c   p. 843
4. b   p. 832
5. c   p. 836
6. d   p. 838
7. a   p. 832
8. d   p. 833
9. a   p. 843
10. b   p. 840

true/false answers

1. F   p. 831
2. F   p. 844
3. T   p. 843
4. T   p. 833
5. F   p. 826

CHAPTER 22
LOCAL GOVERNMENT AND POLITICS IN TEXAS

Chapter Goals and Learning Objectives

Most students who have grown up in this country have, no matter what level of previous governmental studies, some intrinsic understanding of constitutions and the three branches of government. Watching TV, sitting through civics class, students hear about national and state government. However, many students have a real sense of what local government is and how it works, except, perhaps, when a student receives a ticket from a city police officer.

Local government are political subdivisions within state governments. There are three basic categories of political subdivisions that can be characterized as local governments: city governments, county governments, and special district governments.

City governments are chartered by the state and most of them can conduct their governmental affairs independently of state government as long as they are not in conflict with the state constitution. County governments are essentially branch offices of state government and act as the local entity that administers and executes state law. Special districts are the fastest growing form of local governments in Texas, serving single government purposes for specific geographic areas, governmental purposes not available in the area from other levels of local government.

This chapter is divided into four sections. The first section examines the historical and constitutional roots of local governments in Texas. The second section explores the structure, role, and function of county governments. The third section addresses the different types of city governments and the historical development of cities' power. The fourth section discusses special districts, giving particular emphasis to two of the most common types of special districts, water districts and school districts.

After reading this chapter, you should be able to:

- discuss how historical and constitutional forces have shaped local government in Texas.
- explain the role, structure, and function of county governments.
- describe different types of city government and the powers exercised by each type of city government.
- define special districts and explain how they differ from city and county governments.

Chapter Outline and Key Points

This section provides you with a basic outline of the chapter. The outline is composed of key concepts and terms.

The Roots of Local Government in Texas

    municipal corporations--

    counties in the Republic of Texas and when Texas joined the Union--

    home rule--

Counties

    number of Texas counties--

    Brewster County--

    Harris County--

    Loving County--

    Texas Association of Counties--

    multiple function of counties--

    Structure of Counties

        four year terms--

        Commissioners' Court

            County Judge--

            Commissioners' Court--

            County Commissioners--

            roads and bridges--

            Avery v. Midland County (1968)--

    District Attorneys and County Attorneys

        District Attorney--

Criminal District Attorney--

County Attorney--

Sheriff

Sheriff--

county jail--

County Clerk and District Clerk

County Clerk--

District Clerk--

Judges and Constables

County Tax Assessor-Collector

Tax-Assessor-Collector--

duties--

ad valorem taxes--

central appraisal district--

Treasurer and Auditor

County Treasurer--

County Auditor--

Auditor appointed by panel of district judges--

Authority of County Governments

Local Government Code--

general ordinance-making authority--

county election authority and procedure--

Finances of County Government

    property tax--

    fee revenue--

Cities

general-law cities--

home rule--

city charter--

Forms of City Governments

    weak mayor-council--

    strong mayor-council--

    Houston--

    council-manager--

    Austin--

    city commission--

    Galveston--

Authority and Functions of City Governments

    multiple functions of cities--

    Texas Municipal League

Finances of City Governments

    municipal sales tax--

    property taxes--

    other taxes and fees--

    water and sewage and capital budgeting--

Municipal Annexation

annexation--

extraterritorial jurisdiction (ETJ)--

Municipal Annexation Act of 1998 and 1999 amendments--

writ of mandamus--

Politics and Representation in City Governments

at-large election--

at-large-by-place election--

single-member districts--

cumulative voting--

proportional representation--

Special Districts

reasons for special district governments--

Water Districts

Water Code--

TCEQ--

School Districts

independent school districts--

school trustees--

Texas Education Agency--

charter schools--

1993 school-finance reform--

Research Ideas and Possible Paper Topics

1. Select two Texas cities that are demographically diverse and that hold two different types of elections, specifically at-large city council elections and single-member districts' council elections. Evaluate the policies supported by the councils according to whether or not the policies address the political interests of the minority ethnic groups in the two cities.

2. Annexation is a politically explosive issue of local government. To gain a better sense of the advantages and disadvantages of the annexation, select a city in Texas that has had direct experience with the issue. Interview city officials about their opinion of the annexation and interview residents who reside in a newly annexed area.

3. Attend an open city council meeting in your city. Identify the city officials who attended the meeting, explain the meeting's agenda, and describe the extent of public participation in the meeting. Then, based on your experience at the meeting, discuss whether or not you think local government is efficient and democratic.

4. Many Texans live in suburbs which use special district governments known as MUDs (municipal utility districts). What are MUDs? What are their function, how are they formed, how are they operated and how do they fund their services?

5. Public school financing in Texas remains a fluid and controversial issue for school districts and state government. What are some of the current problems surrounding public school financing in the state and in your local ISD?

Websites

Most **cities** in the state of Texas have websites. To access a city's website simply type in the name of the city in the "name" section of the following URL:
   www.ci.name.tx.us

Most **counties** in the state of Texas have websites. To access a county's website simply type in the name of the county in the "name" section of the following URL:
   www.co.name.tx.us

The Texas Association of Counties maintains a website that offers users information about the Association's membership, activities, publications, legislative bills related to counties, and more.
   www.county.org

The **Texas Association of Regional Councils** serves as a coordinating entity for the local Councils of Government (COGs) in Texas. Texas COGs are regional planning boards in Texas to assist local governments in the given regions to coordinate local services. The TARC's website

provides local government information, including information regarding special district governments.
www.txregionalcouncil.org/index.htm

The **Local Government Code** for the State of Texas is available on-line.
www.capitol.state.tx.us/statutes/gtoc.html

The **Texas Education Agency** website provides information about Texas schools and links to all independent school districts in the state.
www.tea.state.tx.us

Practice Tests

MULTIPLE CHOICE QUESTIONS

1. Most large cities in Texas abandoned at-large elections in favor of either

    a. cumulative voting or proportional representation.
    b. proportional representation or a mixed system of single-member districts and cumulative voting.
    c. single-member districts or a mixed system of single-member districts and some at-large.
    d. cumulative voting or single-member districts.

2. Special district governments are often used rather than multifunction governments such as counties and cities in Texas because

    a. some policy areas must be addressed on a larger basis than cities or counties.
    b. constitutional limits on counties make it difficult to take on new tasks.
    c. some functions are better served by a single-focus governmental entity.
    d. all of the above

3. Council manager is a form of

    a. city government.
    b. county government.
    c. special district.
    d. state government.

4. In Texas, _____ are granted the power of annexation.

    a. County governments
    b. City governments
    c. School districts
    d. Water districts

5. In Texas, _____ are granted general ordinance-making authority while _____ are not.

    a. cities/counties
    b. counties/cities
    c. special districts/cities
    d. state governments/local governments

6. In a council-manager form of city government, the

    a. city council hires a city manger to run the city.
    b. mayor hires a city manager to run the city.
    c. city council and the mayor hire a city manager to run the city.
    d. the voters elect a manager to run the city.

7. Unlike home rule cities, general law cities do not have

    a. city charters.
    b. city governments.
    c. city elections.
    d. all of the above

8. In county government, the _____ is responsible for keeping the records for the district court.

    a. county commissioner
    b. district attorney
    c. county clerk
    d. district clerk

9. A form of city government in which elected members serve on the legislative body and also serve as head administrators of city programs is called

    a. weak mayor-council.
    b. city commission.
    c. strong mayor-council.
    d. council-manager.

10. _____ elections are not likely to produce results that closely reflect a city's population.

    a. At-large
    b. Single-member district
    c. At-large-by-place
    d. all of the above

TRUE/FALSE QUESTIONS

1. The district attorney is an elected official who prosecutes criminal cases.

2. The county treasurer is an official appointed by a district judge to audit county finances.

3. Strong mayor-council city governments do not hire city managers.

4. In 1999, amendments adopted to the 1998 Texas Municipal Annexation Act granted county governments the power of annexation.

5. Special districts are unifunctional.

COMPARE AND CONTRAST

- City governments and county governments.

- School districts and water districts.

- Weak mayor-council and strong mayor-council.

- Council-manager and city commission.

- Home rule cities and general law cities.

ESSAY AND SHORT ANSWER QUESTIONS

1. Discuss the political philosophy behind annexation and offer an argument opposing or supporting the political philosophy.

2. Discuss the reasons behind the adoption of home rule and explain how home rule cities differ from general law cities.

3. Discuss the authority and functions of county government.

4. How do special districts differ from county governments?

5. In your opinion, which form of city government is more preferable: weak mayor-council or strong mayor-council?

ANSWERS TO STUDY EXERCISES

multiple choice answers

1. c   p. 869
2. d   p. 870
3. a   p. 860
4. b   p. 867
5. a   p. 857
6. c   p. 861
7. a   p. 858
8. d   p. 856
9. b   p. 860
10. a   p. 868

true/false answers

1. T   p. 854
2. F   p. 856
3. T   p. 860
4. F   p. 867
5. T   p. 870

CHAPTER 23
THE TEXAS LEGISLATURE

Chapter Goals and Learning Objectives

Back in 1866 Mark Twain said, "No man's life, liberty, or property is safe while the legislature is in session." The same is oft said these days every two years of the Texas Legislature when it rolls into Austin in January in odd numbered years for a 140-day regular session.

A part-time body whose members are paid $7,200 a year for their services, this so-called "citizens legislature" was conceived for a rural state in 1875 by Texans angry over heavy-handed Reconstruction rule by Carpetbagger Radical Republicans from the North. Those angry Texans eviscerated the governorship and met their desire for a weak legislature in the Constitution of 1876 so as never to suffer a powerful government over them again.

Some would said that their efforts were quite fruitful if, indeed, the goal was to create a government of inefficiency in general and control by the wealthy elite in particular. The Texas Legislature reflects the Old South concept of protection of the wealthy landholder. Once controlled solely by conservative Democrats, the institution in now run by conservative Republicans, both groups often taking their direction from powerful special interest groups which serve as the institutional memory for the body every two years.

The dominance of the Republican Party in Texas from a minority party to the majority party is illustrated in changes in the Texas Legislature. The legislature is not structured along minority/majority party lines because of the post-Reconstruction dominance of the Democratic Party. There was no need to organize the legislature by party membership because the vast majority of the membership was Democratic. Today, both the Texas House of Representatives and the Texas Senate are lead and dominated by Republicans.

This chapter describes the structure and membership of the Texas legislature as well as its key leaders. It describes the legislative process and how members of the Texas legislature make legislative decisions. It examines the relationship between the Texas legislature and the governor. Finally, it explores changes in the legislative branch including changes in the power granted to legislative leaders and changes in the demographics of legislative members.

After reading this chapter you should be able to understand

- the roots of the legislative branch, including the constitutional changes in the legislature over Texas history.
- how the legislative membership attempts to represent the public.
- how the Texas Legislature is organized and how laws are made and budgets are set.
- how legislators make decisions and how the legislature works with the governor.

Chapter Outline and Key Points

This section provides you with a basic outline of the chapter. The outline is composed of key concepts and terms.

    constitutional amendments--

    redistrict--

    impeach--

    Sharpstown scandal--

    Dirty Thirty--

The Roots of the Legislative Branch

    bicameral Congress under the Constitution of the Republic of Texas--

    African-American representation during Reconstruction--

    white supremacists regain power over the legislature after Reconstruction--

The State Constitution and the Legislative Branch of Government

    size of Texas Senate--

    size of Texas House--

    bill must pass both houses--

    responsibility of initiating action to raise revenue--

    responsibility of approving gubernatorial nominations--

    impeachment process--

Constitutional Provisions Affecting Legislators

Length of Terms

    Senate--

    House--

Compensation

legislative pay

per diem--

Texas legislators' compensation compared to other states--

Sessions of the Legislature

biennial legislature--

regular session--

special session--

Legislative Membership: Representing the Public

Variables Affecting Members' Elections

Redistricting

single member districts--

redistricting--

census--

approximate size of Senate district after 2000 census--

approximate size of House district after 2000 census--

gerrymander--

U.S. Voting Rights Act--

Legislative Redistricting Board--

Reelection Rates and Turnover of Membership

incumbents--

reelection rates after redistricting--

average tenure of incumbents in Texas Legislature--

term limits--

Personal and Political Characteristics of Members

Occupation, Education and Religions

see Figure 23.1 and 23.2--

Gender, Race, and Age

see Figure 23.1 and 23.2--

Political Party

see Figure 23.1 and 23.2--

Ideology

conservatives and libertarians--

liberal, populist--

How the Texas Legislature is Organized

Leaders

President of the Texas Senate--

Pro-Tempore (pro-tem)--

Speaker of the House--

Committees

committee--

standing committees--

procedural committees--

substantive committees--

power of Lieutenant Governor and Speaker to appoint members to committees--

Organizing for Power and Influence in the Legislature

legislature party caucus--

legislative lingo (table 23.4)--

Leadership and Opposition in the House

    Gus Mutscher--

    Bill Clayton--

    Gib Lewis--

    Pete Laney--

    Tom Craddick--

Speaker's Race--

    speaker's race--

    speaker's lieutenants--

    speaker's team--

House Leadership and the Political Parties

    party nominees for speaker--

    personal and factional groupings--

    conservative Democrats--

    bipartisanship--

Speaker's Influence over Committees

    assignments as rewards--

    pledge card extortion--

House Opposition and Political Parties

    not along party lines--

    House Republican Caucus--

    bipartisan committee leadership--

Organizing in the House Through Nonparty Caucuses

    nonparty legislative caucus--

House Study Group--

House Research Organization--

Texas Conservative Coalition--

Legislative Study Group--

Leadership and Opposition in the Senate

1999 amendment requiring election of Lieutenant Governor from within Senate if vacancy in Senate Presidency--

Rick Perry and Bill Ratliff--

David Dewhurst--

Role of the Lieutenant Governor

term of office--

stepping stone--

Texas has one of the most powerful lieutenant governorships in the country--

Coalition Building in the Senate

Bill Hobby and Bob Bullock--

Rick Perry--

Senate two-thirds rule

The Lawmaking and Budgeting Function of the Legislature

legislative process--

What Is a Bill? What Is a Resolution?

bill--

joint resolution--

simple resolution--

concurrent resolution--

Rules, Procedures, and Internal Government

    housekeeping resolutions--

How a Bill Becomes a Law

    public and formal hearings--

    referral to subcommittee--

    reported from committee--

    The House Calendars Committee

        Calendars Committee--

    The Senate Calendaring Function

        intent calendar--

        Killer Bees--

    Bill Reaches the Floor

        quorum--

        first, third and second readings--

        filibuster--

        germane--

        engrossed bill--

The Bill Into One: The Final Stages

    concur or not concur--

    conference committees--

    Approval of the Final Document

        enrolled bill--

The Budgeting Process

    biennial budget--

Legislative Budget Board--

balanced budget--

deficit spending--

debt--

budget execution authority--

How Legislators Make Decisions

backscratching and logrolling--

Growth of Legislative Staff

staff roles--

individual, institutional and group staffing--

Staffing for Technical Assistance, Specialized Information, and Political Assistance

Legislative Council--

Legislative Budget Board (LBB)--

committee staff--

House Bill Analysis Office--

Relations With Lobbyists

open government measures--

lobbyists registered with Texas Ethics Commission--

The Ethics of Lobbying

Frank Sharp--

Brilab--

Bo Pilgrim--

officeholder accounts--

lobbyist and campaign finance--

The Legislature and the Governor

veto--

governor and special sessions--

length and agenda of special sessions--

Research Ideas and Possible Paper Topics

1. Select a bill and track its progress through the legislature. Explain why the bill was successful or unsuccessful. (Information regarding past and current bills can be accessed at the Senate's and the House of Representative's websites. For further information on these websites, see the websites section for this chapter.)

2. Although Anglos have dominated the membership of the Texas legislature, the legislature is becoming more ethnically and racially diverse. Do you think this change in the demographics of the legislature's membership will affect the type of legislation produced by the legislature, especially around matters concerning minorities?

3. If you wanted to be elected Speaker of the House in the next legislative session, how would you run your "speaker's race"?

4. Examine the role of the Lieutenant Governor of Texas as President of the Texas Senate. Compare his powers as President of the Senate to the powers of the Vice-President of the United States as President of the U.S. Senate. Why are the Lieutenant Governor's powers over the Texas Senate so significantly greater than those of the Vice-President's over the U.S. Senate?

5. Examine the role of campaign finance as an influence over the decision-making process of Texas Legislators. Why and how are lobbyists so powerful and influence over the legislative process in Texas that they are called often the "fourth branch" of Texas government? Who are some of the most significant lobbyists in Austin? Are they former members of the legislature or former key staff members?

Websites

The Texas House of Representatives maintains a website that provides information about bills, committees, members, and more.
www.house.state.tx.us

The Texas Senate maintains a website that provides information about bills, committees, members, and more.
www.senate.state.tx.us

Texas Legislature Online is a website that provides users with legislative information and resources as well as links to the websites of agencies associated with the Texas Legislature, such as the Texas Legislative Council and the Legislative Budget Board.
www.capitol.state.tx.us

Texas Legislative Council provides the Texas Legislature and legislative agencies with bill drafting and research services. They also provide Texas' state agencies with information.
www.tlc.state.tx.us

Texas Legislative Reference Library provides research and reference assistance to the Texas Legislature, other state agencies and the public.
www.lrl.state.tx.us/library/about.html

A clip from the 1996 documentary "Vote for Me" shows how votes are won inside the Texas Legislature by lobbyists. The 8.48 minute video clip introduces views to Texas lobbyists, many of them former Texas legislators who can use their political connections to influence and *practically write* bills for legislators. However, the lobbyists are paid a lot, a lot more than the legislators. Perhaps that is why many legislators become lobbyists after retiring or being defeated. The video clip is hosted on the website **Best Practices in Journalism** and is worth 8.48 minutes of your time to see how the Texas Legislature *really* works.
http://www.bpjtv.org/video/index.cfm?videodoc=intro&clipname=cnam_lobbyists

The **Texas Ethics Commission** hosts a searchable data base of lobbyists registered to work to influence the Texas Legislature.
http://www.ethics.state.tx.us/dfs/loblists.htm

Texans for Public Justice has prepared a report entitled "Austin's Oldest Profession: Texas' Top Lobby Clients & Those Who Service Them," a scathing examination on the tremendous influence big money lobbyist have over the Texas Legislature.
http://www.tpj.org/reports/lobby02/index.html

Practice Tests

MULTIPLE CHOICE QUESTIONS

1. The lieutenant governor serves as an officer in the

    a. executive branch and the Senate.
    b. Senate and the House of Representatives.
    c. executive branch and House of Representatives.
    d. legislative and judicial branch.

2. A _____ is formed if the Senate and the House of Representatives cannot agree on a single version of a bill.

   a. standing committee
   b. interim committee
   c. special committee
   d. conference committee

3. An enrolled bill is a bill that has been

   a. rejected by the governor.
   b. approved by the Senate and the House of Representatives.
   c. rejected by the Senate and the House of Representatives.
   d. approved by the House of Representatives, but rejected by the Senate.

4. The _____ provides legal advice, bill drafting, and other services to members of the Texas legislature.

   a. Legislative Budget Board (LBB)
   b. Pro-Tempore Council
   c. Legislative Council
   d. Texas Municipal League

5. Budget execution authority may be exercised during

   a. a special session.
   b. a Regular session.
   c. a Crisis session.
   d. an interim.

6. A legislative action that either proposes an amendment to the Texas Constitution or ratifies an amendment to the U.S. Constitution is called

   a. a joint resolution.
   b. an amending resolution.
   c. a mark-up.
   d. a concurrent resolution.

7. A simple resolution goes through

   a. both chambers.
   b. only one chamber.
   c. both chambers and the governor's office.
   d. one chamber and the governor's office.

8. The Senate two-thirds rule requires that

   a. every bill must win a vote of two-thirds before it can be considered.
   b. only bills dealing with budgetary matters must win a vote of two-thirds before it can be considered.
   c. every bill originating from conference committees must win a vote of two-thirds before it can be considered.
   d. every bill dealing with procedural matters must win a vote of two-thirds before it can be considered.

9. With regard to term limits for Texas Legislature, voters in Texas

   a. approved term limitations for members of the legislature.
   b. rejected term limitations for members of the legislature.
   c. have never voted on term limitations for the legislature.
   d. approved term limitations for members of the Senate, but not the House of Representatives.

10. Historically, most legislators have been

    a. Anglo and Hispanic males.
    b. Anglo males and females.
    c. Hispanic males.
    d. Anglo males.

TRUE/FALSE QUESTIONS

1. Standing committees can be procedural or substantive.

2. A bill is a legislative document that can create a law, but not amend a law.

3. A quorum is the minimum number of votes a bill needs to pass the Senate.

4. The Legislative Budget Board and the Governor's Budget Office prepare separate budget proposals.

5. The governor is in complete control of the agenda of a special session.

COMPARE AND CONTRAST

- Rules in the House of Representatives and the Senate.

- Leaders in the House of Representatives and the Senate.

- A joint resolution, a simple resolution, and a concurrent resolution.

- First reading, second reading, and third reading.
- Special session and regular session.

ESSAY AND SHORT ANSWER QUESTIONS

1. Discuss changes in the demographic profile of the legislature in the past 30 years.

2. Explain how term limitations and single member districts affect legislative members' elections.

3. Briefly identify the different types of legislative committees and their functions.

4. How does the Senate two-thirds rule work to protect minority rights in the Senate?

5. Why are special sessions necessary and what powers does the governor have over special sessions?

ANSWERS TO STUDY QUESTIONS

multiple choice questions

1.	a	p. 895
2.	d	p. 902
3.	b	p. 902
4.	c	p. 907
5.	d	p. 906
6.	a	p. 897
7.	b	p. 897
8.	a	p. 897
9.	c	p. 886
10.	d	p. 888

true/false questions

1.	T	p. 891
2.	F	p. 897
3.	F	p. 901
4.	T	p. 903
5.	T	p. 909

CHAPTER 24
THE GOVERNOR AND BUREACURACY AND TEXAS

Chapter Goals and Learning Objectives

When George W. Bush campaigned for the presidency in 2000, he oft touted his record of executive leadership as Governor of Texas, laying claim to improving education, cutting taxes, and increasing important state services. To put it charitably, he was really stretching the truth. Of course, politicians on the stump are want to fib egregiously if not caught, and few caught Mr. Bush's big ones. He got away with the fibs because few folks understand that Texas' governor is not a true chief executive, responsible for managing the ship of state, but is, indeed, one among many in the Texas plural executive model. And his actual powers over the legislature are weak as well. Too bad for Al Gore that he had not taken a Texas government class like you are now doing.

This chapter examines Texas' plural executive form of government. The strong executive or single executive model exists on the federal level, while the Texas Constitution of 1876 constructs a plural or weak executive model. Power in the executive branch is divided among elected officials, appointed officials, and more than 100 executive boards and commissions. Texans, angered by the iron hand of the Republican Reconstruction administration of E.J. Davis, took the Texas governorship and placed it under the mallet of the Texas Constitution of 1876, smashing it as one might smash a ripe tomato, spreading its power about as far as fruit of the tomato would splatter.

While the Texas governorship is not without power and certainly not without prestige, it is, nevertheless one of the weakest governorships in the nation. Yet, candidates spend millions every four years to win the office. This chapter will examine why, and what the governor really can do, despite what the candidates are willing to tell you.

After reading this chapter, you should be able to

- discuss the historical development of the plural executive.
- identify the roles and powers of the governor.
- list the key officials in the executive branch and their power and duties.
- describe the structure of bureaucracy.
- discuss legislative efforts to make bureaucracy more accountable.

Chapter Outline and Key Points

This section provides you with a basic outline of the chapter. The outline is composed of key concepts and terms.

Perry's "Father's Day Massacre"--

Perry's veto of the prompt-pay-bill--

plural executive--

The Roots of the Executive in Texas

From President of the Lone Star Republic to Governor of Texas

effects of Constitution of 1876 on governor--

Sam Houston--

Terms of Office

length and number of terms--

salary--

impeachment--

Jim Ferguson--

Miriam Ferguson--

succession--

Rick Perry--

The Constitutional Roles of the Governor

chief of state--

chief executive officer--

commander-in-chief--

chief budget officer--

largely ceremonial powers of governor--

clemency

governor's message to the legislature--

The Development of Gubernatorial Power

Characteristics of Gubernatorial Power

scale to measure the power of governors--

where strong governors are found in U.S.--

Restriction of Governor's Power

reaction to Reconstruction--

anti-administration legislature and new constitution--

Comparing the Texas Governor with Other Governors

cabinet system--

plural executive in Texas--

Texas tied for the weakest state governors--

personal power of governors--

The Governor's Power to Appoint Executive Officials

gubernatorial appointments--

Texas Senate approval of governor's appointments--

senatorial courtesy--

lame duck appointments--

overrepresentation--

underrepresentation--

governor appoints contributors and political allies--

The Power of Staff and Budget

nineteenth century governor's staff--

Office of the Governor--

budget for staff, housing and other activities--

The Governor as Policy Maker and Political Leader

wielding political power--

"Chief Persuader of Texas"--

Public Opinion Leadership

Relationship with the Legislature

state of the state message--

special sessions of the Legislature--

veto power--

pocket veto--

line-item veto--

The Plural Executive in Texas

many Texas state executives elected by people of Texas--

Attorney General

chief civil council to state government--

little authority in criminal law--

Deceptive Trade Practices Act--

Hopwood--

Attorney General's Opinions

Jim Mattox--

Dan Morales--

John Cornyn--

Greg Abbott--

Comptroller of Public Accounts

chief tax collector for Texas--

subsumed Texas Treasure's duties in 1996--

revenue-forecasting function--

Bullock's Raiders--

John Sharp--

Carole Keeton Rylander--

Land Commissioner

oil leases and revenue--

fund for schools and universities--

Veterans Land Program--

Bob Armstrong--

Garry Mauro--

David Dewhurst--

Jerry Patterson--

Agriculture Commissioner

Texas Department of Agriculture--

weights and measures--

pest-control regulations--

Jim Hightower--

Rick Perry--

Susan Combs--

Railroad Commissioners

Texas Railroad Commission--

oil and gas industry regulation--

regulation of trucking and mining--

captive of the industry--

railroad regulations primarily job of federal government--

State Board of Education

state education policy regulated by fifteen member board--

Texas Education Agency--

religious conservatives and the State Board of Education

Modern Texas Bureaucracy

implementation and execution--

legislatures make policy, bureaucracies implement it--

rule making--

regulation, and provision of services and products--

Administrative Procedures Act--

two basic patters of how Texas executive agencies are organized--

Secretary of State

keeper of state records--

Texas Register--

chief elections officer--

Myra McDaniel--

Gwen Clarkson Shea--

Public Utility Commission

PUC--

quasi-judicial--

Texas Natural Resource Conservation Commission

TNRCC--

TCEQ--

Insurance Commissioner

State Board of Insurance--

Commissioner of Health and Human Services

Department of Health and Human Services--

Public Counsels

captured agencies--

public counsels--

Boards and Commissions

Board of Criminal Justice--

six years, staggered--

governor may appoint but cannot independently remove appointments--

Making Agencies Accountable

The Sunset Process

sunset law--

good government--

Staff and Size

full-time equivalent workers--

Regulating the Revolving Door

revolving door--

regulators turned lobbyists--

Regulating the Relationship Between Agencies and Private Interests

executive agencies in policy-making roles--

iron triangle in Texas--

Research Ideas and Possible Paper Topics

1. Several of the constitutional revision efforts addressed in Chapter 21 involved reforms aimed at the executive branch. How would you reform the executive branch and why?

2. The first Sunset Commission strongly supported the idea of good government. Select two agencies and evaluate their performance according to the standards outlined by the first Sunset Commission.

3. Compare Governor Clements and Governor White in terms of their ability to exercise public-opinion leadership. Which governor do you think was more successful in his use of this power and why?

4. Article 4, section 9 of the Texas Constitution requires the governor to deliver governor's messages to the legislature. The messages emphasize policy goals, budget priorities, and more. Write the speech that you would deliver to the legislature if you were governor.

5. There are several elected offices in the executive branch. Select one of the offices (except that of governor) and explain why you would want to be elected to that office and what you would do if you were elected.

Websites

The website of the **Texas Governor** offers users information about the governor's legislative priorities and information about divisions in the executive branch.
www.governor.state.tx.us

The Texas Library and Archives Commission website offers users a comprehensive list of links to websites for Texas agencies and commissions.
www.tsl.state.tx.us/trail/agencies.html

Texas Legislature Online provides a gateway to the executive, legislative, and judicial state agencies.
www.capitol.state.tx.us/tlo/resources/resources_state.htm

The *Texas Register,* the bulletin of Texas administrative rule making, is published and maintained on-line by the Texas Secretary of State.
http://lamb.sos.state.tx.us/texreg/index.html

| **Practice Tests** |

MULTIPLE CHOICE QUESTIONS

1. The practice of senatorial courtesy is associated with

    a. the governor's power to appoint executive officials.
    b. the House of Representatives' power to appoint Speaker of the House.
    c. the Senate's power to appoint the Majority Leader of the Senate.
    d. the legislature's power to approve executive judicial appointments.

2. Elections for _____ are on a staggered basis.

    a. Agricultural commissioners
    b. Railroad commissioners
    c. Land commissioners
    d. Insurance commissioners

3. Governors' appointees tend to overrepresent

    a. Hispanic males.
    b. Anglo males and females.
    c. Anglo females.
    d. Anglos and males.

4. The most significant elected state officials are the attorney general,

    a. the governor, and the land commissioner.
    b. the lieutenant governor, and the Railroad commissioner.
    c. the governor, and the lieutenant governor.
    d. the governor, and the agriculture commissioner.

5. The length and number of terms for the governor are

    a. two years with a two-term limit.
    b. four years with no term limit.
    c. four years with no term limit.
    d. two years with a four-term limit.

6. The state official appointed by the governor to be the keeper of the state's records is the

    a. secretary of state.
    b. state clerk.
    c. attorney general.
    d. chief of state.

7. The land commissioner is

    a. appointed by the governor.
    b. elected by voters in the state of Texas.
    c. appointed by the governor and approved by the Senate.
    d. elected by voters in various land districts.

8. Captured agencies resulted in the need for

    a. sunset laws.
    b. more elected offices in the executive branch.
    c. public counsels.
    d. more elected offices in the bureaucracy.

9. The key players in the iron triangle model are

    a. executive agencies, private interests, and the legislature.
    b. the governor, the legislature, and private interests.
    c. executive agencies, private interests, and the courts.
    d. the governor, the legislature, and the courts.

10. Texas executive agencies may be headed by

    a. one person.
    b. a board.
    c. a commission.
    d. all of the above

TRUE/FALSE QUESTIONS

1. Unlike the governors of other states, the Texas governor lacks line-item veto power.

2. The land commissioner is more significant in Texas than in most states because the state owns so much land.

3. The Populist movement in Texas is largely responsible for the creation of the railroad commissioner.

4. Sunset is a concept of establishing a date at which agencies will cease to exist unless the legislature renews them.

5. Texas does not measure its number of employees in units known as full-time equivalent (FTE) workers.

COMPARE AND CONTRAST

- The powers of the Texas governor with that of other governors.

- Underrepresentation and overrepresentation in governors' appointees.

- The governor as policy maker and political leader.

- Land Commissioner, agricultural commissioner, and railroad commissioner.

- Public counsels and executive agencies.

ESSAY AND SHORT ANSWERS

1. Why were Sunset laws needed and have the laws been successful?

2. Describe the role and authority of the land commissioner, and explain why the land commissioner is so important in the state of Texas.

3. Discuss how the length of term, number of terms, and salary for the governor has changed during the 1900s.

4. Explain how the governor uses his or her constitutional powers and non-constitutional powers when working with the legislature.

5. Discuss patterns of overrepresentation and underrepresentation in governors' appointees.

ANSWERS TO STUDY QUESTIONS

multiple choice answers

1.	a	p. 926
2.	b	p. 936
3.	d	p. 927
4.	c	p. 933
5.	b	p. 920
6.	a	p. 941
7.	b	p. 935
8.	c	p. 944
9.	a	p. 950
10.	d	p. 940

true/false answers

1.	F	p. 932
2.	T	p. 935
3.	T	p. 936
4.	T	p. 946
5.	F	p. 946

CHAPTER 25
THE TEXAS JUDICIARY

Chapter Goals and Learning Objectives

You may never meet the Governor. You may never shake hands with the Texas Attorney General. You might one day meet your state senator or representative. But it is probable, in fact, down right likely, that one day you will meet a state judge in a Texas courtroom. Maybe for a traffic ticket dismissal. Possibly for a child custody hearing or a divorce proceeding or a will contest. You could end up as a witness in a civil trial or sit on a jury in a capital murder trial. But it is likely that you will one day be in a Texas court. And if you watch local television news, you will far more often be exposed to the trials of murderers, robbers and frauds in state courts (or even the will contests of former Playboy centerfolds, such as Anna Nicole Smith in a Harris County Court) covered by local reporters where you will hear about the trials and tribulations of your governor and state legislators.

The judicial is that branch of government that interprets the law and adjudicates disputes under the law between individuals and the community (the criminal law) and between private individuals or groups (the civil law). The Texas judicial system is divided into civil and criminal approaches to the law. It is also divided into trial and appellate courts. It is a complex and fascinating system for it reflects the passions and drives of human beings in conflict. Rather than take your disputes to the streets, you may take them to court where the weapons are facts in evidence as opposed to fists, guns or knives.

This chapter examines the structure, operation, and responsibilities of Texas courts throughout history; describes the judges and the judicial selection; evaluates criticism of the judiciary system in Texas; and describes the basic steps in the judicial process.

After reading this chapter you should be able to

- describe the structure, operation, and responsibilities of Texas courts.
- discuss the characteristics of judges and how they are selected.
- explain and evaluate criticisms of the Texas judiciary.
- describe basic steps in the judicial process.

Chapter Outline and Key Points

This section provides you with a basic outline of the chapter. The outline is composed of key concepts and terms.

The Roots of the Texas Judiciary

roots in English tradition with some features of Spanish law--

The Structure of the Judiciary

Local Trial Courts (Fig. 25.1)

municipal courts--

justice of the peace courts--

County Courts

constitutional county court--

probate cases--

trial *de novo*--

county courts at law--

misdemeanor criminal cases--

District Courts

district courts--

civil jurisdiction--

felony criminal jurisdiction--

Intermediate Courts of Appeal

fourteen Texas Courts of Appeal--

en banc--

The Supreme Courts

Texas Supreme Court--

Texas Court of Criminal Appeals--

writ of *certiorari*--

Petition for Review--

Application for Discretionary Review--

per curiam--

Judges and Judicial Selection

all but municipal judges are selected by partisan elections--

Judicial Qualifications and Personal Characteristics

judicial qualifications (table 25.1)--

Judicial Selection

partisan election process--

vacancies from death or resignation filled by gubernatorial appointment--

Texas Trial Lawyers Association--

Texas Civil Justice League--

Republicans replace Democrats on Texas Supreme Court--

Chief Justice Thomas Phillips--

Criticisms of the Judicial Branch

Reforming the Court Structure

Task Force on Judicial Reform--

Reforming Judicial Selection

merit selection--

Reforming Campaign Finance

limits on campaign contributions to judicial candidates--

Increasing Minority Representation on the Bench

straight ticket Republican voting in judicial elections has virtually eliminated minority judges--

The Judicial Process in Texas

capital felony, three degrees of felonies, state jail felony, three classes of misdemeanors (see table 25.2)--

The Criminal Justice Process

Arrest and Searches

arrest and search warrants--

probable cause--

arrest without warrant based on what?--

warrantless searches--

automobile searches--

consent--

Booking

station house bail--

Magistrate Appearance

examining trial--

Grand Jury Indictment

grand juries (only for felonies)--

true bill--

no bill--

indictment--

Arraignment

arraignment--

no public defender system in Texas - attorney appointed by court for indigent--

plea-bargains--

Pretrial Motions

motion for jury or bench trial, continuance, competence, venue change, etc.--

Jury Selection

venire--

voir dire--

challenge for cause and peremptory challenges--

Trial

guilt innocence phase and punishment phase--

charge to the jury--

unanimous verdict required for guilty or not guilty--

mistrial--

capital cases--

Appeals

death penalty verdicts automatically appealed directed by Texas Court of Criminal Appeals--

appeals court reviews for reversible error--

discretionary review--

The Civil Justice Process

Pretrial Procedures

petition by plaintiff--

answer by defendant--

Trial

district court, ten of twelve jurors must agree

county court, five of six jurors must agree--

Research Ideas and Possible paper Topics

1. Judicial candidates must file disclosure reports with the Texas Ethics Commission. Select the reports of a judicial candidate who successfully ran for office. Examine the rulings the candidate made once he or she became a judge. On the basis of your research, do you think judges' rulings are affected by campaign contributions?

2. The Texas Constitution guarantees defendants certain basic rights, such as the right to a fair and speedy trial and an individual's right to a court-appointed attorney if the individual is indigent. In your opinion, do the problems with the Texas courts (overlapping jurisdictions, lack of qualified court-appointed attorneys, etc) affect a defendant's constitutional rights?

3. If you were appointed to a judicial reform commission, what reforms would you advocate and why? Talk to a local lawyer to see, from his or her experience in court, if he/she agrees with your assessments.

4. Examine the claims of "tort reform" advocates who wish to restrict citizens' rights to civil courts. What are the bases of their claims. Are the cases claimed to be "frivolous" actually unjustified? What procedures do Texas judges use to eliminate frivolous lawsuits before they ever go to trial? What groups are behind the "tort reform" movement in Texas?

5. The death penalty has come under criticism from many citizens and groups recently. Texas is one of the leaders in the nation in putting prisoners to death. What are some of the arguments against the death penalty and some of the arguments for?

Websites

Texas Judiciary Online is a state judicial system website that offers information on a variety of topics: the structure of the judiciary, judicial agencies and groups, judicial records, resource materials, and much more.
    www.courts.state.tx.us

The **Texas State Government** home page offers a list of links to the websites of various courts, state laws, court rulings, and much more.
    www.state.tx.us/category.jsp?language=eng&categoryId=8

The **Texas Supreme Court** home pages provide attorneys and the public with information about Justices, opinions and orders, and information about cases before the court.
    www.supreme.courts.state.tx.us

The **Texas Court of Criminal Appeals** maintains a website that provides information regarding opinions and rules of procedure and practice for attorneys and court reporters.
    www.cca.courts.state.tx.us/

3. Justices of the Peace must

    a. possess a law degree.
    b. be a registered voter.
    c. be twenty-five years of age.
    d. all of the above

4. Procedures in the civil justice process

    a. are more formal than procedures in the criminal justice process.
    b. as formal as the procedures in the criminal justice process.
    c. less formal than procedures in the criminal justice process.
    d. cannot be compared to the procedures in the criminal justice process.

5. The Texas Supreme Court has appellate jurisdiction over

    a. civil cases.
    b. criminal cases.
    c. civil and criminal cases.
    d. criminal cases involving fines of over $1,000,000.

6. In a criminal trial in state district court, in order to find a defendant guilty or not guilty, what type of jury verdict is required?

    a. 10 out of 12 in agreement
    b. 5 out of 6 in agreement
    c. a simple majority
    d. unanimous vote for either guilty or for not guilty

7. In a capital murder trial,

    a. defendants have the right to an attorney if they cannot afford one.
    b. defendants do not have the right to waive the right to a jury trial.
    c. defendants' cases will automatically be reviewed by the Texas Court of Criminal Appeals.
    d. all of the above

8. Except for municipal judges, Texas judges are

    a. appointed by the governor and approved by the Senate.
    b. appointed by the governor and approved by the legislature.
    c. elected in partisan elections.
    d. elected in nonpartisan elections.

The **Texas Trial Lawyers Association** is the professional organization for civil trial lawyers in Texas and works to keep the civil courts open to citizens in the face of the "tort reform" onslaught by business and corporate interests.
www.ttla.com

The **Center for Economic Justice** is a non-profit organization that works to increase the availability, affordability and accessibility of insurance, credit, utilities, and other economic goods and services for low-income and minority consumers. Its website includes a page debunking the arguments of "tort reform" advocates.
http://www.cej-online.org/tortrefo.php

Texans for Lawsuit Reform is an organization created and funded by big business and corporate interests promoting the "tort reform" agenda in Texas.
http://www.tortreform.com/

The **Texas Criminal Defense Lawyers' Association** is the professional organization for criminal defense lawyers. Its website provides a great deal of information about the criminal justice system in Texas and governmental threats to civil liberties.
http://www.tcdla.com/

Practice Tests

MULTIPLE CHOICE QUESTIONS

1. The state's highest appellate courts are

    a. courts of appeals.
    b. the Supreme Court and the Court of Criminal Appeals.
    c. district courts.
    d. county level courts.

2. _____ judges on the Court of Criminal Appeals must agree to review a case before it will be accepted for review.

    a. Five
    b. Six
    c. Four
    d. Nine

9. Faced with the cost of judicial campaigns and its effect on the judiciary's imputed fairness, the legislature

    a. created the Judicial Campaign Fairness Act of 1995.
    b. barred judicial candidates from receiving campaign contributions.
    c. required judges to run in non-partisan elections.
    d. all of the above

10. _____ and _____ are the two major categories of county courts.

    a. district courts, constitutional county courts
    b. district courts, county courts of law
    c. county courts of law, justice of the peace courts
    d. constitutional county courts, county courts of law

11. A trial de novo would not take place in a _____ court.

    a. justice of the peace.
    b. district court.
    c. county court.
    d. appeals court.

TRUE/FALSE QUESTIONS

1. A petition for review is a request for Court of Criminal Appeals review.

2. Courts of Appeal do not involve testimony or juries.

3. Municipal judges may be elected or appointed by the city council.

4. The Judicial Campaign Fairness Act of 1995 does not contain the loopholes that earlier acts contained and therefore is more effective than previous acts.

5. Texas judiciary has its roots in both English tradition and Spanish law.

COMPARE AND CONTRAST

- The Supreme Court and the Court of Criminal Appeals.
- County trial courts and local trial courts.
- The highest appellate courts and intermediate appellate courts.
- Judicial qualifications for municipal judges and justices of the peace.
- The Criminal justice process and civil justice process.

ESSAY AND SHORT ANSWER QUESTIONS

1. Why do supporters of judicial reform want to make district courts the state's only trial courts?

2. How do the demographics of judges compare to the demographics of the legislature?

3. Should qualifications for municipal judges and justices of the peace be increased and rendered more consistent across courts?

4. How does a case move from a county court to the Supreme Court?

5. Should Texas judges be selected according to merit?

ANSWERS TO STUDY QUESTIONS

multiple choice answers

1. b   p. 959
2. c   p. 965
3. b   p. 967
4. c   p. 979
5. a   p. 964
6. d   p. 979
7. c   p. 966
8. a   p. 972
9. d   p. 963
10. a   p. 963

true/false questions

1. F   p. 965
2. T   p. 964
3. T   p. 961
4. F   p. 972
5. T   p. 959

CHAPTER 26
POLITICAL PARTIES, INTEREST GROUPS, ELECTIONS, AND CAMPAIGNS IN TEXAS

Chapter Goals and Learning Objectives

Political parties and interest groups link citizens to government; however, the goals of the two entities differ. Political parties seek to control government and interest groups seek to influence government. Elections are the mechanism through which political parties gain control of government and campaigns bind together political parties, interest groups, candidates, and the public.

This chapter describes the structure of political parties in Texas and how political parties operate in Texas. It also explores the types and roles of interest groups, as well as their impact on Texas politics and government. Finally, it examines elections and political campaigns in Texas.

After reading this chapter, you should be able to

- describe the structure of political parties in Texas.
- explain how political parties operate in Texas.
- discuss interest groups and their impact on Texas politics and government.
- describe elections and political campaigns in Texas.

Chapter Outline and Key Points

This section provides you with a basic outline of the chapter. The outline is composed of key concepts and terms.

The Roots of Political Parties, Interest Groups, Elections, and Campaigns in Texas

era of one-party Democratic dominance in Texas--

Political Parties in Texas

Party Organization

Formal Organization

temporary party organization--

precinct convention--

county convention--

state senatorial district convention--

state convention--

permanent party organization--

precinct chairperson--

county chairperson--

county executive committee--

state executive committee--

state party chairperson--

Susan Weddington--

Molly Beth Malcolm--

Functional Organization

Democratic Party Unity

liberal influence since 1976--

Ralph Yarborough--

Jim Mattox, Jim Hightower, Garry Mauro, Ann Richards--

conservative Democrats becoming Republicans--

Republican Party Unity

pragmatists or economic conservatives--

ideologues or social conservatives--

Christian Coalition--

Kay Bailey Hutchenson--

David Barton--

2002 Republican platform--

Party Effectiveness

two ways state party's performance measured--

local party's task is getting voters to polls--

Party in the Electorate

party attachment--

change in party affiliation--

increase in independents--

party realignment in Texas--

party dealignment in Texas--

contemporary party coalitions--

Republican coalitions--

Democratic coalitions--

Party in the Government

In the Executive Branch--

In the Legislative Branch--

In the Judicial Branch--

Interest Groups in Texas

Types of Interest Groups

Business Groups and Trade Associations--

Professional Associations--

Labor Groups--

Racial and Ethnic Groups--

Public Interest Groups--

Political Activities of Interest Groups

   Lobbying--

   lobbyist registration--

   two trends in characteristics of Texas lobbyists--

   principal job of lobbyists, according to lobbyists--

   personal friendships with legislators--

   lobbying legislative staff--

   technical information from lobbyists--

   expert testimony--

   top-down strategy--

   lobbying agencies and departments--

   grassroots lobbying--

   Astroturf lobbying--

   Electioneering--

   PACs--

   preference for incumbents--

   Litigation--

Elections and Political Campaigns in Texas

   Types of Elections

      primary elections--

      must win primary by majority--

      run-off elections--

      participation low in primaries--

      special elections--

general elections--

Tuesday after the first Monday in November of even-numbered years--

win general elections by plurality-

non-presidential year elections--

local elections--

municipal elections and special district elections are non-partisan--

Political Campaigns in Texas

money in elections--

in 2002 Perry spends $24 million and Sanchez $64 in general--

few restriction in Texas--

Media: Linking Candidates and Voters--

importance of TV in Texas campaigns--

political consultants--

Marketing: Selling the Candidates--

benchmark poll--

tracking polls--

campaign consultants--

The Voters' Decisions

Voter Turnout--

legal requirements for voting in Texas--

motor voting--

early voting--

lower Texas voter turnout--

The Vote Choice: Parties, Issues and Candidates--

Research Ideas and Possible Paper Topics

1. Select two different types of interest groups operating in Texas and compare the type of activities in which they engage. How are the activities different and why are they different?

2. Voter turnout in Texas is quite low. If you were a member of the legislature, what type of legislation would you support to increase voter turnout in Texas?

3. In 2000, Republican candidates won every statewide election. What forces contributed to this victory?

4. Media is as significant a factor in elections as anything in modern politics. What factors come into play with regard to media campaigns? What role does television play in statewide and local campaigns? Is radio useful to a candidate? What about newspapers and direct mail? Does the Internet play a role yet?

5. What are some of the factors in the growth of the Republican Party in Texas over the past thirty years? What happened to the Democratic Party, once dominant in Texas, in terms of elected officials and voter identification? What can the Democratic Party in Texas do to regain parity with the Republicans?

Websites

The Secretary of State's Elections Division website offers voter information, election returns and forms, election law information, and election reports.
www.sos.state.tx.us/elections/index.shtml

Texas Democratic Party maintains a website at
www.txdemocrats.org

The **Republican Party of Texas** maintains a website at
www.texasgop.org

The **Texas Libertarian Party** maintains a website at
www.tx.lp.org

The **Reform Party of Texas** maintains a website at
http://www.texasreformparty.org

Based in Houston, the **Texas Politics Resource Page** is hosted by Texas political consultant George Strong, and presents facts and gossip about Texas elections and politics. An outstanding links page for current political candidates across the state.
http://www.political.com/

Practice Tests

MULTIPLE CHOICE QUESTIONS

1. The most important function for the party organization is

    a. gaining the support of interest groups.
    b. winning elections.
    c. making sure conventions run smoothly.
    d. finding delegates for conventions.

2. Evidence for realignment in Texas is derived from the following indications:

    a. young voters are more likely to identify with the Republican Party than the Democratic Party
    b. some Democrats are switching to the Republican Party
    c. in 2000, Republican candidates won every statewide election
    d. all of the above

3. Litigation was practiced extensively by _____ and _____ interest groups in the 1950s and 1960s.

    a. professional, labor
    b. business, professional
    c. civil rights, environmental
    d. professional, environmental

4. Special elections are held in Texas to

    a. fill vacancies in state legislative offices.
    b. approve local bond proposals.
    c. fill vacancies in U.S. congressional offices.
    d. all of the above

5. A _____ election determines which candidate a political party will endorse.

    a. special
    b. primary
    c. general
    d. bond

6. The effect of the motor-voter-registration system has been to

   a. increase the voter turnout.
   b. increase the number of individuals registered to vote.
   c. increase the number of individuals registered to vote and increase the voter turnout.
   d. none of the above

7. The permanent party organization consists of

   a. chairpersons and committees.
   b. conventions and committees.
   c. chairpersons and conventions.
   d. temporary chairpersons and committees.

8. The party in government includes the party in the

   a. judicial branch.
   b. executive branch.
   c. legislative branch.
   d. all of the above

9. The temporary party organization consists of

   a. chairpersons and committees.
   b. conventions.
   c. conventions and chairpersons.
   d. committees.

10. The purposes of a precinct convention are to select delegates to the party's

    a. county convention and adopt resolutions.
    b. state convention and adopt resolutions.
    c. national convention and adopt resolutions
    d. city convention and adopt resolutions.

TRUE/FALSE QUESTIONS

1. Voter turnout in primary elections is very low.

2. Some local elections generate high voter interest, but most do not.

3. General elections determine which candidate a party will endorse.

4. In Texas, political parties and interest groups developed early and quickly.

5. Interest groups participate in lobbying, electioneering, and litigation.

COMPARE AND CONTRAST

- Interest groups and political parties.
- Primary elections, special elections, and general elections.
- Dealignment and realignment.
- Permanent party organization and temporary party organization.
- Party in the electorate and party in the government.

ESSAY AND SHORT ANSWER QUESTIONS

1. Do you think Texas has undergone a realignment or dealignment?
2. Explain the roots of intraparty conflict in the Republican Party.
3. Describe the different political activities performed by interest groups.
4. Describe the three types of elections.
5. How does money affect political campaigns in Texas?

ANSWERS TO STUDY QUESTIONS

multiple choice answers

1. b   p. 988
2. d   p. 994
3. c   p. 1006
4. d   p. 1007
5. b   p. 1006
6. b   p. 1014
7. a   p. 990
8. d   p. 998
9. b   p. 998
10. a   p. 988

true/false questions

1. T p. 1007
2. T p. 1008
3. F p. 1007
4. F p. 989
5. T p. 1001